THE
EVOLUTION
OF
AMERICAN
TELEVISION

THE EVOLUTION OF AMERICAN TELEVISION

George Comstock

SAGE PUBLICATIONS
The International Professional Publishers
Newbury Park   London   New Delhi

For information address:

SAGE Publications, Inc.
2455 Teller Road
Newbury Park, California 91320

SAGE Publications Ltd.
6 Bonhill Street
London EC2A 4PU
United Kingdom

SAGE Publications India Pvt. Ltd.
M-32 Market
Greater Kailash I
New Delhi 110 048 India

Printed in the United States of America

Library of Congress Cataloging-in-Publication Data

Comstock, George A.
    The evolution of American television / George Comstock.
        p.   cm.
    Bibliography: p.
    Includes Index.
    ISBN 0-8039-3552-8. — ISBN 0-8039-3553-6 (pbk.)
    1. Television broadcasting — United States — History.   I. Title.
PN1992.3.U5C64   1989
384.55′4′0973 — DC20

                                                            89-33253
                                                                CIP

SECOND PRINTING 1990

Contents

88887

For Nora Irene Misiolek

Preface

It has been almost a decade since I wrote *Television in America,* a task as enjoyable as the subsequent experience of seeing the book go through a number of printings. So much has happened since then within the business of television and to the technology on which television depends, as well as within research on the mass media and human behavior, that a new and much larger volume was required. *Television in America* was intended as a classroom text, and as a précis for the knowledgeable scholar. It was adopted at several dozen universities, and enough colleagues were kind enough in their remarks to permit at least the illusion that the book served both purposes.

The Evolution of American Television has similar goals, although it is directed somewhat more forcefully toward students. The prospective reader, whatever his or her status, should be warned that it has three minor and one major theme. The three minor ones:

There is much to be learned about television from the study of psychology and social psychology, political behavior, sociology, communications, and other social and behavioral science disciplines and fields, both directly (when television or other mass media are their subject) or indirectly (when their subject is thought or behavior with some pertinence to the use or influence of the media).

The role and influence of the mass media, and of television in particular, are, with rare exceptions, better understood as an evolutionary process dependent on technology than as one or more revolutions brought about by technology.

The application of the social and behavioral sciences to television requires a search for evidentiary patterns, the use of theory, and a willingness to speculate. It is configurations rather than singular findings that are most likely to be meaningful, and sets of facts, even "scientific findings" when apart from ideas, are not particularly informative.

The major theme is that television is neither simply entertainment nor, for fewer hours, simply news, but an institution that is some of both at all times which, for that reason, influences our lives. It achieves this influence by the time it consumes, by the incursion of that time on other activities and competing media, and by the content of what it disseminates. The content, in turn, is the product of the medium's economic character and social role.

The empirical study of this institution has provided confirmation for some suppositions and disconfirmation for others. Such formal evidence is the foundation for everything that is said. However, it would be foolish to pretend that "research," given the resources that have been devoted to any particular question, will consistently reply with compelling, definitive answers, or that there are not some questions that are difficult or impossible to confront directly in any sound way by available methods and techniques. We should not be afraid that empirical evidence will mislead us as much as we should be careful that we do not discard what it can tell us by subjecting it to unrealistic or inconsistent standards. The broadcasting and advertising businesses—the "industry"—naturally apply very harsh criteria when they find results unpleasant, and quite different criteria when they seek guidance toward their own ends, as in program testing and evaluation. We should not be so silly.

The research is covered by genre, topic, school of thought, and major contributor(s). There are plenty of citations. Those whose works have been pioneering, especially intriguing, unusually perspicacious, or possess particular authority certainly are named, and principal sources are acknowledged. Nevertheless, there has been no attempt to be exhaustive or comprehensive either in citations within the text or references at the end.

The analysis is intended to be provocative. Shifts from empirical evidence to theory and speculation are intentional, and (it is hoped), the dividing lines clear. When we combine empirical findings with the theories they have helped shape, we are able to say much more that is meaningful than when we do not go beyond the so-called hard evidence. Because these theories have been shaped by empirical investigation and because many of the predictions to which they lead have been empirically confirmed, these theories are not simply speculation, but plausible, fact-rooted interpretations of events and behavior that give us some understanding of what research has not specifically encompassed, including the future. Speculation is a further step toward embracing larger and more elusive questions that do not fall clearly within the net of either empiricism or theory, but is far from guesswork because it draws on these bases. The heart of this volume is the confluence of these modes of thinking: empiricism, theory, and its extrapolation beyond that which has received substantial support.

George Comstock

Acknowledgments

This volume owes much to the author's previous writings and thus to the persons whose help made them possible. For the material drawn from *Television in America,* the most prominent are: Steven Chaffee, Robin E. Cobbey, Marilyn Fisher, Natan Katzman, Maxwell McCombs, Donald Roberts, and Eli A. Rubinstein. For material added since then, there are my editorial and research assistants, Nora Misiolek and Hae-Jung Paik; the editors of the collections in which my work has appeared: Erik Barnouw, Arnold Goldstein, Jack P. Gibbs, Stuart Oskamp, and Edward Seidman; and the contributors to the first two volumes of the series I edit, *Public Communication and Behavior* (1986a, 1989a): Brandon Centerwall, Thomas Cook, Thomas Curtin, Dennis K. Davis, Brian Flay, Susan Hearold, Aletha Huston, Shanto Iyengar, Donald Kinder, Neil Malamuth, William McGuire, W. Russell Neuman, Stuart Oskamp, David Phillips, John P. Robinson, and John Wright. A special debt is owed to J. Ronald Milavsky, a sociologist, whose knowledge and insight in regard to media research gained during his many years with the National Broadcasting Company continuously have made him an invaluable informant and, occasionally, a splendid antagonist. The S. I. Newhouse School at Syracuse University provided two crucial elements: an amiable environment and necessary resources.

It is pretentious to reach too far in behalf of an undertaking as modest as this, yet neither the author's career nor this volume would exist in their present configuration were it not for five individuals. They are:

11

Richard F. Carter, Merrell Clark, Roger Levien, Nathan Maccoby, and the late Wilbur Schramm.

Portions of this volume in a different form have appeared as journal articles, as chapters in collations, and as papers commissioned or invited by Action for Children's Television; the Center for Afro-American Studies at the University of California, Los Angeles; the East-West Communications Institute at Honolulu; the Ford Foundation; the International Encyclopedia of Communication; the Kaiser Foundation; the Michigan State Mental Health Association; the Society for the Psychological Study of Social Issues in conjunction with the Columbia Broadcasting System; and the World Book Encyclopedia. The author is grateful for their encouragement and support. None is responsible for what was then or is now said.

The chapter on children and television draws extensively on the monograph commissioned by the Educational Resource Information Center at Syracuse University, *Television and Children: A Review of Recent Research* by George Comstock and Hae-Jung Paik. The author is grateful for the assistance of Ms. Paik in that endeavor, and any merit bestowed on that chapter must be shared with her, while the author must accept responsibility for errors, faults, or omissions here.

Michael Cheng prepared the author and subject indices. Yanmin Yu assisted. The book thereby has been made more useful and the lives of several parties — readers, the author, and those cited — made better.

1

The Paradigm

The paradigm as a means of explaining continuities was made famous by Thomas Kuhn (1962) in his account of the evolution of science, *The Structure of Scientific Revolutions.* He presented the concept as representing the typical rationale and mode of inquiry within a field. At any given time, one or another paradigm is paramount; that is, widely accepted. At such a time, scientific inquiry is limited by the wide subscription to the same paradigm, and there is continuity. Change, and significant progress in looking at things in new ways, comes only when a new paradigm begins to gain acceptance. In effect, there is a revolution as old rules are abandoned for new. Kuhn thus saw science as advancing knowledge and breadth of understanding within paradigms, and changing toward superior comprehension through the revolutionary abandonment of one paradigm for another.

The concept is equally useful in understanding continuities in society. The nuclear family consisting of mother, father, and children is a paradigm that is under challenge by the increase in single-parent households. The division of federal power between the executive, legislative, and judicial branches is a paradigm that helps to explain the stability of our government through changes in issues, popularity of parties, and major events. Television in the United States, although changing in many important ways since its introduction four decades ago, also has exhibited a remarkable degree of continuity, and that is attributable to the particular paradigm within which it has evolved. That paradigm can be described succinctly by three terms: nonpaternalism, entertainment, and competition.

Nonpaternalism

Broadcasting in the United States is the creature of federal regulation. Its character derives from the conditions to which it responds, and these are largely the product of policies adopted by the federal government. These policies, proclaimed in legislation, applied over the past decades by the Federal Communications Commission (FCC) and, to a lesser degree by the Federal Trade Commission (FTC), and continually dulled or sharpened by the mood of the current Congress, are responsible for the number of television stations, the relative strengths of public and commercial broadcasting, and the way both public and commercial stations behave.

The fulcrum for the federal role is the principle of obligation in exchange for privilege. The privilege, in this case, is economic in the form of a license that permits a television station to operate. The value of a commercial station depends not upon the equipment it possesses, which, like a used car, certainly will bring some return in the marketplace, but upon the flow of income made possible by its broadcasting license. Behind licensing is the belief that the resources of a given community can be equitably and properly mined by a selected few.

Obviously, as is the case for all media, there is a limit on the number of television and radio stations that a particular community can support. Licensing imposes a further restriction on the stations that can operate within a geographical area. No such artificial limitation holds for print or other media. Thus we have come to treat broadcast media differently.

Television stations are licensed to ensure that signals will not conflict. The license requires, in the language of the Federal Communications Act of 1934, that the station serve the "public interest, convenience, and necessity." To justify such a requirement, the airwaves are designated as public property. It could just as easily be said, and many observers regularly do, that because the airwaves *are* public, licenses are imposed and service required. The logic flows equally strongly in both directions — from regulation to the status of the airwaves, and from the status of the airwaves to regulation. However, the first is the sounder explanation because it is a principle of sociology and of the way societies are managed that attributes and labels are assigned to achieve ends rather than to dictate them. In principle, the purpose of regulation is to make sure that the delivery of service to the public is not impeded by the chaos that might result from open competition.

Because of the very high demand for commercial time on the part of advertisers, the limitation of licenses to channels that will not interfere with each other means, in effect, that license holders have a fair guarantee of a profitable business. In exchange, television stations are expected to act to an arguable degree in accord with the conception of the public interest held by the FCC and Congress, whether or not doing so maximizes profits.

Despite these circumstances, American television is thoroughly non-paternalistic by the standards of much of the world. Public broadcasting, like commercial broadcasting, exists because of the licenses made available by the FCC. However, it has not so far received sufficient financial support to give it much weight in the totality of television viewing by the American people. In most areas on most evenings, public television attracts less than 5% of the audience viewing television. The estimate that nationally 95% of what Americans watch daily on television is commercial programming would overestimate the magnetism of public television.

In most countries, if there is a system of broadcasting dependent on advertising, it must compete with a strong system operating free of such support. Elsewhere, in countries industrialized or not, Western, Soviet, Asian, Third World, or "other" in orientation or location, we find broadcasting systems created to serve a programming philosophy. In some cases, these systems are government-run; in other instances, as with the British Broadcasting Corporation (BBC), the system is independent of the government and insulated from its direct influence. These systems are supported by taxes, fees levied on television set owners, or both. The puny role in America of broadcasting independent of commerce is the exception, not the rule — although hardly discreditable by that fact.

This proportionately minuscule share of attention devoted to public television by the public is the product of the meager and generally uncertain financial support allocated to such broadcasting. The framework, although certainly open to an expanded place for non-commercial public radio and television, was constructed in the first days of radio and made firm by the Communications Act of 1934. From the beginning, the priority was given to broadcasting conducted as a business, deriving its income from the sale of time to advertisers. Such time, the analogue of space in newspapers and magazines, naturally increases in value as the size and purchasing power of the audience increases. William J. McGill, president of Columbia University and chairman of the second Carnegie Commission on the Future of Public Broadcasting (1978) was correct a decade ago in remarking with the release of the Commission's report, *The Public Trust,* that much of the fate and character of American broadcasting had been settled long ago. "We couldn't go back 50 years and change everything," he said, perhaps wistfully, in explaining the Commission's argument for much stronger financing for new programming rather than for the creation of a new national network or for the shift of many public stations from the difficult-to-receive UHF to the far superior VHF frequencies occupied by commercial broadcasters.

What happened, simply, is that the federal government aligned itself with the values of private enterprise in devising a system of broadcasting, and then, in accord with the deep-rooted American distrust of those same values, established a means to temper the outcome. Among the numerous exemplifications of this same duality are anti-trust legislation, the Federal Drug Administration, and the Environmental Protection Agency. There is probably justified self-suspicion in the 1934 Act's prohibition against the FCC stipulating program content, yet the obligation to review the performance of broadcasters at regular intervals implies unambiguously a concern over content. The solution has been various requirements that presumably shape but do not mold content:

- The recently (and conceivably temporarily) abandoned Fairness Doctrine, requiring full and balanced treatment of controversial issues;
- The preference for local ownership, which ostensibly enhances the likelihood of public service;
- The policy that public service is incomplete without news;
- A hostility to concentration of ownership within a community of broadcast outlets and newspapers on the grounds that single ownership threatens the diversity of viewpoints to which the public has access; and
- A concern that broadcasters take community opinion into account in devising their schedules.

What immediately and largely determines content, however, is the invisible hand of economics – and in this instance, it has forever tied programming to popularity. In the American system of broadcasting, the first step was not a conviction about the effort programming should make to serve the country, but the adoption of a means by which any handwringing over such a conviction could be evaded. The decisions are made based on what reaps a profit. That was true for radio. It became true for television.

This technological innovation, the country's primary medium of entertainment today, the scourge of Presidents, adored by children, and so successful that it is journalistic practice to wisecrack that a television station entails a license to print money, was first placed on display as a curiosity at public events in the United States in the latter half of the 1930s. Partly because of the delay in development caused by World War II, it remained an exotic novelty until the early 1950s, when the television set quickly became a common item in American living rooms.

Today, almost every household reports to the U.S. Bureau of the Census that its possessions include one or more television sets, and over three-fourths of households have color sets. On any fall day in the late 1980s, the set in the average television-owning household was on for about eight hours. Between eight and nine p.m. on a typical fall evening, the audience would be about half the people in the country – over 100 million persons. Such extraordinary presentations as the Super Bowl (which transforms football from a team and league sport to a test of "the right stuff"), Alex Haley's *Roots,* and debates between presidential aspirants can attract from 75 to more than 100 million viewers.

There are about 1,450 licensed television stations in operation. About 1,100 stations are managed as privately owned, profit-seeking ventures and they annually broadcast more than seven million hours of programming. About 340 public and educational stations supported by contributions and subsidies add about 2.2 million hours. Most homes, even in remote areas, have access to several stations. About 40% of all homes are able to receive 11 or more stations and an increasingly larger proportion, currently estimated at approximately 55% of all homes, subscribe to cable or pay-TV services for additional programming (By the numbers, 1989).

The three giant television networks – the American Broadcasting Company (ABC), the Columbia Broadcasting System (CBS), and the National Broadcasting Company (NBC) – are the nervous system of

American television. Just as American television is almost synonymous with commercial television, commercial television has been to a substantial if decidedly decreasing degree synonymous with major network television. About 55%, down markedly from the 90% of a decade ago, are affiliated with one of the three, which provide about two-thirds of their programming. The rest of commercial programming—on nonaffiliated stations and in time not covered by the networks—is either locally produced or, far more frequently, obtained from outside sources. Much of this programming is made up of network reruns, thereby enlarging the presence of the major networks in American television.

The government's principal involvement in commercial television has been through the FCC. This agency, authorized by the Communications Act of 1934, literally determines the structure of American television by setting the rules to which broadcasters must conform. It allocates uses of available spectrum space (such as commercial versus public television); determines the privileges (until in some instances, halted by the courts) that commercial "open air" broadcasters, cable, pay-TV, and other communications operators enjoy; and licenses television stations. In principle, the FCC could revoke a station license under periodic review, but in practice it seldom has done so, although license renewals have been challenged frequently by would-be broadcasters and dissatisfied citizen groups. The FCC requires that a station broadcast a "reasonable" amount of news and community-oriented programming, and if this vague criterion of public service has not been scandalously violated, the renewal of a license is not in jeopardy.

Both the language of the authorizing statute and the free speech guarantee of the First Amendment constrain the agency from interfering in programming. Many have argued that the FCC could exercise extensive influence over programming by increased scrutiny during license renewal. The premise is that the obligation to oversee the public interest conveys the power to reject a broadcast schedule without implying that the commission has authority over any specific element of that schedule. Under such reasoning, the FCC could evaluate stations on the emphases on and divisions among various programming categories in their schedules. By so acting, the FCC presumably could increase the programming directed at any conceivable social category: children, families, ethnic minorities, the elderly, or viewers seeking news, information, education, or culture. Court rulings on the whole imply that the

FCC has such power. However, the FCC has made no more than the feeblest of gestures in such a direction. Thus, the precise boundaries of its authority over programming remain uncertain. They can only be fixed by a court test — an event contingent on a disputed FCC action — and in regard to programming, the FCC has taken few if any steps that could be termed sizeable, much less bold.

Many would hold that the FCC has been at least as adept at the sidestep as at the forward step. Precisely for that reason, Barry Cole and Mal Oettinger chose the title *Reluctant Regulators* (1978) for their account of the FCC. Cole is a professor who spent several years at the FCC; Oettinger has closely followed broadcast regulation as a journalist. They describe an agency made hesitant because of lack of expertise, inadequate data, and continual and close association of its staff and commissioners with the businessmen on whose behavior they are supposed to pass judgment. Reluctance is enhanced by the frequency with which these officials find subsequent lucrative careers in some field of communications. Vincent Mosco (1979), a sociologist who served as a Fellow at the now-defunct White House Office of Telecommunications Policy, reinforces such a view in his analysis of the treatment of the four major broadcasting innovations of the television area: FM, UHF, cable, and pay-TV. In each case, he concludes that the FCC opted for the status quo and for that which had been demonstrated to be readily feasible — to the profit of the broadcasters in place and to the detriment of new entrepreneurs, technological innovation, and, arguably, the public.

There are several exceptions where the federal government has become involved in the content of what is broadcast. Two became the concern of the FCC because of the provisions of the 1934 Act and its revisions: (1) The Fairness Doctrine, requiring full and impartial treatment of controversy, and (2) the Equal Time Law, requiring that candidates for public office be given equivalent opportunities for broadcast exposure. The Fairness Doctrine, which demanded of broadcasters that they cover not only important public issues but all sides of issues as well, was the foundation for the obligation imposed on radio and television to provide news and public affairs programming. Its broadest application occurred in regard to cigarette commercials before they were banned by congressional statute. The Fairness Doctrine was interpreted (after the requisite legal challenges) as requiring that broadcast schedules with cigarette commercials also had to contain public service announcements (PSAs) warning of the health risks of smoking. "Smoking" was thus defined as a controversial public issue. This left the tobacco companies with a sharply diminished interest in television advertising since, in effect, they would be subsidizing anti-smoking advertising. Thus, the congressional ban was far from wholly unwelcome.[1]

Recently, Congress abolished the Fairness Doctrine on the grounds that the quantity and diversity of media available to the public, electronic and otherwise, eliminate the necessity of such a requirement. However, many argue for the doctrine's reinstatement on the grounds that the size of the audience for broadcast news and the news' importance makes the availability of alternatives irrelevant as long as spectrum space is limited.

The Equal Time Law continues to impose fairness in what is offered to political candidates, but it does *not* affect how candidates are treated on a day-to-day basis since news coverage is specifically excluded on the grounds that newspeople are free to decide what constitutes news and candidates are unlikely to be equal in their ability (or misfortune) to create news. Thus, the law imposes equity of opportunity, not balanced coverage.

A third exception involves the FTC. This agency has had the responsibility to protect viewers from deception and misleading commercials, and it is because of such authority that the FTC joined with the FCC in 1979 in conducting extended hearings on the propriety and influence of advertising directed at children.

Children's programming illustrates the impotence that besets the FCC in regard to broadcast content. The agency's 1974 policy statement advanced a number of auspicious phrases as guidelines for broadcasters, such as "diversified programming," programming that would "further the educational and cultural development of the child," "age-specific" programming for preschool and school-age children, and more programming during weekdays. Five years later, a special staff assigned to study children's programming concluded that these admonitions had largely been ignored. In effect, the staff admitted that a policy statement that goes against economic interest without including forceful means of implementation is not policy, but wishful thinking.

The staff proposed that a major option open to the agency was to require a certain number of hours per week of programming for children. Specifically, it suggested that broadcasters be required to present five hours per week of "educational or instructional programming" for preschool children and two-and-one-half hours for school-age children weekdays between 8 a.m. and 8 p.m. The broadcasters vociferously dissented, for their economic interest lies with entertainment programming which draws from as wide an age spectrum as possible. The large and sometimes huge audiences that make broadcasting profitable can be assembled only by attracting a diversity of viewers at any given time. Narrowly-defined audiences of youngsters, such as those attracted to *Sesame Street*, are unacceptable to profit-minded broadcasters.

The broadcasters challenged the evidence that they had failed to comply, the desirability of behaving other than as they had, and both the value and legitimacy of new stipulations. By the mid-1980s, the FCC had abandoned any effort to influence the television programming created for children. The chairman at the time, Mark Fowler, had preached against any but market forces as criteria for broadcasting and he made it clear that, in his view, programming for children was no exception. Under the Republican administration of Ronald Reagan, the FCC had emphasized deregulation. Yet, that story is as much one of powerlessness and temerity as of altered direction because at no time did the FCC ever take decisive action in behalf of a category of programming. Even had the staff's recommendation been followed, the agency could not have guaranteed the quality of what was presented as cultural and educational. Thus, the agency's eventual declaration rose to a note of humility — and urged Congress to do more for children's television through public television and a National Endowment for Children's Television. Congress, of course, has done neither. In fact, legislation similar to the FCC staff proposals or authorizing funding for non-commercial production have languished year after year.

Programming policy thus falls largely to the broadcasters themselves. It is formulated implicitly in the numerous decisions that are made that transform an idea — or, more formally, a "concept" — into a scheduled program. This is the process that determines the evening series and miniseries, the made-for-TV movies, the specials, the documentaries, the news and information programs, game shows, and day-time soap operas from which viewers can choose. It is literally the making of American television.

Todd Gitlin (1983), a sociologist at the University of California at Berkeley, interviewed more than 200 producers, directors, writers, and executives about what takes place, and the story he tells has a number of distinctive elements: (a) a highly imperfect system — although it employs many techniques of the social and behavioral sciences — for estimating what will become popular coupled with a fast and accurate means of measuring the degree of popularity achieved by any given broadcast; (b) unique contractual practices that make the assembling of a "deal" for a particular broadcast product the truly creative element in programming; and (c) a commitment to making highly popular entertainment accompanied by beliefs about what constitutes such entertainment that so strongly favors the status quo, proven success, and the familiar format that periodic revolutions brought about by novel successes are inevitable. In this milieu, the "recombinant" principle holds by which new programming is created by combining elements from past successes, innovative programming is limited in how far it can go and tends to regress toward conventionality, and the fate of any given program rests on dozens of decisions. The overall result is that most television is much the same.

As Gitlin   concludes (not perhaps without a touch of irony and cynicism):

> So the networks do just what they set out to do. They are not *trying* to stimulate us to thought, or inspire us to belief, or remind us of what it is to be human and live on the earth late in the twentieth century; what they are trying to do is "hook" us. Meanwhile, the government regulatory agencies have been persuaded that "the marketplace" is its own regulator, which means that no interest that cannot be expressed in Nielsen numbers counts (*Inside Primetime*, p. 334).

The absence of a public, formal declaration of intent beyond the acknowledged desire to attract as many viewers as possible does not imply a lack of overall uniformity or coherence to what is broadcast. It only means that policy emerges from the structure of broadcasting rather than being imposed by those who rule it.

Historically, policy has been explicitly made in the formulation and enforcement of codes and standards to which broadcasters declare their allegiance. Such guidelines have set standards in regard to violence, portrayals of sexual relations, obscenity, the occult, advertising, and other content. They have specified what is unacceptable, and thus have made policy by proscription rather than by prescription. When enforced, these guidelines have resulted in the fine-tuning of the broadcast product to minimize any possibility of harm or offense to the public.

Of these, the priority has gone to the latter for two reasons. First, most people, including those who work in television, believe they have a clearer notion about what might offend than what might do harm. Second, from a sociological perspective, one of the major purposes of such guidelines is to protect an institution from intervention by the government, harassment by politicians, and complaint from the public. Because of the ambiguities of harm, offense is more likely to evoke such behavior. Even if totally ineffectual on both counts, expressed codes and standards at least are available for display.

For many years, the most publicized of these shields was the Television Code of the National Association of Broadcasters (NAB). It was primarily a symbol, because the only sanction imposed by the NAB for violation was denial of the offender's right to display the NAB seal. It died more than a decade ago by judicial decisionmaking and Justice Department opinion. The formal, cooperative subscription by NAB member stations to an external standard was deemed a violation of the federal antitrust statutes. That is, stations must individually make their own judgments. The important point is that the demise of the code had no discernible effect on program content. Broadcasters simply have lost a convenient political tool with which to protect themselves from criticism. Broadcasting is like any other business: Self-regulation is the first defense against undesired intervention by government.

The important codes have been those formulated and enforced by each of the three networks. This is because there has, in fact, been some effort at enforcement. Over the past few decades, a specialized staff of substantial size at each network has been assigned the duty of applying the codes. Concepts, scripts, film footage, and other aspects of video treatment have been scrutinized to maximize conformity. The earlier term "fine-tuning" was not used in disparagement of this undertaking, for it has been an attempt by the networks to go about their business of attracting audiences in a responsible way. The intention has been good, if the results are sometimes trivial or open to ridicule, and this effort — serious, if modest — has set network broadcasting apart from the other technologies by which programming is brought to the home television screen.

Decisions about whether some specific element of content is appropriate for broadcast, whether based on an articulated code or some less formal, more intuitive *ad hoc* criterion, occur in a context of asymmetry of approval and approbation in regard to the mass media in general and television in particular. Approval is largely influential only when in the form of popularity, which in the case of television means ratings (the proportion of the possible viewing audience) and shares (the proportion of those viewing who are tuned to a particular program). Praise from the prominent or ardent applause from some small segment of the audience are welcome but do not typically become strictures for future programming. Being liked by a few is irrelevant to profitability. Offending any part of the audience, however, is generally avoided except when offense to a few may seem the price of popularity. The reason is simple: Outrage by the prominent or the many involves the broadcaster in conflict when he would prefer to do business. The codes are designed to minimize such conflict by symbolizing pure motives, minimizing offense, and precluding actual harmful effects.

If in practice the networks function as monitors of broadcast quality, in theory and in law the responsibility falls entirely to the individual stations. It is the individual station that is licensed, not the networks. This implies that it is the individual station that is responsible for what it offers, regardless of the original source. Furthermore, not only have the courts concurred with this perspective, but they have held that the station cannot compromise its independent responsibility by subscription to a code devised by an external source. The judicial occasion was the "family viewing" litigation of the mid-1970s. In response to pressure from Congress, then-FCC Chairman Richard Wiley informally — by telephone, letter, and meeting — induced the networks, the NAB, and their member stations to subscribe to a code eliminating violent and sexually provocative programming that would be considered unsuitable for young viewers between 7 and 9 p.m.

The Hollywood writers and producers challenged this step on three grounds: violation of the First Amendment; failure to follow the ordinary safeguards of hearings and votes; and, the absence of due process in reducing the value of previously-produced television by barring it from a significant time segment. The judge concurred with the plaintiffs. Eventually, the courts remanded the issue to the FCC for whatever action it might wish to take (on the grounds that the FCC could not be said to have acted beyond its powers until it attempted to do so using its conventional procedures) where it has been ignored ever since.

The major lessons are that: (a) responsibility lies with, and cannot be evaded by, individual stations; (b) external codes are collusive; and (c) the one significant federal attempt to reform programming available to children faltered and was abandoned.

By the end of the 1980s, the result was a move for federal legislation exempting the television business — networks, stations, cable operators, and other entities — from the anti-trust strictures that preclude joint efforts, as exemplified by an industry-wide code and the family viewing experiment, to establish standards for programming and especially to reduce violence. Even with such legislation, any notable change is doubtful. In its brief history, the family viewing accord was accompanied by about the same amount or a minor decrease in violence within the 7-9 p.m. period, while violence after 9 p.m. remained much higher after increasing decidedly the previous year (Gerbner, Gross, Eleey, Jackson-Beeck, Jeffries-Fox, & Signorielli, 1977; Comstock, 1982a). This qualifies as a net gain only after some astringent arithmetic because there are as many teenagers in the audience the hour after as the hour before 9 p.m., and while the proportion of children 2-11 in age in the audience is much greater before than after 9 p.m., about one-fifth are still in the audience by 10 p.m.

The federal government has been a major financial contributor to public broadcasting, but its influence over programming on both commercial and public television largely has been limited to enforcement of the Fairness Doctrine and the Equal Time Law. The principal exception has been federal financing for programming intended to have cognitive, motivational, or behavioral effects on some subset of the larger audience such as children, teenagers, parents, or an ethnic minority. Here the federal role has ended in helping to make such programming available. Examples, although not all entirely federally financed, include *Sesame Street, 1-2-3 Contact, Vista Alegre, Carrascolendas, Freestyle,* and *Over Easy*. As a whole, these programs are best thought of as special education rather than as attempts to intervene in or reform television broadcasting.

The advantage of the American system is, of course, the minimization of the use of television by the government for its own purposes. In the United States, there is no voice of officialdom to cajole, threaten, or mislead over the airwaves. Profits, not politics, have compromised the news by limiting the amount of time the affiliated stations are willing to cede to the networks for the evening newscasts. Nevertheless, the networks continually have lost money with the news they do broadcast, so news can hardly be called a victim of profits. Controversies over news coverage, in which critics of television news are usually aligned with an offended administration, make it clear that the temptation to meddle in the news, whether commercial or public, is great. Certainly, within the system most vulnerable to federal meddling, public television, there have been various efforts over the years to bring its coverage more in line with the desires of an incumbent administration. A system that has strong safeguards against such manipulations of the media has much to recommend it, whatever its other deficiencies.

The report of the Carnegie Commission on the Future of Public Broadcasting (1978) a decade ago responds to this danger by advancing numerous proposals for increasing the insulation of public television from government. What the report also makes clear is that the American system is unusual in its reliance on business success:

> The United States is the only Western nation relying so exclusively upon advertising effectiveness as the gatekeeper of its broadcasting activities. The consequences of using the public spectrum primarily for commercial purposes are numerous, and increasingly disturbing. The idea of broadcasting as a force in the public interest, a display case for the best of America's creative arts, a forum of public debate — advancing the democratic conversation and enhancing the public imagination — has receded before the inexorable force of audience maximization. (*The Public Trust*, p. 21)

Entertainment

The consequence of the means by which nonpaternalism has been achieved is television's pervasive emphasis on entertainment. The arbiter of commercial broadcasting — and because it is so dominant, of American television itself — is its pursuit of the audience. It is audience size and character that determine the profit for the broadcaster. Popularity is the goal, with size modulated in importance by the desire to attract viewers in the 18 to 55 age bracket who constitute the principal market for consumer goods. Popularity does not simply rule entertainment — it makes entertainment the principal dimension of commercial television. This is true from two perspectives: (1) Entertainment dominates the schedules of networks and individual stations, and (2) the other two major categories of programming, sports and news, are held to the same criteria as entertainment with attracting as large as possible an audience the first priority.

Public television differs from commercial television by devoting more of its schedule to information, although much of that information does not concern public affairs, but private events — hobbies and interests. Over the years, public television also has increased the proportion of its schedule devoted to entertainment. This tendency for public television to follow commercial television is the result of its susceptibility to the idolatry of popularity. *Of course* the entertainment purveyed by public television is typically different from that offered by the networks; who would argue otherwise? *Of course* network television frequently offers programming risky in audience appeal and as adventuresome, serious, and cultural as anything attempted by public television; no sensible person would say differently. The point is that entertainment is surer than information to attract an audience, and thus the dominance of entertainment in American television is inevitable. J. Mallory Wober (1988), the British social psychologist, makes the case succinctly based on research in numerous countries, times, and places: "[T]he almost thermodynamically determined laws of viewing behavior . . . indicate that less demanding and more arousing material will be more readily viewed by more people than will more demanding and less arousing material" (p. 210).

Entertainment is a very broad concept. We can try to distinguish it from art, but this ignores the fact that the social and psychological functions served by the two — that is, the enjoyment derived — is to some degree much the same. At the same time, the eminent Columbia University sociologist, Herbert J. Gans (1974), goes too far in his absurdly egalitarian claim that no meaningful distinctions can be drawn between the "low-brow" and the "high-brow" or between presentations of greater or lesser quality because of this fact. What he ignores is that while the social activity necessary for their consumption may appear the same, the psychological, cognitive, and intellectual rewards may vary considerably, and holding people's interest enjoyably, even to an equal degree, does not imply equivalence of artistic motive or goal, which may vary sweepingly both as to the magnitude and degree of actual achievement. The fact that there is often disagreement about precise ranking does not invalidate belief in a hierarchy of worth based on something other than popularity, or make less ludicrous the idea that public attention implies any value other than itself. That television is entertaining is hardly a failing. At issue in evaluating the medium is the kind and quality of entertainment it provides.

The significant failure of television entertainment is not that it shares qualities with other entertainment, but that it serves primarily as a vehicle for advertisers. The interest of broadcasters in their programming is secondary to their interest in its attractiveness to audiences. The intrinsic characteristics of that programming are not of much importance to advertisers, for these characteristics only achieve their value in the degree of popularity attained. Even being popular is not enough, as it might be for a novel or a play, for the pitting of program against program in the same time slot leaves no ambiguity about superiority, and superiority by the criterion of garnering the largest potential market for goods to be hawked is what will bring the greatest revenue from advertisers. Broadcasters, hardly fools, would certainly acknowledge that what is good for advertisers may not be good for the public, but by their actions they rate the interests of television and advertisers as identical.

Erik Barnouw (1975), the Columbia University professor acknowledged to be the leading historian of broadcasting, recounts many tales of how advertisers have gone beyond mere appeal in shaping programs to their ends. Sponsorship by one cigarette maker in the early days of the medium meant that there could be no smoking by villains, coughing by anyone, or fires anywhere, for any one of these might reflect unfavorably on the product. Such product protection has been common when programs — once the rule and now the exception — have been sponsored in part or wholly by a specific advertiser. By the same rationale, controversy typically has been avoided. During television's "golden age," one drama based on a real-life instance of white resistance to a new black neighbor was transformed into an all-white story of inexplicable hostility toward a new resident — until at the very end it is revealed that he is an ex-convict. Decades later, Gitlin (1983) records his top level producers, writers, directors, and executives as acknowledging the norm of avoiding controversy. Taking a position and being controversial are seen as identical in the ethos of the business of television. The somewhat peculiar view of the ideological landscape held there is well expressed by the head of entertainment for one of the networks:

> I don't think that we should advocate on television any one particular point of view: social, political, whatever. I think that we ought to examine both

points of view. And by examining both points of view, we have conflict, and conflict is the essence of drama or comedy . . . (*Inside Primetime*, p.230)

When asked by Gitlin whether this was a "moral" or "market" position, the reply was:

I think it's basically what I think is marketable. I mean, I have my own values. Everybody has their own values. The guy who is making Chevrolet cars, let's say, may have Cadillac tastes, but he's making Chevrolet cars because he knows that that's what's marketable. And that's basic. Business is business. We are out to reach the most number of people in a wholesome manner. (*Inside Primetime*, p.250)

What makes these comments particularly telling beyond their naiveté — exemplified in the beliefs that the "two sides" good for television drama and comedy embrace the complexities of the world and that values as a factor in television programming are analogous to the aspirations of auto workers — is the context within which Gitlin presents them: The failure of television to deal with the Vietnam War other than on the news until well after such "breakthrough" movies as *The Deerhunter* and *Apocalypse Now*. As a topic, it could too easily tumble out of the trench of safety. It thus becomes easy to understand that blacklisting during the McCarthy Era became for sponsors simply a sensible means of not risking offense, and thus they became conspirators in the denial on the basis of political affiliation, rumor, and innuendo of the opportunity to work in or appear on television.

Barnouw suggests that drama that has emotional truth, a realism quite distinct from the accuracy of police procedure or geographical setting, is incompatible with commercial television because, by contrast, it would emphasize the triviality of commercials; in his word, they would seem "fraudulent" (p. 163). He further argues that the very themes and substance of television entertainment derive from the needs of the U.S. nation-state — from the game shows honoring lust for possessions, thereby promoting consumption, to the action and adventure series in which the strength, skill, and subterfuge necessary to defeat powerful, ruthless enemies symbolically justify nuclear stockpiles, high levels of defense spending, and covert actions.

The quiz shows of the late 1950s exemplify the hand of the advertiser at work. Several primetime programs gained great popularity by pitting contestants against each other for huge prizes — as the names of two,

The $64,000 Question and *The $64,000 Challenge,* made clear. Then Herbert Stempel, a deposed contestant, confirmed rumors that the contests were fixed to ensure suspense and audience-pleasing participants. Investigations by a New York grand jury and a congressional committee followed. Charles Van Doren, a Columbia English instructor who won $129,000 and, in so doing, became a highly paid television personality, confessed that he had been fed answers in advance. Behind the manipulations was the desire of the sponsor for a hit show. As Van Doren told the committee, dishonesty was argued to be permissible because it was "only entertainment."

As a result of the scandal, the networks began to take a larger role in programming rather than leaving everything to advertising agencies and the sponsors. Today, series no longer are manufactured to the specification of a single sponsor, and commercial time is sold for inclusion in programming produced to the expressed demands of the networks. Yet, what the quiz show scandal represented is no relic, for at its roots was the organization of broadcasting around the principle of maximum popularity.

Competition

Television in America is a business of unabashed competition. So, one might remark, are all businesses. Competition in television differs, however, because of the gladiatorial aspect imposed by the character of the medium and by the way it is organized. The consequence is a drive by each of the three networks and of the stations within a market to be first in the value to advertisers of the audiences assembled for their programs.

As Les Brown (1971) of *Channels* emphasizes so astutely in his account in one season's struggle among the networks for dominance in the ratings, television only appears to be in the business of entertainment, sports, and news. In fact, it is in the business of vending the attention of the public to parties interested in selling their products to that public. Properly perceived, the product is not programming but audiences. Size of audience, modified somewhat by its predilection for consumption, is the determinant of profits.

Economists bicker over whether the proper criterion for assessing the rate of return to broadcasters is capital investment, a standard by which broadcasting becomes one of the most lucrative businesses in the

United States, or regular investment in new programming, by which it simply becomes a very healthy business. However, there is no doubt that over the years the three networks and most of the many hundreds of stations have amply enriched their operators. To be "numero uno" in the ratings means tremendous return to a network.

For example, when ABC became the profit leader for the first time in 1977, it reported an increase in one year of almost 100%, rising from $83 million in profits before federal income taxes to $165 million. In recent years, even to be third among the networks in ratings has assured a substantial profit. The system, however, only gives comfort to being first. There are not only the demands of the network organization itself (where jobs and salaries are dependent on financial success) and of the stockholders (who, like stockholders everywhere, want increased dividends and rising share values), but of the affiliate stations, whose profits derive to a large extent from the success of network programming in attracting audiences.

Television is a mass medium that can enter almost every home in the country at any moment. Because of the continuing and pervasive measurement of audience size — most prominently by the A. C. Nielsen Company, but also by others — the division of spoils at any given hour is seldom in doubt. The untended set, the inaccurate report, the straying of viewers' attention to other activities — these anomalies may nurture the carpings of journalists about the accuracy of audience figures, but the measures undeniably provide a reliable currency for comparing performance. The dependence of profits on audience means that for any one competitor, station or network, it always is more desirable to attract as large a body of potential consumers as possible, thereby maximizing the price that advertisers will pay for access to them, than it is to expand the total audience in any given hour by offering something appealing to a smaller audience composed of individuals who would not ordinarily watch television.The strategy dictated by the system is to offer widely popular fare that divides the audience for mass entertainment, not adventuresome programming that would attract otherwise indifferent viewers.

Competition in television means a struggle each hour for dominance. The incentives discourage diversity, for a network audience of 10 million is not as valuable as an audience of 20 or 30 million, even if that 10 million were made up of viewers who otherwise might turn to something other than television. The capacity of the medium to reach almost everyone, and the fusing of profits to appeal, leads to programming that tends to be much the same across outlets. Television operates like a game in which each player's return takes precedence over the total return to all players. There is an inevitable narrowing and homogenization of what is offered, coupled with the frequent head-to-head scheduling of the medium's starships of greatest interest. The system thus ignores millions, yet squanders its best programming.

The 1970s will be recorded as the decade in which competition escalated from hard-fought to frenzied. The upward rush of ABC on a calculated appeal to the teenagers given control of the set by blasé adults ended a ratings hierarchy that seemed to have the permanence of the pyramids. The third network, now first, had established strength in sports dazzlement before riding situation comedy to primetime preeminence. Later, it would turn to news as a still stationary front. Warfare became a good metaphor for what was taking place. The increasing production of made-for-TV movies, the emergence of miniseries, and the ever-handy "special" made showboating a common term in television and something desperate always done by the other guy. Series were turned over as fast as cards at blackjack. The season for which programming was scheduled, once stretching from fall to spring, became two seasons which dissolved into hasty replacements and rearrangements. The success of such a phenomenon as the miniseries *Roots,* which set a record for audience size, seemingly would have encouraged innovative programming, yet the breakup of stable schedules probably has reduced habitual viewing and second chances for series have become as rare as second acts in American lives were thought to be by F. Scott Fitzgerald. Many wondered if a series such as *All in the Family,* which took more than a season to build an audience, could survive in the new atmosphere.

That atmosphere probably exacerbated the inevitable tensions between network broadcasters and the Hollywood "hyphenates" — so-called because their jobs so frequently combined some portion of being a producer-director-writer — over the quality of programming. The Hollywood community, already beset by network-imposed restrictions on violence, fiercely deplored the confinement of serious drama to luxury display for "boutique" programs. The broadcasters spoke of business as usual.

The 1970s were new in the intensity of competition, but the values and interests of those who broadcast and those who create what is broadcast never have been and never will be in perfect congruence. The broadcasters are essentially businessmen. The Hollywood people frequently bring to their jobs artistic, literary, narrative, and journalistic intentions. It is hard to imagine how otherwise they could perform adequately, however often these intentions must be made subordinate to marketability. The Hollywood community — or at least its more creative segment — would prefer a system that evaluates the program, not the audience; that encourages innovation, not convention; that rewards originality, not imitation; that accepts controversy as well as conflict; that presents realism as well as fantasy, and that makes it possible to try to say important things about important topics. By the standards of the so-called "golden age" of television when live drama of the sort ordinarily found on the stage was offered nightly, such prospects continually dimmed through the 1960s and 1970s.

The golden age of television began in the late 1940s and ended about 10 years later. The list of participants — writers, directors, actors, and actresses — who would go on to distinction and fame is long. Numerous plays presented were remade into acclaimed movies. The era ended precisely because television is a business. When television was new, sets were first purchased by those with higher incomes and greater education. Diffusion was extremely rapid. With television in almost every household, the audience became more heterogeneous and dominated by the less educated. Advertisers became skeptical of selling consumer goods by commercials which promised quick solutions in the context of dramas portraying problems conceivably without solution. Live drama became expensive to produce, and less expensive alternatives proved as, or more, successful in attracting viewers. Serious live drama became noncompetitive. The weekly series, and in particular, action-and-adventure series (of which westerns were, at first, among the most popular), became the staple of evening television. As Marshall McLuhan (1964) has pointed out, new media typically borrow formats from old media. Television at first borrowed from the stage, and to a lesser degree, from movies (which is why so many of its early original dramas were made into movies). Later, television found its *metier* in imitating certain aspects of radio. The action-adventure series met the criteria of quick and comparatively inexpensive production, audience popularity, and advertiser satisfaction. Thus, television's first three decades can be described as: The 1950s — live original drama; the 1960s — the repetitive filmed serial; and the 1970s — the breakup of old patterns by fierce competition with the serial joined by the made-for-TV movie, the special, and the miniseries. The consequence was that by the end of this period, many in Hollywood, while enjoying greater prosperity and turning out the programs as always, had begun to express doubts about the value of the business of which they were a part and about whether the medium was what it could and should be.

The 1980s brought further change. The question about the nurturance of novel programs was answered almost immediately by *Hill Street Blues.* This hour-long, noisy, realistic, fragmented, intense portrait of an urban police station was renewed at the end of its first season with conceivably the lowest ratings of any show ever renewed. By the end of the year, it had received considerable critical acclaim and swept the Emmys with an unprecedented 21 awards. It went on to become not only NBC's highest rated program, but the highest rated among all regularly broadcast programs. It demonstrated that a program unlike anything regularly broadcast at the time could receive sufficient network patience to find an audience. It also has a claim to being the exception that proves the rule. Examples of such programs continued to be rare. *Hill Street Blues* cast off many of its novel aspects in the search for popularity, and by the time it was cancelled late in the decade, its surviving elements had become accepted conventions of television drama.

Another question was answered by *The Cosby Show,* a program rejected at least once by each of the three networks. NBC eventually decided that the star's drawing power perhaps would be sufficient to rescue a format that no longer was supposed to have audience appeal, family situation comedy. It quickly became the top-rated program in the country, and helped bring about another revolution in the standings among the networks when last-rated NBC established itself as the most popular. *The Cosby Show* not only demonstrated that the knowledge and rules by which network executives make programming judgment are faulty, but that the usefulness of format in predicting popularity is limited. The shift in network standings demonstrated again how the dominance that is imputed to one or another is a superiority that rests on the sands of programming decisions and changing audience tastes. Such standings inevitably are impermanent because they rest on no firm capital of advantage, such as lower costs, superior labor supply, or nearness to markets.

However, the major changes of the 1980s were more pervasive and had implications for the future. The network share of the audience continually declined, while the audience for television as a whole increased. The deficit was attributable to the many alternative sources of programming that developed, with the increase in the appeal of independent stations probably accounting for the largest share, with the additional signals, and especially broadcast signals, made available by cable probably next. Network influence over production lessened somewhat as the independent stations and various consortiums of stations offered new means of distributing programs outside of the network system.

The VHS videocassette recorder (VCR) became by far the preferred means of in-home playback and recording, vanquishing the video disk to educational applications and the Beta-tape to circumstances in which picture quality has high priority. The VCR probably contributed only slightly to the decline in network audience share. More importantly, it almost certainly sharply increased video use by attracting comparatively infrequent users of broadcast television.

Finally, the competition not only among the networks but between the networks and other programming sources had a liberalizing effect on programming. In the search for new formats, social issues became popular. In fact, the most watched program was *The Burning Bed,* a true account of a battered wife who killed her husband by setting him on fire and who was found not guilty of a crime by a jury. Such programs had conflict but were also controversial. Television dramas became more gritty, more realistic, more decidedly "television." The most notable example was *Miami Vice,* with its lurid photography and specialized musical scores. Competition was not the only factor responsible. The sources on which the recombinant principle could draw had multiplied; *Miami Vice,* for example, had MTV (Music Television) as well as *Hill Street Blues.* The medium itself had also become more accepted on its own terms rather than as a vehicle which should more widely disseminate something more particular to another medium. Thus, the 1980s could be said to be the decade when television became itself and when the faintest imprint of what its future might hold could be discerned.

The adversarial posture is everywhere in television. It is as prominent in the programming of news and sports as it is in entertainment. News and sports must compete like other programming for a share of the audience, and personalities, formats, and programs will become defunct if they do not maintain adequate popularity. Entertainment programs begin their journey from concept to final cut many months before they are broadcast. En route, they are continually revised, accepted, or rejected on the basis of intuition, conformity to written and unwritten standards, and research on their appeal. Of these, the most important by far is intuition. News and sports undergo a similar honing. Anchorpersons, reporters, commentators, and personalities are picked to attract viewers not fully enamored of the competition—so as one network or station finds a place in the minds and time budgets of viewers, others will reshape their presentations by juggling age, sex, demeanor, and set decor to find a sentiment uncaptured.

Public television shares the pervading values of commercial television. Audience attraction universally has become accepted as the measure of the medium. Public television must justify its governmental and private funding by demonstrating that it serves a need which is compatible with and economically feasible to be met by the deployment of broadcast television. If mass appeal is in conflict with its proffered goals, a negligible appeal is inconsistent with survival. Although the people who run public television often will explain to a critic that it is not intended to be popular, in fact it strains constantly in accord with the urgings of critics and friends alike to attract more and more viewers. Thus, there should be no surprise at public television's trend toward entertainment over the years. It is only being true to its medium.

Local production for local commercial programming is rare except for news and variants on informational programming, such as coverage of leisure opportunities. Commercial programming has been produced largely by organizations independent in ownership from the networks, although the latter are their major customers. This separation, although clouded by a history of network control and involvement in the honored proclivity of healthy firms to consume their suppliers, is the result of the application of the federal antitrust statutes to broadcasting. Ownership of production companies by the three major networks was construed to infringe on competition, for what sensible oligopolist would buy from other than his own company? In practice, however, the networks determine to a large degree what will be produced in two ways. First, they remain the principal consumers of the product in question, and therefore constitute the demand which suppliers must meet. Second, they are involved very closely in the development of programs, with the go-ahead on production at every stage contingent on and at the mercy of network approval.

As the 1990s began, the emphasis on network responsibility for programming that started with the quiz show scandals became heightened by strong economic incentives and new opportunities. Deregulatory policies made it possible for networks to make more of what they broadcast, including series. Economics dictate a strong presence of the networks in such production because large revenues are generated when successful series are syndicated to independent stations and network affiliates for broadcast outside of times when they are carrying new programming. These are profits in which the networks in the past did not share, but now they can do so. Increased direct involvement in production seems certain. Similar policies now make it possible for production companies and studios to own outlets — theaters, cable companies, television stations, and video stores. The result is a trend toward vertical integration, with those who once principally disseminated (networks and broadcasters) taking on ownership of production facilities (companies and studios) and those who once principally produced taking on ownership of the means of dissemination.

The antitrust action may have added vigor to business, but not necessarily to the home screen. The demands of the networks, canny if not always accurate in estimating popularity, not only influence first-run network-disseminated programming, but also the rest of programming — for non-network television, whether from an independent station or during the open hours of an affiliate, consists to a considerable degree of reruns.

News and sports programming, unlike entertainment, are entirely the products of the disseminators. Networks and local stations make their own. News would appear to be different in that the daily decisions are made autonomously of management. In fact, both news and sports programming are hybrids in that they are expected to meet the same criteria as entertainment programming — that is, to attract bigger, and from the advertiser's viewpoint, more lucrative audiences than the competition. Sports coverage would appear to differ from coverage of general events by not raising questions about bias, ideology, or balance. In fact, many such questions do arise when sports coverage focuses on individuals. Private matters of public figures are pursued righteously in the "public's right to know" whether their fame rests on politics, sports, or some other means of notoriety. What is missing in the case of sports coverage, and what gives the illusion of difference, are major public issues. News and sports resemble entertainment in that none of the three categories of programming can escape the values of management. Journalists may manufacture the news and commentators present sports in their own lights, but management manufactures both journalists and commentators in its light. Management sets the policies to which news and sports programming conform. Formats and personnel are the creatures of management, as is the budget to do the job. The three categories are alike in being tailored to the exigencies of competition.

McLuhan (1964) designated television as a "cool" medium. He was right to argue that media have characteristics that impose some meaning of their own on what is conveyed, and possibly apt in his metaphor; however, he could not have found a less accurate term for the way television transacts business.

The Future

The three terms — nonpaternalism, entertainment, and competition — will continue to describe American television despite the many changes certain to occur. The paradigm will continue because the factors which create it will remain the same. Any recasting of the Federal Communications Act will change the way broadcasting does business in the 1990s and beyond, but not the underlying pattern of broadcasting. The basic principle of obligation in exchange for privilege will survive; regulation, whatever the precise form, will continue as a gently applied hand; and the marketplace, defined much as it is today, will continue to dictate the content of television. The trend is toward a loosening of federal stipulations, not the abandonment of the system.

Even if the Carnegie Commission's proposals were followed resolutely, there would be no change in the preeminence of television designed to serve the needs of advertisers. The increasing of federal financial support for public broadcasting, the production of more new programs on the basis of expert advice about their cultural desirability, and the insulation of decision-making from federal influence would dress up the public television schedule, expand the audience, and offer programs that generally would not survive the gauntlet of commercial television — but they would not bring about a revolution in taste or business conduct. After a three- or even four-fold increase in the public television audience, television viewing by the public would remain almost 90% the product of commerce.

The principal source of change will be neither an altered federal posture nor the blooming of public television, but the technological developments that are changing the communications environment. There will always be television available free to viewers because of the revenues derivable from the sale of advertising. Despite inevitable declines in audience, networks will continue, for national programming will remain popular enough to serve as a vehicle for advertising. Nevertheless, there is a shift toward greater choice that is quantitatively large enough to suggest the beginning of an upheaval in mass media not unlike that which followed the introduction of television. The diffusion of that innovation was so rapid that what occurred approximated a revolution, even though its effects on the whole were slow to evolve. The increasing availability of cable television with its many channels; the use of satellites to feed cable systems, which makes possible a "super station" such as WTBS in Atlanta, and station consortiums that buy and present non-network programming, reach millions of homes nationwide with distribution systems that compete with the networks; pay TV, an apparent financial success in its few trials; and videocassettes and in-home playback and recording systems — these innovations mean that the seeker of entertainment and information no longer will be confined by the behavior of network and local broadcasters. The consumer will have many more alternatives. Their availability, in turn, will stimulate new sources to supply them. To some degree, television will come to more closely approximate book and magazine publishing in satisfying a variety of tastes and nurturing interests found among the few while in other ways maintaining its status as a mass medium for a mass audience. Even so, the step from technological capability to widespread actuality will be a long, and in some ways, a slow one. The disappearance of network television by the end of the 1990s was predicted in the late 1970s and early 1980s. Such prophecy has proved premature. The increased cost to the consumer of alternatives coupled with the high cost of producing quality programming place a ceiling on the extent to which television can deliver programming other than by broadcasting to mass audiences. We would be quite mad to think that the new technology means the end of television as we have known it, and madder still to believe that television's impact will be lessened by innovations that in fact make the tube more appealing. What we look forward to is not revolution but evolution.

Note

1. As long as there were some cigarette commercials on the air, anti-smoking PSAs also would have to be broadcast. The tobacco industry would have found it difficult to restrain cigarette advertising without risking violation of the antitrust statutes on the grounds of collusion. If one company used television, others would feel it necessary to do so. Thus, the legislation achieved by law what otherwise would have been prohibited by law. A victory for health and consumer groups also was a victory for their opponent, for the federal ban brought about what the opponent sought in the circumstances — a reduction in anti-smoking PSAs.

2

The TV Experience

There is no more clearly documented way in which television has altered American life than in the expenditure of time. It has not only changed the way the hours of the day are spent, but the choices available for the disposal of those hours. In doing so, television has brought the age of the mass media to maturity.

For a brief time when television was a novelty, people thought they would cluster around the set and give it their full and continuing attention. This did not come to be so. Rapt attention, of course, is hardly unknown. Nevertheless, "television viewing" as measured in hours and minutes means something quite different. It is an experience that, while sharing much with consumption of other media, also has a claim to being unique.

In the early 1960s, advertising researcher Charles Allen (1965) placed time-lapse movie cameras in 100 homes in Kansas and Oklahoma and took about a million photos at the rate of four per second. About 10 years later, Robert Bechtel again continuously monitored people watching television (Bechtel, Achelpohl, & Akers, 1972). This time, video cameras relayed their images to constantly-manned mobile units parked in the yards of 20 Kansas City families, and cameras simultaneously recorded (a) behavior in front of the screen and (b) what was on the screen.

Allen found that for about a fifth of the time, the set entertained an empty room. For another fifth of the time, whoever was in the room was not looking at the set. He reported that children "eat, drink, dress and undress, play [and] fight . . . in front of the set" and that adults "eat, drink, sleep, play, argue, fight, and occasionally make love . . . " Bechtel and colleagues observed similar divided attention, ranging from doing housework to reading to dancing while watching television. Some people mimicked what they saw.

Surveys in the United States and abroad that have asked people to recall what they did while watching television also make it clear that the metaphor of a theater in the home does not fit television. Most often it is housework of one kind or another — washing, ironing, cleaning, and cooking — that accompanies viewing, but there is also plenty of talking, eating, and other activities.

The Kansas City films by Bechtel of people in their living rooms not only documented that television often plays to an indifferent house, but that attention varies with what is shown. Attention wavered most for four categories of programming:

- Commercials
- Sports
- News
- Daytime soap operas

It was decidedly most constant for movies, with children's programs and suspense tales scoring somewhat better than the remaining categories: religious, family, game, and talk shows. Because there is no obvious reason to expect that attention would vary consistently by program category, the range of attention can be said to be substantial — from between 55% to 60% of program time for the four categories receiving the least attention to 76% for movies. In fact, one might argue that sports, news, and daytime soap operas should be among the highest in attention scores because their viewers ostensibly are dedicated fans.

The explanation is that the four least-viewed categories are episodic, highly familiar in format, and comprehension seldom depends on having *seen* what has just occurred. Commercials, sports, and news consist of independent episodes; soap operas are produced so that whole episodes, much less portions, can be missed without losing track of the plot. Commercials have a high degree of redundancy because they are certain to be aired again or to have been seen before. Sports, news, and soap operas have similar if somewhat less strong aspects of redundancy, for nothing that is shown probably cannot be experienced at another moment (the replay), in another source (the sports news, or a competing news show), or at another time (the next episode). All four can be readily followed by audio alone. Movies, in contrast, have sequential plots and vary much more within formats so that viewer familiarity in advance is comparatively low (although high enough for the members of these families to ignore the screen one-fourth of the time), and the visual is often more important or even crucial. Children's programs, because of their fast action and the naivete of the child audience, and suspense tales, because they consist of climactic incidents to whose enjoyment the viewer is led by following what came before, similarly claim higher than average attention. What emerges is a principle of television consumption: Attention rises and falls with the need to understand what will come next.

Finally, the fact that commercials have about the same appeal as sports, news, and soap operas deserves comment. Given the frequent criticism of commercials over the years for their absurdity, banality, consumption of program time, stereotyping, and venality, one might expect them to fall far below other categories in attention. That this is not the case hints at two other principles for which we will find some support later: Public opinion about television is not a particularly strong predictor of television consumption, and television is to a sizable degree consumed as a medium in blocks of time with moderate variations in attention within those blocks.

Television viewing typically is discontinuous. It is frequently non-exclusive. It is often interrupted. It changes with the type of program. All of these are encompassed in the figures so lucratively vended by the A. C. Nielsen Company.

Viewing versus Monitoring

The "novelty hypothesis" was proposed soon after the advent of the medium, and lingers on despite four decades of failure. People no longer often say that television viewing will decline as the novelty wears off, but offer an alternative version — that it will decline as alternatives become more popular, such as participant sports, hobbies, travel, or cultural and sports events. History has proven and is proving otherwise. What few people in the late 1940s would have predicted has occurred —

television viewing, measured by hours of set use in the average household, has risen steadily.

At the beginning of the 1960s, the figure was slightly less than six hours a day. By the end of the 1970s, it was about seven hours. By the end of the 1980s, about eight hours. These are fall and winter figures; summer viewing is about 15% lighter.

This upward trend has been accompanied by a number of persistent patterns:

- Substantial variations in television consumption by demographic categories.
- The secular (or long-term) convergence of differences in television consumption associated with demographic attributes.
- Differences in television consumption associated with race.

The influence of demographic factors is easy to catalogue and has not changed for four decades. Television viewing is greater among:

- children in the elementary school grades or younger than among teenagers in high school or young adults in college;
- adults age 55-plus than among those ages 18 to 54 (the age breakdowns used by the major audience measurement services);
- adult women than adult men;
- those of all ages socioeconomically less well off; and
- blacks and those of Hispanic background than among whites.

Conversationally, we can say that television, by the measure of exposure, is particularly popular among children, older and elderly adults, the poor and less affluent, and minorities.

These differences demand interpretation. First, several of these categories consist of persons with a greater than average likelihood of being in the vicinity of an operable television set on any day. These include children, women, and the elderly. Second, several consist of persons with a motive for vicarious involvement or an arguable need for information because their firsthand association with others is somewhat limited. These include the elderly (who are less likely to be in the labor force) and women (who are also less likely to be in the labor force or, if elderly, less likely to have obligations outside the household). Third, for some — blacks and those of Hispanic origin — there is arguably an analogous motive to learn about or experience the majority culture. Fourth, several include those for whom leisure options may be restricted — the elderly (by age and income), the less affluent (by education and income), and minorities (by education and income). All of these explanations have a good claim to validity. However, the first is especially important because it represents the influence of a powerful and pervasive factor that enhances not only the understanding of why someone views more or less television, but the very nature of the medium and its role in American society.

What the first represents is time available. If we examine television viewing over the lifespan or among demographic categories, we find that it is greatest where the opportunity to view — or, time available — is greatest. If we examine television viewing during the course of the year, we find it is greatest in the fall and winter when outdoor leisure activities and vacation travel are at a minimum (given the supposedly greater appeal of new programming in fall and winter, what needs to be explained about lower summer viewing is not the discrepancy but why it is so modest). If we examine television viewing during the course of the day, we find that it rises and falls with the availability of the viewer; from the viewer's perspective, time available.

Two eminent British social scientists, Patrick Barwise and Andrew Ehrenberg (1989) who have studied audience behavior in Great Britain, the United States, and many other countries, make clear the crucial importance of time in their examination of several thousand viewers in New York and Los Angeles. Their focus was the degree to which "repeat viewing" occurs — that is, how frequently do persons who view one episode of a series view the next? They found that the average repeat viewing for both programs shown every weekday (Monday through Friday) and those shown weekly was 50%. Some news and some soap operas were somewhat higher in repeat viewing, but by no means overwhelmingly so. They then found that when people were viewing at a given time *they almost always* watched the program they had watched previously in the same time slot. That is, the deficits in repeat viewing were not attributable to shifts in viewer preference or exploration of the choices available, but to non-availability of the viewer. The viewers were elsewhere. Thus, even in the daily schedule, time is a powerful predictor of television viewing. The extraordinary importance of time is perhaps most dramatically made clear by the failure of *Monday Night Football* — by commonsense expectation the focus of a loyal audience of regular viewers — to escape the average deficit in repeat viewing for all programs.

These varied facts lead to some principles of television viewing:

- Viewing is primarily a function of time available in the vicinity of an operable television set.
- Program content will play a large part in choosing what to view, but the predominance of time over program availability means that major changes in the overall television schedule would not affect total audience size much.
- The comparative and frequent (although certainly not invariable) predominance of time over program availability means that the decision to view television typically precedes the decision over what to view.

Television viewing is the reciprocal of obligations, whether they are biological, educational, familial, or voluntary. It is what people do when there is nothing else they must, should, or want to do.

A remarkable aspect of viewing, despite many observable differences among identifiable subgroups of the population, is how much alike so many are. When in 1970 set use was 6.8 hours a day in households whose head had less than one year of college, it was 5.6 hours a day in households headed by someone with more years of schooling (Comstock, Chaffee, Katzman, McCombs, & Roberts, 1978). That is the maximum discrepancy recorded between these two groups. In earlier and later years, the typical discrepancy is less than 45 minutes. Yet, even that 1.2 hours, substantial as it is both absolutely and as a proportion, does not constitute two different worlds, but varying degrees of a common experience. And, as we shall see, what people choose to view is much more alike than one would guess from differences in their backgrounds and in what they think and say about television.

Television viewing always has been greater among those lower in socioeconomic status, with education making a greater difference than income. Education means many things, including more imagination in disposing of time and greater capacity to exercise that imagination. The term "book culture" was employed by the sociologist Rolf Meyersohn (1965) to describe the cultural allegiance of the better-educated which left them, in its earlier years, less interested in television. By the end of the 1970s, this socioeconomic difference appeared to be lessening. Television consumption was becoming more similar across socioeconomic strata. Two reasons were that the time available for viewing began to be exhausted among the less educated and the more educated became more accepting of the medium.

Probably no small role has been played in this convergence of consumption by the entry of the first television generation and those succeeding into the legion of the college-educated. These are adults for whom television held none of the ominous qualities that it did for some of their parents. At the same time, we should not think of the greater acceptance of television by those with lower education as reflecting simply a lack of leisure opportunities. Television meant participation in American life, although of a new kind, and viewing among the less educated was greater, not lesser, for those with more hobbies and interests. Thus, it was the comparative absence of conflicting leisure preferences and the greater congeniality of mass audience programming for their tastes and interests that made television more popular among those of lower socioeconomic status. It was not simply greater leisure opportunities that set the better educated apart, but leisure of a particular character — "book culture," and everything that phrase implies.

Blacks and those of Hispanic background would be expected to view more on the average than whites because of the larger proportion of households low in income and education. They do view more. However, at least among blacks, socioeconomic status falls short as an explanation. Far fewer data beyond amount of viewing are available on those of Hispanic background, so we shall speak now only of blacks. What occurs in their case is quite rare. Ordinarily, differences among racial groups are illusory in that they are attributable to differences in socioeconomic status or something else commonly measured, such as rural vs. urban residence. In this case, ethnic background, and not the differences in income and education related to it, are at work.

The facts are simple. Blacks on the average view more than do whites when socioeconomic status is equivalent. Blacks typically have more favorable attitudes toward television. The inverse relationship between education and attitudes favorable to the medium observable among whites does not characterize blacks. Educated blacks tend to be as favorable or more favorable toward television than those less educated. Blacks also have shifted toward using television as a major source of political information more rapidly than have whites.

The explanation almost certainly involves a number of factors operating sometimes independently and sometimes in concert, depending on the individual. The overall result is that blacks think more highly of television than do whites and watch more of it. Unlike whites, greater education is not a sure predictor of more negative attitudes and less viewing among blacks.

There can be no argument that there was not much particularly pertinent to blacks in the available general audience media in the late 1940s and early 1950s. National magazines and local newspapers largely ignored them. Many have argued that the failure of newspapers to cover problems and events within black communities contributed to the urban riots of the 1960s. By being new, television escaped the antipathy toward older national media. By being national, it escaped antipathy toward local media. Television also arrived just in time to give prominent coverage to the civil rights movement. Thus, the medium capitalized on prevailing attitudes and historical events. At the same time, blacks generally were conceivably less imbued with the "book culture" promoted among whites by white-run institutions of higher education; years of education (the social science measure of "education") simply may not have quite meant the same thing for blacks as for whites in this particular respect. Blacks, because of integration, also would have been particularly curious about the white society portrayed on television. Finally, many blacks, because of racial bias as well as economic deprivation, had limited leisure opportunities.

The appeal of television for blacks is somewhat ironic. Except for the news coverage of the civil rights movement in the South, television too largely ignored blacks in the early years. Even in the late 1960s, when the networks adopted policies of greater black exposure in entertainment and commercials, the proportion visible has never been more than trivially or transiently greater than their proportion in the population. That is why the black television audience is a fascinating puzzle requiring a multi-part solution.

Persons of Hispanic background on the average also watch more television than do whites, and probably a somewhat similar set of explanatory factors apply. In any case, the affinity of a minority for the medium aimed at a mass audience is compelling testimony to its ability to develop programming acceptable to everyone. In doing so, in this case, television becomes a symbol and a means by which the mass media take a role in the acculturation of minorities to the majority or dominant culture.

These varied data on audience behavior come chiefly from the various audience measurement services, of which the A. C. Nielsen Company is preeminent. They are not produced for scholarly interest, but to serve the needs of advertisers and the television business in establishing the price to be charged for advertising time. This principal purpose of television audience measurement is far less famous than its byproduct — the ranking of programs so that those not popular enough to command acceptable prices can be cancelled. By occupying the territory so prominently, these services have established the definition of television viewing: Time spent in the vicinity of an operating television set that the individual in question or someone else recording the datum classifies as time spent watching television. The audience measurement services simply obtain electronically from representative samples of households data on the programs or other uses for which sets are in employ and data on which of the occupants of those households are using the television from the occupants themselves.

These self-estimates are in blocks of time, and as the research of Allen (1965) and Bechtel and colleagues (1972) make clear, much of this time is spent not watching television but often doing something else. Television viewing is not analogous to attending a concert, play, or theater movie. As University of Maryland sociologist John Robinson (1977), a foremost student of the way people spend time, has made abundantly clear, estimates of television viewing vary markedly with the means by which they are obtained. "Viewing" is not a fact, but a creation. Estimates based on queries of how much television is viewed on the average day, how much was viewed yesterday, which programs were viewed yesterday, and viewing yesterday by quarter-hour segments all will be different (and typically in descending order) and will differ from those obtained by the audience measurement services.

At first glance, it would seem puzzling that parties with such venal interest would trade with such an inflated and inaccurate metric. The answer is that a substantial degree of inattention is accepted as inherent in the phenomenon of viewing television, and discounts for amount or variation by program category are made subjectively. What is important is that unpopular programs can be discarded (and overall prices protected) and programs ranked (within categories) by popularity (so that prices vary with audience size). Accurate estimates of audience size in conformity with the audience measurement definition of viewing for these purposes are satisfactory; it is irrelevant that an overestimate of attention is implied, since a more accurate estimate would not affect the decisionmaking of those buying and selling the commodity involved — audience attention.

A psychologist at the University of Massachusetts at Amherst, Daniel Anderson (1985), has added to the research of Allen and Bechtel by charting attention by age. His findings:

Age 1 — 10 percent
Age 3 — 50 percent
Age 13 — 80 percent
Adults — 60 percent

He argues that the early, sharp increase represents the increasing ability to understand what is being presented. He is almost certainly correct. We would add that it also represents, because of this understanding, an increasing need to see what has come before in order to comprehend what will come next; in effect, a motive for attention has been created. We would thus interpret the decline among adults as increased mastery of the medium. They are less dependent for comprehension on visual attention than those 13 years old.

Anderson, along with psychologists Aletha Huston and John Wright (1989) at the University of Kansas, have found that audio plays a large role in viewer behavior. Children quickly learn the conventions of television production. Music, sound effects, and sound level signal turns of the plot or the importance of what is being presented. Verbal content provides knowledge of what is portrayed, whether or not the visual portion is attended to. Children shift their attention between television, playthings, and people in accord with these cues. Additional cues are provided when other viewers in the room pay attention. Adults surely behave similarly.

Television is not lightly termed an audio-visual medium. It is the audio portion combined with the ever-continuing programming and free home availability after set purchase that makes possible the peculiar activity called "viewing." An alternative term would be "monitoring," which replaces the attention to the screen that is connoted by "viewing" with the use of cues from a multiplicity of sources to maintain a desired degree of attention to what is being emitted from a television set. It is highly accurate for a great deal of television consumption, and we will understand better the television experience if we think of it as made up at different times and in different circumstances of either viewing or monitoring, but for most viewers most of the time, of monitoring.

Leisure

In the mid-1960s, the Hungarian sociologist Alexander Szalai (1972) conducted an extraordinary investigation of modern times for the United Nations Educational, Social, and Cultural Organization (UNESCO). He directed teams in 12 countries in western and eastern Europe and in the western hemisphere, including the United States, in surveying how men and women in moderate-size cities spent each day. The result is a comparative international portrait of the amounts and proportions of time expended on work, sleep, travel to the job, cooking and eating, child care, mass media, and other activities.

These data, analyzed by Szalai (1972) and the American opinion researchers John Robinson and Philip Converse (1972), reinforce many impressions about the place of television in American life. The principal findings:

- Among the 12 countries, which included France, East and West Germany, Belgium, Yugoslavia, Poland, Hungary, the Soviet Union, Bulgaria, Czechoslovakia, and Peru, Americans were the most likely to view some television during a day. Americans who watched, on the average, viewed for more hours than viewers elsewhere. If Japan had been included, only the Japanese would have outranked Americans in devotion to television.

- In the United States, television was the third greatest consumer of time, behind only sleep and work. These were the top three out of 37 activities exclusive of each other that people described as their primary activity at any given time.

- Television as a primary activity accounted for a full third of all leisure time, and the figure increased to about 40% when viewing described as secondary to some other activity, such as eating, was included.

- Television was first among all leisure activities. Even socializing of all kinds, including conversations at home and away, did not challenge television's domination of free time; it accounted for only about a fourth of leisure. Reading, study, and other use of mass media accounted for only about 15%. Going somewhere and doing something — hunting, hiking, attending the opera, the Washington Redskins — made up only about 5% of leisure.

Television had become the principal component of discretionary life in America.

The UNESCO data also crudely approximate the results of a gigantic experiment, for in many societies television saturation was incomplete and television set owners could be compared to nonowners. The groups otherwise were much alike, and the fact that comparisons could be made across several societies, as if a single experiment were replicated again and again, adds confidence that the results are not happenstance. The principal findings:

- A major effect of television appeared to be reduced sleep. Set owners in these various societies on the average recorded 13 minutes less sleep per night.

Set owners also reported spending less time:

- socializing away from home,
- listening to the radio,
- reading books,
- conversing,
- attending the movies,
- attending religious ceremonies,
- engaging in miscellaneous leisure,
- traveling in behalf of leisure, and
- engaging in household tasks.

Dust mice proliferated; other media suffered.

There was also a marked *increase* in one kind of activity — total time each day devoted to the mass media. Many other media suffered because of television, but the fascination of television itself was enough not merely to compensate for the time drawn from other media, but to move the mass media to a far more central position on the social stage. This is one of the medium's most significant effects. It achieved it immediately upon introduction, and the rise in the daily use of television since then has further increased this new centrality of the media.

Mass Media

The stunning rise of television turned public life newly and sharply toward the mass media. The UNESCO studies estimate that television increased daily attention to the mass media by one full hour. Newspapers, magazines, books, radio — Gutenberg began *his* revolution in the fifteenth century, and Marconi started his at the beginning of the twentieth, but it was with the diffusion of television in mid-century, 500 years after the invention of cast metal type, that the mass media became an occupying invader in everyday life.

Television shrank, destroyed, or changed other media, so that the larger role for the mass media was in fact command seized by television. That new hour spent on the media was spent in television viewing. Given the nature of television, this meant watching more entertainment, more stories and images acceptable to people all over the country with all sorts of backgrounds, and more attention by people to words and pictures and the symbols they constitute that were the same for everybody.

The mass media in the United States will never be what they were before television. Radio once not only held listeners for many more hours a day, but it was a medium resembling television. Huge, heterogeneous audiences tuned to comedy, drama, variety, music, and news programming disseminated by three major networks. Bob Hope is still prominent, but the big stars of those days have faded to nostalgia — The Great Gildersleeve, Amos 'n' Andy, Jack Benny. Radio became a largely local medium with each station aiming at a relatively homogeneous segment of the audience. Appeal is precise — Top 40, progressive rock, jazz, talk, news, foreign language. Critics declare radio for the most part a vendor of music, operating as an adjunct of the record industry. In a big market such as Los Angeles, there is even room for a station dedicated to the music of the big bands, thriving, surviving, and defunct. By adding moving pictures to words, television has replaced radio as the national medium of daily entertainment.

Movies changed, too. The UNESCO studies found that television set owners spent less time at the movies. The motion picture industry found that this was indeed true. By 1970, annual movie attendance was about 19 million, compared with 41 million ten years earlier and 82 million in 1946. Closed theaters sometimes capable of seating several thousand adorned every business district. Movie attendance began to decline before the introduction of television as people turned to other activities — such as spectator sports and pleasure driving — which had been suspended by World War II, yet television made certain that there would be no reversal of the trend. At first, television was a dumping ground for movies that had exhausted their theater audience, but by the 1970s television had become a major source of income for moviemakers through primetime screening of features and made-for-TV movies. Today, theater movies are an important part of American culture and entertainment, and the old theaters have been replaced by complexes housing several theaters, each seating a few hundred people at most, but total annual movie theater admissions are a modest fraction of what they were before television. What permits the movie industry to enjoy record annual revenues is increased admission prices, which are many times greater than what they were in the 1940s.

Television also helped to refashion the American film. By becoming the center of family entertainment, television reduced to comparative insignificance one of the big movie audiences. Yet, by being a home medium, television had to be more restrained in what it dared to show. In the competition between the two media, movies became increasingly more violent and sexually provocative as they sought an audience of teenagers and adults. Television followed in their wake. Violence became a staple of programming. Sexual provocation became progressively more frequent and explicit. The two media took advantage of increasingly liberal public standards, but they also contributed to this permissiveness by what they displayed in their struggle.

The movie industry discovered that a major portion of its post-television audience was made up of teenagers and young adults as older adults on the whole found themselves satisfied with what television could (and in the case of broadcasting theater movies, eventually would) bring them while for young persons, movie-going served social and personal ends — to get out of the house, to get away from family, to be with friends, to date — unmet by television. The result is a dichotomy between the demands placed on these interlocked and seemingly similar media: Television programs seek to be acceptable to everyone to increase their probability of attracting a large enough audience, while movies frequently attempt to be acceptable to 14 year olds to have a chance at attracting a profitable portion of movie-goers.

The magazine business was transformed. At the end of the 1970s, several long-dead giants of earlier decades — *Life, Look,* and the *Saturday Evening Post* — were resurrected, but their editorial ambitions were hesitant and their readerships small compared with pre-television days. Television, as these magazines once did, appeals to a broad range of tastes — the mass audience heterogeneous in makeup. Television reduced the time available for magazine reading and undermined the magazines aiming at a mass audience by taking away advertising revenue. The big four of American general audience magazines — *Life, Look,* and the *Saturday Evening Post,* plus *Collier's* — folded up. The multicolor, full-page spread intended to sell America became the TV commercial. The demise of these magazines made available pocket change and time among consumers. Magazines appealing in depth to narrow tastes — *Gourmet, Yachting, Road and Track, Cosmopolitan, Travel and Leisure* — prospered as readers and advertisers converged on the sharp focus not congenial to television.

Comic books surrendered many of the action- and humor-seeking young readers to television. Sales were 600 million in 1950; 20 years later, with the potential audience vastly expanded by population growth, they were half that. Television supplied the same kind of entertainment in a cheaper, more convenient, and arguably more entrancing manner.

One might expect book publishing to be largely unaffected by television. One must guess again — and it was not only a matter of television consuming time that might be spent reading. One unambiguous effect of television's introduction was to lower per capita library circulation. It is important to notice, however, that of the two major title categories, fiction and nonfiction, only fiction was markedly affected. This is an example of media substitution based on function. Television did not then, and does not now, well serve the many and varied interests that lead people to nonfiction books, although at times it touches on many of them — history, literature, hobbies and crafts, science, computers, and the like. It has always been a medium immersed in fantasy, entertainment, and storytelling, so of course it might reduce demand for another medium dealing in the same content. This dampening effect on similar content in other media was further reflected in the titles favored by book publishers. During television's first two decades, titles of imagination and fantasy — fiction, poetry, and drama — declined from 22% to 13% of all trade books.

Publishers also began to think of television as a means of promotion for books and began to select titles based on their suitability as the topics of talk shows. The novel that becomes famously popular is an ideal servant of two masters, giving the publisher access to television and television talk shows a topic. Equally suited to the medium are books about the body, the mind, possessions, and money. They exploit self-interest and anxiety, and labeled as factual, they give the unimaginative — those who think that a dull account of something that actually happened is more truthful than something made up that is psychologically or sociologically valid — the assurance that there is some truth inside.

The celebration of fame and the passage to an inner circle of personal and material privilege became two preoccupations of television. The materialism and narcissism that seemed to pervade life in the latter part of the century and that was celebrated by such phrases as the "me generation," "self actualization," and the slogan on the license plate frame (arguably most frequently encountered on Porches in California), "In the Game of Life the One Who Has the Most Toys Wins," was partly packaged by television's literary sideline.

New Yorker writer Thomas Whiteside (1981) describes how television has affected the evolution of publishing. Nonfiction is superior to fiction for television promotion because a talk show host can get by with staff briefings on the former, while only reading ordinarily will do for the latter. Thus, publishers favor nonfiction properties. Books by famous people are excellent, but the personal motives of viewers make self-help books by unknowns just as promotable. Whiteside's exemplary title: *Your Erroneous Zones.* Fiction has a chance primarily when the author can talk about the factual or real-world experience behind the work, either that of the author or the characters, or when the novel widely is believed to be based on celebrities or prominent people. In the latter case, the author either can talk about these personages or deny that they are the basis of the story. Either way, the discourse is comprehensible to a mass audience.

Television also has become the model for expanding sales. Whiteside suggests that television and the supermarket are especially "attuned" to one another. In any case, books have come to be marketed in supermarket fashion with chain bookstores accounting for increasing proportions of sales. These stores mimic the audience measurement procedures of television by compiling by computer the equivalents of ratings and shares so that shelf space, future orders, and editorial planning for future endeavors will be in line with expected audience behavior. Finally, the show business package has become common in which television is often one element in a sequential media strategy. The center of the package is a "project," which is the translation of an entertaining idea or concept into concrete form. Whether a book or theater movie, that project becomes the first step in what will be a series of sales promotions. Thus, a hardbound best-seller may be followed by a miniseries, with the release of the paperback timed to coincide with the broadcast of the series. Supermarket paperback racks thus function as billboards for television, and television promotions as sales pitches for the paperback. The made-for-television or theater movie can serve the same function as the miniseries. In still another variant, the initial project may be a miniseries with a coincidental paperback promotion. What distinguishes the show business package from the ordinary promotions of several decades ago is two-fold: (a) its origination in a concept devised artfully and practically for exactly such exploitation (the idea precedes the scheme instead of the book or movie preceding the promotion), and (b) the interrelated, sequential nature of its components. Thus, television has not only become a factor in the selection of which books to publish and a means of book promotion, but a model and participant in the making of books into a truly popular mass medium.

Newspapers at first sometimes refused to print TV schedules for fear of aiding a competitor. They soon learned that television was something people wanted to read about as well as watch. Leo Bogart (1972), careful analyst of trends in media popularity, concluded after two decades of television that daily newspaper circulation had not been seriously affected, although census bureau statistics indicated a small decline in per capita circulation. If circulation was not sharply affected, time spent reading newspapers almost certainly declined. Big-city dailies did fold one after another as people moved to the suburbs after World War II and labor and distribution costs rose, but it was these factors, and not television, that were responsible. New dailies emerged to serve the increasing populations outside the urban cores. Circulation thus increased almost evenly with population growth. Local newspapers could provide information through news and advertising unsuited to the brevity of television news and television commercials.

Nevertheless, television and its technological evolution pose a continuing threat to other activities dependent on disposable time and income, such as newspaper reading. Although circulation was affected only modestly compared with apparent early effects on other media, there are many reasons for concern among newspaper publishers. Per capita circulation has not increased over the years, as one might expect with rising levels of education and the proportion of persons with college degrees. The proportion of households subscribing to more than one newspaper has declined. The time available to peruse the newspaper has been further reduced by increases in television consumption, as well as by competition from other activities for discretionary time, reducing somewhat more, the value to an advertiser of newspaper space. Furthermore, since the mid-1970s, per capita circulation has shown new signs of decline.

In sum, readership in the sense of amount of exposure probably was adversely affected early, but not enough to affect circulation markedly. Circulation probably did not grow as it would have in the absence of television, but it did remain stable. There were greater inroads on readership as television viewing increased, and finally circulation appeared more clearly to be adversely affected. Newspapers remain valuable properties, and in some instances, circulations are enormous. Nevertheless, while not an endangered species, as a business, they are engaged in long-range contention to maintain their share of the media market dollar.

The character and content of print media have changed in their attempts to compete with television. Media are adaptable and malleable. When the mix changes, so too do the individual components. One example is the asymmetrical coverage of television by newspapers and magazines. Television has become news to the print media; print media only makes news on television with big stories, exclusives, and scoops. Television is accepted as part of the environment on which the media, all media, are to provide surveillance; print media are not. The striking fact is the extraordinary amount of attention that the print media give to television. Familiarity has obfuscated its scope. For example, the two pages that the typical newspaper devotes daily to television, rivals the space given to editorials and commentary, often equals or exceeds the coverage given to business exclusive of stock market statistics, and equals a third or more of daily sports coverage. The most prominent example of print media coverage of television is the magazine whose sole justification is that medium, *TV Guide.* Its weekly circulation of 22 million is the largest of any periodical in the United States.

People and *Us* early represented the transubstantiation of the sensibility, topics, and people of the television talk show into print: brief treatment; no demand on sustained attention; the famous or prominent, especially those from entertainment; an emphasis on personal experience; and the verities of sex, success, wealth, and eccentricities. The captions and headlines take the place of the talk show host's opening sally, the text substitutes for the conversation, and the photos are the screen stilled. The most prominent recent instance is certainly *USA Today.* This national newspaper — which covers events, lifestyles, money, and sports — is modelled after television news, with stories that almost never require more time to read than that displaced by the average television news item (about one and a half minutes) and graphics that substitute for film footage. The cycle became complete in the late 1980s when *USA Today* syndicated *USA Today: The Television Show,* a nightly news summary with a four-focus format: life, money, sports, and "U.S.A."

There are many other ways in which television was additive or subtractive in regard not only to media, but to other leisure alternatives. Television adversely affected some activities as it did some media, but it also drew attention to and enshrined others. The nightly entertainment at home and coverage of glamorous sports events turned the minor league diamonds ghostly, with attendance falling from 42 million in 1949 to 10 million 20 years later (Bogart, 1972). Other sports gained. Professional football became so popular that Congress was called upon to mandate the televising of games once a sell-out was assured, and television created a new national holiday with the "Super Bowl."

The many changes in media popularity and character occurring during the first four decades of television can be looked upon as cultural change imposed by transactions involving the attention of audiences. Television changed radio, movies, and magazines by changing the behavior of audiences. The new behavior brought about by television at first resulted in deficits in attention to other media. Some deficits were permanent. Examples include comic book reading, movie theater attendance, and total amount of radio listening. But this new behavior also created opportunities by changing conditions under which media entrepreneurs competed. Specialized magazines found audiences profitably large because television is not economically viable when aimed at a narrow audience, and when directed at a mass audience, it fails to serve the needs and interests of subgroups. In some instances, deficits were transient because other factors — such as increasing affluence and rising levels of education — were increasing audience size. Book publishing and libraries, for example, have not only done well in a television society, they have flourished, with increasing per capita figures over the past four decades. While time spent reading almost certainly has been suppressed by television — it would be considerably greater in the absence of the medium — the magazine business has prospered. An analogous claim can be made for radio; despite the suppression by television of time spent in radio listening, radio has prospered with formats compatible with the television-dominated mix of media. The character of media enterprises was changed, but they were not destroyed.

When an old medium is wholly or partially replaced by a new medium and when that can be attributed to public preference for the new medium as serving the functions of the old medium in ways either less expensive or more satisfying, the process is called "functional displacement." This is clearly what occurred with radio, comic books, and to stretch the concept of a medium, minor league baseball, and to a lesser degree with general audience magazines. When it can be attributed to such extrinsic factors as the drawing away of advertising revenues, which figured importantly in the demise of general audience magazines, or the geographical movement of the audience along with rising labor costs, as occurred with major urban newspapers, the process calls for another label, "economic and market forces." What usually accompanies either of these is a third phenomenon, in which the media transform themselves in order to survive. This process could aptly be called the "repositioning of functions."

The overall result of these three processes has not been uniform replacement of other media by television, but the creation of an environment in which many media are represented. Theodore Caplow of the University of Virginia and his sociological colleagues make this very clear in their return in the mid-1970s to the community that had served as the subject of famous examinations of American social patterns in the 1920s and 1930s by Robert and Helen Lynd in *Middletown* (1929) and *Middletown in Transition* (1937). Caplow and colleagues (Caplow, Bahr, Chadwick, Hill, & Williamson, 1982) write of "the intrusion of the media" but actually describe a remarkable accommodation to all the media can offer. Television broadcasting began in 1946 with two hours a day on a single station. By 1975, five stations were available from broadcast and four by cable. Demographics and amount of consumption were similar to those of the nation; so, too, was the practice of doing other things, such as housework, while ostensibly "viewing" television. Motion picture theater attendance was adversely affected, but by 1975, the actual number of theaters, and thus the variety of offerings, had increased. Compared with 1925 and 1935, newspaper circulation appeared to have increased. Diversity of coverage was greatly increased by the availability of out-of-town papers. Per capita library circulation remained unchanged, but with fewer card holders taking out more books. By 1975, in accord with a television effect, nonfiction had come to account for a higher proportion of books circulated. Book reading clearly increased markedly, however, since in 1975 there were numerous outlets for book sales while in 1925 and 1935 reading largely had been confined to library books.

Any further increase in television set use attributable to the greater variety of offerings made available by cable, additional pay options, and in-home recording and playback will impose a further curtailment on time. The greater ability of cable to reach small, selected audiences on behalf of local advertisers may undercut the revenues on which newspapers depend. Book publishers and book clubs may find the world one of scarcity in the coming years. The profitable pop novels about life at the top, espionage capers, and sweeping moments of history are precisely the subjects most suitable to miniseries and made-for-television movies, to which the networks are increasingly likely to turn to win audiences attractive to advertisers. Even more threatening is the competition from cable, pay options, and VCRs. They essentially package the same vicarious excitation as best-selling fiction and extract fees for access that can only reduce the amount of money available for expenditure for the same type of diversion from print sources.

Television, by directing attention, has become an arbiter of the success of others. When television draws attention to something far better than what is at hand in real life, the real life suffers. Live, minor league baseball could not compete. When it draws attention to something of which people might want more, real life benefits. In England, for example, television apparently markedly increased attendance for horse racing, horse jumping, and major soccer confrontations by making these events newly important to the public. The same thing occurs repeatedly not only with sports, but with the rest of that 5% of leisure that is devoted to doing something or going someplace — culture, live entertainment, the outdoors.

With sports, however, television has established an uneasy symbiosis. It guarantees some financial success from the fees paid for televising the event. Conceivably, it could be the architect of greater popularity. Nevertheless, it also can destroy a sport by exhausting public interest. Professional boxing presents a cyclical example. In its early days, the televising of major bouts drew attention to the sport and helped make such fighters as Floyd Patterson widely popular. By presenting nationally ranked fighters, it also sharply reduced attendance for local bouts. As a result, boxing withered and disappeared from the television screen. The dramatic championship confrontations of Mohammed Ali demonstrated that there was a latent market for spectacles by their closed circuit popularity. Broadcast television soon readopted boxing as a staple, but now it became a sport at the national level dependent not on live attendance but on dissemination by various forms of television.

Colleges now consider televised sports synonymous with endowments and alumni gifts as sources of income. College as well as professional sports and the medium have thus entered into a never-ending nervous dance. Every televised basketball, football, or other sports encounter brings many thousands of dollars to the participating schools. The revenues for bowl or championship encounters range into the millions of dollars. The talented college athlete, the effective coach, and the successful athletic program because of television have become one of the major financial assets of American educational institutions. Television, in effect, has helped to professionalize college athletics in behalf of the economic welfare of American education.

Most people, if asked how television viewing affects their lives, would say that it seldom interferes with anything important. They would be wrong. Sleep, social interaction, and reading would be said to be unimportant by few, yet they have been reduced by television. Television has also severely altered the available options for the expenditure of time. Increasing set use implies more, not less, of these kinds of influence.

What the Public Thinks

Television occupies an ambiguous place in the American mind. It increasingly has gained attention over the years. This is so whether the measure is what's in other media, what's on people's minds, or what people are doing with their time. Nevertheless, television has fallen in expressed public esteem. People watch more but think less highly of it. Those who criticize it apparently often fail to act in accord with their words. Television thus holds its detractors in the same spell as its fans.

In 1963, Gary Steiner conducted a wide-ranging examination of public opinion about television, drawing on two-hour interviews with a representative national sample of about 2,400 adults and more in-depth study of a few hundred adults in a single city. In 1970 and again in 1980, Robert Bower (1973, 1985) did much the same thing. These three sets of data, reflecting opinion across three decades, are landmarks in the understanding of public opinion about television. However, because the media constantly seek information about themselves to better their market positions and because scholars frequently have inquired into public response to the media, these data are only the core of a wide range of evidence from which we can draw conclusions.

Foremost of these is that the data at times appear to be in conflict. This is a vital point, because it implies (a) that many conclusions must explain apparently contrary information, and (b) that the contrariness of the information may, itself, be highly informative.

The public by any absolute measure remains very favorable toward television. A sizable majority of the public will endorse television as interesting, exciting, informative, wonderful, and imaginative. About half concur that it is "generally excellent." And again, about half will say it is getting better — a figure that takes on a cheerier cast when it is placed beside those for radio, which is about two-thirds as great, and for newspapers and magazines, which are only about a third as great.

Nevertheless, there has been a definite decline in public satisfaction since 1960. Fewer people will endorse such statements today. Increasing numbers believe that television is getting worse. With each passing decade, the expression of public opinion favorable to television has declined.

This shift is not as incongruous with the upward trend in hours of television consumed per day as it first appears to be. Television's ubiquity may have encouraged a few to be more stringent in what they demand. More importantly, the increase in consumption represents changing norms about the acceptability of television viewing. Turning on the set, whatever the hour, has become more frequently the equivalent of switching on the lights. As the public with each passing year increasingly has accepted television as a constant glow in the household, it also has become more jaded about it. There is an important lesson here, and it is that public opinion about the media is a very poor predictor of the public's consumption of them.

The change in the status of the medium, from forefront to background, is exemplified by the motives the public declares for viewing. A decade later, about the same proportions as in 1960 would declare that they viewed television to enjoy a favorite program, to see something they considered special, just to watch television, or to learn something. Far fewer designated television as "a pleasant way to spend an evening" (Bower, 1973). Over the years, television has become less often the nightly focus of life and more a medium of passive acceptance. In fact, "the acceptance medium" describes its place in American life quite well.

The fluctuating ratings and the enormous audiences occasionally assembled for spectacular presentations would seem to belie the notion that many people simply watch television without much regard for what they are watching, but this is precisely what takes place. In recognition of this fact, broadcasters have applied the phrase "least objectionable programming" to the most popular offering at any hour. Of course, there is extensive selectivity as viewers attempt to find the most acceptable program once they are watching. The harsh competition among broadcasters would be justified, even if only a small proportion of viewers could be diverted from one program to another, for a single point in the ratings represents several million viewers and a substantial difference in what advertisers can be charged. Nevertheless, a very sizable proportion of the audience at any given time on a typical evening watches a program because it appears on the channel to which the set already is tuned or because someone else in the household desires to watch the program. About three or four out of every 10 viewers admit to such indifference. The broadcasters exercise canniness in thinking about audience flow and the funneling of viewers from a popular program to subsequent offerings, but their success rests on dividing, not increasing, the spoils. Typically, television is consumed as a medium and the decision to view ordinarily takes precedence over the selection of what to view. Total audience size depends on the first; network and station success on the second.

Despite its inclination to offer itself passively to television, the public places a positive value on its viewing. When asked to explain the reasons for their viewing the night before, a large majority will advance reasons positive in tone, such as "to be entertained," "to be diverted," and "to relax." Very few will offer a derogatory phrase such as "to kill time." Yet there is not much enthusiasm. In such querying of the public, about four out of five viewers will assert that they liked what they saw, but only about half as many will designate what they saw as "really worth watching." Nor, as the filming of viewers in their homes indicates, do they give close attention to what they view. About a fourth of those who say they watched a program will confess to not following it from beginning to end, and about a third the next day will be unable to give an accurate account of what transpired. Television is a medium accorded not only high acceptance but great indifference (Bechtel et al., 1972; LoScuito, 1972; Robinson, 1972a, 1972b).

Despite the degree of passivity associated with viewing, the public discriminates not only enough to produce the well-known volatility in programming popularity that makes American television what it is, but also reacts quite differently to the programs it watches. Roderic Gorney, a Los Angeles psychiatrist, and his colleagues David Loye and Gary Steele (Loye, Gorney, & Steele, 1977) assessed the psychological rewards that subscribers to a cable television system believed they received from programs they agreed to watch. They found that the extent to which programs were judged as satisfying or arousing in regard to intellectual, emotional, aesthetic, or moral reward varied greatly, as did the degree to which they were said to be arousing or satisfying as entertainment. J. Mallory Wober (1988), the British social psychologist, reaches a similar pair of obvious and nonobvious conclusions: Large and small audiences may be equal in their degrees of appreciation for the program viewed (obvious), and audiences of about equal size may differ greatly in the degree of appreciation (nonobvious). The latter occurs because people do not have rigid or absolute but only comparative standards about what is acceptable so that viewing may be accompanied by a comparatively low level of appreciation.

The widespread passivity also does not imply a homogeneous reaction to programming. Not only does amount of viewing differ by socioeconomic status, sex, age, and ethnicity, but the audience consists of various groups distinguishable by somewhat different interests. Ronald Frank and Marshall Greenberg (1980), two marketing researchers, analyzed the interests, characteristics, and viewing behavior of a sample of about 2,500 Americans 13 years of age or older. They found that it was possible to identify 14 nonoverlapping mini-audiences on the basis of interests held in common by their members. These mini-audiences varied markedly from one another in demographic makeup and in media consumption. Among the 14, there were three consisting predominantly of adult men, four consisting predominantly of adult women, three representing young adults and adolescents (one male, two female), and four evenly balanced between men and women. Each could be said to have a distinctive set not only of interests but of needs and lifestyles, and these together were reflected in differences in both amounts and types of programs viewed. For example:

- *Adult Male,* "Mechanics and Outdoor Life." Consists almost wholly (96%) of young males (average age, 29). Usually blue-collar workers. Interested in activities not directly competitive with others, but have high needs for escape and creative accomplishment. Camp, fish, and repair autos. View sports less frequently than the average viewer. Above average in viewing programming that features heroes who triumph — science fiction, adventure, crime, and movies.

- *Adult Women,* "Family Integrated Activities." Consists largely (87%) of women in the prime of life (average age, 35). Frequently have young children. Give high priority to activities involving the family. Seek out television that parents and children can view together, and use television to enrich relationships between parents and children.

- *Young Adult/Adolescent,* "Competitive Sports and Science/Engineering." Consists almost wholly (95%) of males (average age, 22). Interested in mechanics, competitive athletics, and personal accomplishment. Above average in the viewing of sports, cartoons, science fiction, and situation comedies. Favor programs that portray conflicts between young persons and parents and other authority figures lightly and with sympathy for the young persons; avoid programs with intellectual or cultural content or strong female figures.

- *Young Adult/Adolescent,* "Indoor Games and Social Activities." Consists almost wholly (91%) of young females (average age, 22). Comparatively low socioeconomic status. High needs to enhance status and to be socially involved with others. Enjoy indoor games. Low interest in most subjects. Above average in viewing of youth-directed programs, daytime game shows, soap operas, and situation comedies. Avoid news, talk shows, documentaries, education, and culture.

These mini-audiences are constructed on the psychological dimension of interests expressed by their members. The fact that the audience can be segmented in this way has *two* major implications. The first is that demographics and interests are two complementary ways of looking at factors that predict media consumption. This is made clear by the strong relationships between those clusters and the sex and age of their members. The second is that the immense audiences that are assembled for popular television programs are not at all homogeneous but coalitions of audience segments that differ in many ways among themselves. This is made clear by the size of these mini-audiences, which each represents only between 4% and 10% of the population so that a popular program must draw significantly from several.

The Frank and Greenberg data do not simply provide a somewhat different way of looking at the television audience. They also provide a sense of why television is unique and why programming for the mass audience involves a certain genius. Primetime television programming is designed to appeal to people who might not seem to have much in common. Daytime programming has a much larger female than male audience, and sports attracts decidedly more males than females. To be a primetime success, a program must draw from a diversity of segments within the larger audience. It can do so by having some element that appeals strongly to everyone, or by having several elements, each of which appeals strongly to some segment while remaining acceptable to other segments. Neither is easily achieved.

Since the first days of commercial television in the United States, better-educated viewers have been more critical toward the medium. Favorable opinions, as well as viewing itself, have been inversely related to socioeconomic status. As television has become more firmly established as part of American life, the differences in viewing have become less pronounced. Attitudes have not so clearly converged. However, the in-depth studies of viewers in selected cities by Steiner (1963) and Bower (1973, 1985) repeatedly demonstrate that what better-educated viewers say is not reflected in what they do. Better-educated viewers will declare that they want more informational programming and entertainment of greater seriousness and cultural quality, but when the categories of programs they choose to view are matched against the choices of those with less education, there is little discernible difference. Education makes little difference in the *way* viewing is divided between popular entertainment and news, information, and culture. The better educated *say* they want more of the latter categories, but they do not devote proportionately more of their viewing to them. They do view less television overall and are somewhat more likely to watch public television, but as a group they do not differ much from those with lesser education in the degree to which popular entertainment is predominant in their viewing. This finding was so startling when it was first reported in the 1960s that it won for Steiner an entry — the only one occupied by a researcher — in Les Brown's *The New York Times Encyclopedia of Television* (1977).

Of course, education and other differences in background shape tastes and preferences in television programming, as the Frank and Greenberg analysis (1980) of mini-audiences documents. Nevertheless, what is least objectionable to the lesser educated often will be least objectionable to the better educated so that differences in underlying preferences may not be observable in viewing habits. The big story is not the obvious one that tastes and preferences will differ somewhat in accord with individual characteristics, but that popular entertainment is as paramount in the television consumption of the better educated as it is in that of the less educated despite what the better educated have to say about television.

People have many complaints about television. Every time survey respondents rate television to some degree as uninteresting rather than interesting, dull rather than exciting, not informative rather than informative, terrible rather than wonderful, not imaginative rather than imaginative, or generally bad rather than generally good, they are registering a complaint. Over the years, however, two topics consistently have been the target of complaints, and they are accompanied by a third focus of disquiet that is better called a concern, rather than a complaint.

The first two are the televising of commercials and the televising of material perceived as unsuitable for children (Bower, 1985). About three-fourths of the public believes that there are too many commercials. About two-thirds thinks that commercials are too long. More than half thinks commercials are in poor taste or annoying. About half the public believes children see things they shouldn't. At the top of the list of complaints, cited by more than a third of the public, are violence, horror, and crime. Next, cited by about one out of six adults, are sexually suggestive or provocative portrayals. About half the public accepts the view that portrayals of aggressive and criminal behavior may encourage young viewers to act likewise.

The concern is the attractiveness of television to children. About a third of the public believes that television may keep children from doing things that would be good for them. More specifically, they believe that watching television "a lot" compared with "very little" is strongly associated with not reading books, doing poorly in school, not growing up as a "better all-around person," being in poorer health, and getting into trouble.

These objections are cancelled as sources of widespread disaffection by attitudes concurrently held by the public. Almost two-thirds also subscribe to the view that commercials are a "fair price" to pay for "free" entertainment, and support for the concept of advertising as a means of financing entertainment has shown no signs of declining over the decades. Those who oppose, for various reasons, advertising directed at children on programming designed for them apparently have been successful in arousing public opinion. A majority of the public, when asked, concur that advertising to very young children and the advertising of heavily-sugared products should be banned or restricted, and that the proportion of time allotted to commercials on children's programming should be reduced. But comparatively few believe that commercials should be banned entirely from children's television.

About two-thirds subscribe to the view that children are "better off" with than without television. When asked about the advantages television provides children, three out of four adults believe that television has educational advantages for children, with only about 20% citing as an advantage the entertainment it provides and only about 10% citing its function as a babysitter. The public believes that watching television "a lot" compared with "very little" is strongly associated with being better informed about world events. While the degree of favorability in these respects as in others has declined over the past decades, these attitudes counterbalance or nullify many complaints, criticisms, and concerns the public has about the role of television in the lives of children.

If behavioral disposition toward television is high in acceptance but low in personal involvement, and attitudinal disposition is favorable but lacking in intensity, then the cognitive activity that accompanies viewing may be said to be frequently low or absent, medium- and not topic-dominated, and much alike for all social strata. This is apart, of course, from the near-autonomic mental activity with its continual drawing of inferences that constitutes monitoring so that the viewing mode may be adopted when cues indicate that it is called for.

These conclusions, which require some explanation, derive from the research of a sociologist at the Massachusetts Institute of Technology, W. Russell Neuman (1982). He decided to investigate not what people think about television, or how they go about viewing, but what they think about while viewing. He focused on the differences that education might make in such cognitive activity in response to television, and he offered three hypotheses:

- *Cultural experience.* Cognitive activity would be positively related to education, which would be in accord with the frequently observed phenomenon that better educated people make more mentally of whatever experiences they have.

- *Polarization.* Cognitive activity would be negatively related to education, which would be in accord with the character of mass audience programming in which the less educated might find more of interest and meaning.

- *Homogenization.* Cognitive activity would be unrelated to education, which is in accord with the medium's goal of wide acceptance.

Neuman interrupted the viewing of everyday television programs with an interview that asked people what they were thinking about while viewing, and went on to probe for more specifics. The results are fascinating:

- About one-fourth replied that they were thinking of *nothing:*
  "my mind was quite blank."
  "A show like this gives me a chance to rest my mind. . ."
  "What thoughts — nothing, nothing really. I was just waiting, you know, for the comedy to happen."

- When the thoughts were divided into *analytic* responses about the program as television (plots, pace, comparisons with other programs, scripts, formulas, production, editing, etc.) versus *interpretive* responses about the implications of the program for real life (political, moral, or religious meaning; relevance to social problems; impact on self and others; intent, motivations behind the program), the analytic responses far outnumbered the interpretive responses.

- For the general population, with education ranging from a college degree down through less than high school, cognitive activity was unrelated to education.

- Only when an elite sample of humanities professors was added to the analysis did education make a difference — these professors generated far more thoughts than the general population sample, but their thoughts, too, were predominantly of the analytic sort.

In sum, cognitive activity while viewing apparently is not very great and for a sizable number of viewers, it is nil. When thoughts were generated, they were far more often about the nature and quality of television than about what it might mean or might imply about the external world. For the general population, television was homogenizing, with all strata responding in a similar fashion despite the educational and experiential gulf that would separate those with a college degree from those who never completed high school. Only the very highly educated sample of professors generated more thoughts, and even they responded more in regard to the quality of television than to its meaning or real life implications. Television for all strata is the provender of escapist, undemanding entertainment, and among all strata, people respond to it as having more relevance to itself than to the external world. Television thus has successfully set the terms for the place it occupies in American society.

The fact is that the public is satisfied with television much as it is. It will endorse various complaints, but it also will endorse views that imply reform is unnecessary. People are inarticulate and unsure of what they want from entertainment until they experience something of which they can say they want more. The public does not place television in any respect high on its agenda of concern. War, unemployment, crime, and similar topics occupy the public but not the media.

It is important to distinguish here between volunteered and elicited opinion. Opinion is volunteered in response to open-ended questions, such as "What are some of the major problems facing the world . . . the nation . . . your community today?" The topics cited as taking precedence over the media represent volunteered opinion. Elicited opinion is the response to such forced choice queries as, "Do you think there is too much violence on television? Agree. Disagree. No opinion." In various surveys over the years, between half and three-fourths of the public have agreed with such a query about television violence. When asked to volunteer topics of concern, not enough people have ever named media violence for it to appear on such an agenda. Television and other media have never obtained a sufficient frequency of response in volunteered opinion as a subject of concern for any percentages to be recorded. Public opinion about television and other media is constituted solely by elicited opinion. The quality of vicarious experience may be paramount to those who create or criticize it, but not to its consumers. The media thus are low in salience as public issues. That the public will nod approval to criticisms of television means that sporadically the few who do care can marshal public opinion, but the conflicting sentiments and indifference of the public also mean that such opinion has no lasting force.

Such an interpretation is strongly supported by the survey conducted by The Roper Organization under sponsorship of the National Broadcasting Company in the early 1980s. Roper (1981b) showed cards each with the name of one of 17 television programs on them to a representative national sample, and asked the respondents what they liked or disliked about the programs. The outcome was volunteered complaints and objections. Sixteen of the programs had been the targets of complaints about "sex and violence" by fundamentalist religious groups and others; the remaining one was *Little House on the Prairie,* about which there presumably would be no such concern and which thereby would provide a baseline of minimal displeasure. Despite the fact that The Roper Organization itself had recorded about 50% of the public replying "agree" when asked if there was too much violence on television, and that other surveys had recorded as many as three-fourths of the public agreeing that there was too much violence and too much sex or that such television content was a serious problem, the highest recorded volunteered figures in this case were 13 and 10% (for violence on *The Dukes of Hazard* and sex on *Dallas,* respectively). The rest were far below that, with the figure for violence 3% or less for 14 programs, and for sex, 5% or less for 11 programs.

In the same survey, Roper also measured fundamentalist religious orientation by a battery of eight agree-disagree items such as, "You were 'born again' — a turning point in your life when you committed yourself to Christ," or "Speaking the word of God to save souls is far more important than leading a good, honest life and helping others." About one-fourth of the public concurred with none, and were categorized as "zero" in fundamentalist orientation. About half concurred with between one and three, and were categorized as "low." About a fifth concurred with between four and six, and were categorized as "high." About 5% concurred with seven or all eight, and were categorized as "very high." The data make it clear that fundamentalist religious orientation is strongly related to objections to media content. The figures for objection to sex on *Dallas* are typical:

- Zero and low, 6%.
- High, 14%.
- Very high, 25%.

Such an orientation is also strongly related to attitudes on social and communications issues, with those high or very high in fundamentalism decidedly more likely to oppose the women's Equal Rights Amendment; to oppose abortion; to favor regulation of the press; to believe that values, ideas, and life-styles of which they do not approve should not be dealt with on television; and to feel that books covering topics of which they disapprove should not be in libraries. As one would expect, such views were most frequent among those very high in fundamentalist orientation.

However, when the behavior and opinions of those very high in fundamentalism were examined, a paradox occurred. Fully one-third had watched *Dallas* in the past month, and one-fourth rated it as their "favorite" or "very good." Only one-fifth thought it was "unsuitable for anyone." That exemplar of secular humanism, *M*A*S*H,* had been watched by 61%, was rated as "favorite" or "very good" by 48%, and was labelled "unsuitable for anyone" by only 6%.

These data offer important lessons beyond differences in volunteered and elicited opinion. They indicate that the media can be better defended by referring to specific instances — this program, that newscast — than in broad terms because people may hold opinions about the media in general that they do not readily apply to specific offerings. These findings suggest that violence and sex on television are not truly salient issues. They also document that while opinions about the media are broadly consistent with basic beliefs and opinions on social issues, behavior, while not necessarily unrelated at the aggregate level, often operates independently. Substantial proportions watched and approved of programs which their religious convictions suggest they should condemn or avoid.

The important implication is that television boycotts have little chance of success through affecting consumption. With television time-dominated and viewed primarily as a consequence of opportunity, and choice among programs at a given time almost always the same, decisions about suitability already have been incorporated in viewing decisions. Those who consider a program unsuitable for viewing already will be absent from the audience. Those who think otherwise will view that program if it is preferable to alternatives, and will continue to do so whenever they are viewing television at that time. One would hardly expect people not to view at all or to change their choice because of outside direction. When boycotts or their threat have some effect, it is generally not through changing audience behavior but because of the fearfulness of advertisers over possible adverse effects on sales or the desire of broadcasters to avoid confrontation or controversy.

3

Evolution Not Revolution

The paradigm that is the basis of American television is likely to remain essentially the same and to a large degree so too will television. As the emphases of the paradigm shift, television will change somewhat. The deregulatory 1980s is an example when compared with the more stringent atmosphere of preceding decades. Yet even such changes affect the way the television business is conducted far more than they affect the medium as attended to by the viewer. While the paradigm is a force for continuity, there are events and trends that make change in the medium inevitable. There have been continual changes in programming as television has responded to public tastes, adopted new formats, through audience measurement discarded less popular programs, and discovered its particular strengths. Beyond these changes, which can be charted by era and season, there are three principal spheres where changes in television can be observed. They are its audiences, the technologies on which it is dependent, and the behavior of the television industry.

Audiences

Two major changes already have been recorded. The amount of viewing per day (or per week or month or year) that people engage in has increased steadily (although there certainly have been occasions when there has been a drop in averages from one year to the next), and the evaluation of television by the public (measured by the phrases or statements chosen to describe it) has declined steadily. These can be further elaborated and others catalogued in regard to three different types of changes in the audience: (a) life-cycle, (b) generational, and (c) secular, or long-term.

The concept of life-cycle changes in the television audience was introduced by the sociologist Robert Bower whose most recent report on trends appeared in 1985, *The Changing Television Audience in America.* Of course, they had long been observed in regard to amount of viewing. Audience measurement data from the A. C. Nielsen Company and other sources present a fairly stable pattern over the years:

- Viewing that is "purposive, selective, and systematic" — a phrase turned by the University of Washington psychologist Andrew Meltzoff (1988) to capture the essence of television exposure — begins between ages two and three, quickly becomes substantial in amount, and remains so throughout the elementary school years. Nielsen data put the figure for ages 2-11 at between 28-30 hours per week, with little difference between ages 2-5 and 6-11.

- Viewing declines by several hours per week during the teenage and, for those still in school, the college years.

- Viewing increases among adults 18 years of age and older to almost approximate that for children, and continues at about this level through the 20s, 30s, and 40s.

- Among adults 55 years of age or older, viewing increases again, and television is the only medium either to remain stable or increase as people pass beyond their mid-50s. Use of some other media (magazines, newspapers, radio) remains stable or declines somewhat, although certain media — theater movies and recorded music — typically have been abandoned many years earlier.

What Bower did was extend the pattern to attitudes, and thus create a framework that encourages the examination of responses to the media in regard to position in the lifespan.

In this case, the life-cycle changes are in accord with behavior. When national samples have been asked whether they personally were most satisfied with cars, TV programs, fashions, popular music, or movies, or which of five things — refrigerator, car, newspaper, telephone, or television — they would choose if they had to do without all but their choice for two or three months, the proportion choosing television increases sharply among those in their 50s and again among those in their 60s over those in their 30s and 40s (Bower, 1985). As adults get older, they become more satisfied with television and less ready to do without it; other things become more readily abandonable.

The generational changes represent differences between age cohorts — that is, persons born within a specified time, usually a decade (i.e. 1950s, 1960s, etc.). A behavioral change is that the amount of television viewing has increased with succeeding cohorts; a dispositional difference is that succeeding cohorts have become more accepting of television viewing, with the most marked shift of this kind probably occurring when the first cohort raised with television became the first parents to have had that experience. Whether the latter change in norms has preceded, followed or simply accompanied the increase in television viewing is moot, it probably was a necessary condition for some of it.

Another, very important generational difference is approval of television news coverage and other treatment of controversial subjects, such as sexual relations, drugs, and racial issues. Older adults are least likely to approve. For some topics, there is a linear trend with decreasing approval with each succeeding cohort; sexual relations is an example. In the 1980s, these differences were modest because social controversies were comparatively muted. In the 1960s, when events such as civil rights protests and the Vietnam War were highly controversial, emotion-laden, dramatic, and divisive, the differences were extreme between the young and the old, and varied stepwise across cohorts. In historical circumstances of that sort, which may never be seen again, television joins the catalogue of social elements over which parents and children and young and old are in conflict.

A secular change is one that is long-term and continuous over the period in question. Two generational differences certainly qualify — the increases in viewing and shifts in norms favoring viewing. Neither has yet reached its limits, but both must be approaching them as the time available, or opportunity, to view television when television is not currently viewed is becoming small for all population groups. Others are major changes in audience composition that arguably have important implications for programming.

The biggest change has been in educational levels. In 1960, almost 60% of the television audience 18 years of age and older had less than a high school education (Bower, 1985). Today, that figure is less than one-third. In 1960, about one out of six had some college education.

Today, that figure is more than one out of three. Accompanying this change has been a shift from blue collar to white collar occupations. In 1960, a modest majority were blue collar. Today, the modest majority are white collar. This reflects the secular shift of the economy from manufacturing to services and information.

Another major change involves age. Between 1960 and 1980, the proportion of young persons between the ages of 10 and 29 increased markedly from about 23 to 31%, while those in the middle category of 30-49 declined from about 41 to 33% and those 50 and over remained stable (Bower, 1985). As the first group matures into the second, and the second into the third, the proportion of the viewing public in the older category will increase.

The decline in the public's evaluation of television, another secular change, is certainly in accord with the upward shift in education, since being better educated and being critical of television go together. Given that shift, the ability of television to retain an overall positive evaluation is at least as remarkable as the decline. The same educational shift would imply greater willingness by the public to attend to news, information, and public affairs. Changes in programming schedules give support to this view. The proportion of such programming available across the broadcast day (ignoring duplicates within time segments) increased from 13% in 1960 to more than double that in the early 1980s. Regular news, however, has remained largely stable in availability. The increase almost wholly has come from entertainment-oriented informational programming, such as talk shows, news specials, and *60 Minutes.* Thus, we find in the 1980s that at every strata of education there is a substantially greater proportion of viewers naming programming in the news, public affairs, and information category as among those shows they "watch regularly or whenever they get the chance" than there were 20 years before, although such endorsements are markedly greater among the most than among the least educated.

The increase in younger viewers probably has similarly encouraged realism and controversy along with conflict in comedies, dramas, and soap operas. They bring to television tastes honed by theater movies and greater approval of the treatment of controversial issues by television.

The forthcoming increase in the proportion of older adults has been interpreted by some as leading to an increase in programming aimed at them or at least particularly pleasing to them. The introduction of elements attractive to teenagers into primetime programming (especially situation comedies) because teenagers often figure crucially in family decisionmaking about what to watch (although they are themselves comparatively light viewers) is an example of exploiting a demographic segment to achieve a mass audience. In the case of older adults, the changes presumably would include a diminution in action-adventure programs, an increase in news and information shows, and an increase in roles featuring or pleasing to older persons.

However, such prognostications almost certainly are unjustified and display little insight into how television operates. Teenagers were useful because by attracting them, the overall audience could be increased. Their attention had some value, but their function as gatekeepers had much more. Older adults have no such comparable status. Today and over the past decades, older adults have viewed greater amounts of television than younger adults. Younger adults have been and will remain the most valuable of all audience segments because they are large both in number and proportions, have substantial amounts of disposable income, and are potential purchasers of the widest possible range of products — from kitchen aids to automobiles, from baby food to cat food, from sports equipment to evening wear. The older adult segment, although larger than in the past, will be in no way comparable in any of these respects. Younger adults are furthermore at greater risk to sources other than broadcast television because they are most likely to be cable subscribers and, if so, to subscribe to additional pay options such as *Home Box Office (HBO), Cinemax,* or *The Movie Channel,* and they are most likely to own VCRs.

Programming, and especially primetime programming, will continue for the foreseeable future to be aimed primarily at young adults. Older adults essentially are a captive audience. Younger adults are not. Thus, rather than programming in the future becoming more attuned to older adults, it will become more attuned to younger adults while attempting what it has in the past succeeded at splendidly — remaining accessible to older adults.

This leads to a little recognized principle of programming: Audience composition determines programming by setting boundaries on who is available to view at a given hour (or, "day-part" in the jargon of broadcasting), but within parts of the day, it is secondary to the function that segments can serve in building a larger audience, the comparative value of major segments to advertisers, and the likelihood that one or another segment will be lost to another medium as contrasted with remaining in the audience because there is no better place to go. In short, it is not only who is in the available audience that matters, but how important they are, how they may add to the inevitable audience, and how vulnerable they are to the competition.

A major set of secular changes have taken place in regard to public television. In 1970, about half the public could receive a public television channel. Today, that figure is in excess of 90%. This is a result of an enormous increase since 1960 in the number of stations operating (from 44 to more than 300 today), a federal requirement beginning in 1962 that all television sets sold be able to receive the UHF signals used by a majority of public stations, and the use of the more readily receivable VHF channels by a substantial proportion of public stations. Attention has grown proportionately so that many more people today report watching public television occasionally or once a week than did so two decades ago. Public television is more often watched by the better educated. Part of the reason is availability. As educational level rises, so too does the likelihood that a public station can be received (because the better educated are more likely to own better sets or live in areas of superior reception). This discrepancy has been lessened by the increases in the availability of public television, but decided discrepancies by education remain. However, even when only those viewers able to receive public television are examined, there is still more frequent viewing by the better educated. Much of the viewing within households of lower educational levels is attributable to children watching *Sesame Street, The Electric Company,* or similar programs. Nevertheless, public television over the years has come to draw somewhat more equally from all strata. Overall, these changes represent enormous growth for this alternative medium, although the proportion of the audience attracted day or night in any market remains very small.

Finally, there has been an important secular change in increased perception by viewers of programs they find "extremely enjoyable." The data presented by Bower (1985) make the trend unmistakable. The average proportion of programs estimated as "extremely enjoyable" by the public has continually increased, and has done so within every stratum of education. At first glance, this finding would appear to conflict with the overall downward trend in the general evaluation of television. However, Bower proposes a convincing resolution. People have become less ready to subscribe to positive labels about the medium because it has, as a medium, declined somewhat in esteem while at the same time they believe that there are more individual programs that are "extremely enjoyable" because of the greater diversity and number of programs that have become available to the average viewer.

Technology

Television has grown and changed because of technological innovations. In a certain sense, it is the creature of technology. Yet such a glib declaration must be severely tempered. Unlike a manufacturing process in which a new technology will be adopted if it increases profits, television involves a human process in which technological innovation is dependent on acceptance by the public. Technology determines the feasible; audiences determine what the medium can or will make of technological developments. The consequences have been unexpected, and to some, disappointing and unwanted. This story can be told in regard to three types of changes in technology: (a) the medium itself, (b) minor improvements, and (c) major dislocations and altered applications.

The medium itself was adopted by the public with extraordinary rapidity. In 1951, the FCC ceased issuing licenses for new television stations until certain technical issues regarding the allocation of spectrum space could be resolved. Within those communities with television broadcasting underway before the ban, the proportion of households with television increased in four years from about zero to over 75%. Within those in which television broadcasting began in 1953, the same degree of saturation occurred within two years. It is hard to think of a comparable rate of adoption. When graphed, the result lines resemble streaks of lightning (Cook & Campbell, 1979).

Minor improvements refer to the many developments that have increased viewer enjoyment in attending to broadcast television. These include the increase in the size of black-and-white screens, the development of color television, the introduction of remote control devices, improvements in television sets that increased the number of channels that could be received (including the federally-imposed receptivity to UHF signals), and generally improved picture quality. The acquisition of the most dramatic of these, the color television, typically increased viewing, and probably each of these contributed in some small way to an increase in viewing. Some of these increases probably represented

temporary enthusiasm, but some also probably persisted and are represented in the ever-increasing levels of television consumption.

Major dislocations and altered applications refer to technological
innovations that might change the way the business of television is
organized and programming disseminated; the diversity, kinds, and
quality of programming available; and, the uses to which television
screens are put and the ways in which viewers behave in regard to them.
Such innovations include cable, its pay options, and satellites; videotext
and its variants; interactive television and the "wired city"; and in-home
playback and recording devices.

Many believed that such innovations, separately to some degree and
in concert certainly, would transform American television from a broadcast to a narrowcast medium. This would be a profound change. Television as a broadcast medium has represented an enormous escalation
among the media in the characteristics identified long ago by the
sociologist Charles Wright (1986) as distinguishing mass from other
forms of communication — the largeness, heterogeneity, and anonymity
of the audience; the rapidity of transmission; the transitory nature of
the experience; the public availability of the message; and the fact that
the communicator is an organization. By these criteria, television is the
ultimate mass medium. The changes made possible by the new technologies for two decades have been projected to occur soon, and certainly
by the end of the 1980s.

If they were to occur, they would change television to a medium in
many ways analogous to magazines and radio, with their age- and
interest-segmented audiences; to motion pictures made for theater release, with their appeal to varied and somewhat distinct publics made
up mostly of those between the ages of 12 and 35; and to book publishing, with its hundreds of specialized clienteles on the one hand and
markets for popular fiction and nonfiction on the other. The culture
disseminated by television would become less popular and more akin
to that promoted or at least tolerated by our liberal arts colleges. The
surveillance of the environment accomplished by news and public
affairs programming would become more specialized in topic and ideology, with programs designed to appeal sharply to specific interests and
decided partisanship. Prescription, such as occurs in newspaper editorials,
would become common. Television would less powerfully reinforce
prevailing social norms because it would no longer be made up of

programming intended to be as universally acceptable as possible. In short, what has been projected is a communications revolution.

Cable, its pay options, and satellites were to create multiple, parallel, but distinctive audiences attending at the same time to such specialized topics as finance, health, the arts, news, made-for-theater movies, science, sports, travel, erotica, nature, food, other cultures, crafts and hobbies, and a diversity of music and musical personalities — rock, jazz, classical, and country and western. There would be a cultural panacea on both the elite and mass levels, with Broadway plays and musicals, as well as experimental drama, brought into the home, and new programming produced to serve popular tastes not popular enough for primetime broadcast television. Videotext and its variants would transmit information tailored to the viewer's specifications onto home screens or in-home printing devices, and this electronic newspaper would bypass newspaper routes, newsstands, delivery trucks, the printing press, and the printed newspaper itself. Interactive television and the concept of the wired city and nation would mean cable linkages rivaling television set ownership in saturation that would deliver an extensive array of public and private services. Examples include access to the meetings of local government, improved crime and fire alarms, medical services, social and psychological counseling, adult education, services from various government agencies, and armchair shopping, banking, and investment. Such a network would link people to services, make information available by request, substitute for errands, telephoning, and the mails, and make possible over-the-screen polling to collect information about public opinion and behavior. The corollary of these varied developments, and in particular those increasing the diversity of what can be viewed on television, was to be the demise of the three major networks by, some said, 1990.

These views of the future have represented careful analyses of technological progress and potential. In fact, they have been uttered when what they proposed already was technologically feasible. Yet, two conclusions are inescapable:

- In many instances, such innovations have been slow to find acceptance, are at risk of being rejected, or have been rejected by the American public.

- In other instances, success or at least continuing presence in the media marketplace has come at the price of a downscaled version of the original vision.

Home Box Office, Cinemax, and *The Movie Channel* have been struggling financially. Cultural programming channels have been abandoned after the loss of billions of dollars. The televising of Broadway productions into the home has flopped. Specialized topic channels for health, finance, children, erotica, and the like have not found firm financial success, and the very visible trend during the 1980s has been their effort to attract more general audiences. Entertainment made for cable has been slow to emerge, occupies little of the cable schedule, and has not looked much different — although there are distinctive nuances here and there — than broadcast entertainment. Cable systems have grown at rates much slower than projected. By the end of the 1980s, only slightly more than half of the nation's households were enrolled. What the systems have experienced typically is rapid early growth, a levelling off with expansion halted at somewhere between a third and somewhat more than half of a community, and an enormous amount of "churn" — the falling away of disaffected subscribers who can be replaced only by former subscribers or from the pool of households whose nonsubscription to date identifies them as likely to be resistant. The interactive QUBE cable system in Columbus, Ohio, expected to be the prototype for many imitators, has abandoned that aspect of its operations as unprofitable and unpopular. Videotext and similar systems as a household information source or a substitute for the daily newspaper have failed in numerous experimental implementations to find acceptance adequate to make them financially viable. Given the half-level of cable penetration, the wired city and the wired nation remain visions.

There can be no doubt that the new technology has changed television by increasing the diversity of programming available, and thereby the pleasure derived by the viewer. The news and sports channels, the local sports coverage, the special interest channels, C-Span, and the pay options that make theater movies and special events available are not on the whole duplicative of broadcast television. The crucial point is that the changes have not been as sharp or sweeping as prophesied.

The sole exception has been in-home recording and playback devices. Of these, the videocassette recorder, and in particular the VHS format, have become overwhelmingly predominant. The lower equipment and software costs have given the VHS format predominance over the Beta system, which presents a superior picture, and the videodisc, whose capacity to locate specific frames for review has made it particularly useful for instructional and archival applications. Everett Rogers

(1986), the University of Southern California expert on the diffusion of innovations, tells the story:

- The rate of diffusion has far surpassed expectations, exceeding that for cable before the end of the 1980s.

- The decision in 1984 by the Supreme Court that there was no copyright violation by videotaping broadcast television in the home assured viewers of an inexpensive program source.

- The major factors responsible for success have been rapidly declining equipment costs, rapidly declining software costs, and an increasing array of software choices.

The record of success of the VCR has been extraordinary, and it probably should be looked upon as analogous to hi-fi and stereo — it gives the individual audience member control over and access to a much wider range of content than is publicly available, and involves gear whose ownership, as with gear that reproduces music, can express expertise, taste, and status. However, it hardly will single-handedly bring about an immediate revolution in television because, while ownership has grown rapidly, the average hours of use per week are not enough to much affect broadcast television, and even some of that use is the time-shifting of consumption of broadcast television.

The error in prophecy is the product of the "technological fallacy" — the belief that because something is feasible, has appealing features, and could be said to be an improvement, it will be widely adopted. Cable for many has failed to improve on broadcast television sufficiently to be worth the price. High production costs have made profitability difficult for television not directed at mass audiences. There undoubtedly are many unmet desires for programming, but they do not sum — from viewers either regular or infrequent — to an audience large enough to support such programming. Electronic distribution of print information to the home may have advantages, but what ends up before the reader, on the screen, or in his or her hands, has neither been able to supplant the daily newspaper nor become a complement to it. The demise of the three major networks has not occurred, and they can look forward to years of health — although in diminished capacity as their audiences are reduced by their increasingly numerous competitors. The older media have not been either wholly or largely displaced by the newer because the latter have failed to provide equivalent or greater satisfactions at more favorable cost or convenience.

The VCR's most significant contribution to change may lie far in the future, and may have less to do with the viewing time consumed by its use than the orientation of the audience toward viewing. One of the reasons for the marginal success of cable's pay options, such as HBO, is the program-dominance that is central to their scheduling. The presentation of feature films and similar "scarce" entertainment assumes that viewing will begin and end in accord with their scheduling, while television to a large degree has been viewed in blocks of time with a considerable degree of program indifference except for the selection of the most desirable option from those available. Viewing by young persons is substantially greater in VCR than in non-VCR households. This implies high VCR use, and their socialization toward using television somewhat differently and demanding a different experience from it. The result could be an audience in the future more demanding and more selective. Conceivably, the VCR could alter television by changing the way audiences use the medium.

Industry Behavior

Technological innovations represent only one way in which television industry behavior has affected the medium. The adoption of new technology has led to a multi-tiered system of dissemination replacing the single-tiered one of broadcast outlets largely fed by networks. Others include the expansion of broadcast outlets, changes in authority over and responsibility for programming, and innovations in audience measurement. These join technological innovations as ways in which changes in the way the television business operates arguably have visibly affected the medium received by the viewer.

The expansion of broadcast outlets has been of towering importance (Bower, 1985; Comstock, 1989b). In 1960, there were 440 commercial VHF outlets. By 1970, the figure was 508. The estimate for 1990 is about 560. Comparable figures for commercial UHF outlets are 75, 183, and 700. These sum to an increase in total VHF and UHF outlets over the past three decades of 145%. In addition, there has been the entry into the marketplace of several hundred "low power," or neighborhood television stations; these entities will not have much effect on overall audience behavior, but they will further the diversity of experiences and presumably increase the amount of community-focused programming available to viewers.

There has been even greater proportional growth in the number of public television stations. In 1960, there were 34 VHF and 10 UHF outlets. In 1970, the figures were 78 and 106. The estimates for 1990 are about 125 and 245. Over the three decades, this represents an increase of 740%.

The importance of the increase in commercial stations is not fully told by the numbers. These additions have not been confined to new communities but frequently have been new entries in markets where the three major networks already have affiliates. These new entries, along with stations previously unaffiliated with the major networks, have become a large pool for *ad hoc* networks transiently powerful in attracting newly large numbers of viewers and for the new if minor Fox network. The independents have become sources not only of network reruns but of new high quality syndicated programming. The result has been a marked increase in broadcast competition for the three major networks.

A major change in television has been the decrease in the share of the audience attending to the three major networks. Their audience share dropped from more than 90% in the late 1970s to about 75% by the mid-1980s, and the estimate for 1990 is about 70%. No one is absolutely sure precisely how to apportion this decline among the competition, but it seems likely from available data that the largest share has gone to broadcast competition from independent stations, with lesser shares going to cable, its pay options, and VCR use, in descending order of magnitude. Given the dissemination of distant broadcast signals by cable, the broadcast component becomes even more substantial. Thus, the myth that network shares are declining because of competition from new narrowcast programming is rebuked by the apparent fact that much of the competition is from the greater availability and diversity of broadcast television.

There have been two major changes in programming authority and responsibility. The first represented a fundamental transfer of power that ever since has affected the making of network television. The second symbolizes fundamental changes in the television business. Both were abrupt, although in retrospect seemingly inevitable.

The first resulted from the confirmation in 1959 by a grand jury and congressional investigations that the charges of quiz show rigging by a defeated contestant were true. In several notorious instances, the sponsor, Revlon, had taken a leading role. The purpose, obviously, was to enhance audience size by keeping contestants with audience appeal in contention. The consequence was that the networks took a far firmer hand in program production, and the common practice of programs being produced by sponsors and their advertising companies ended.

Les Brown in his *The New York Times Encyclopedia of Television* (1977) describes a widening pool of other effects. A network president (although not directly implicated) was dismissed. Several producers were exiled from television; some never returned and others did only years later. Quiz shows such as *Twenty One, The $64,000 Question,* and *The $64,000 Challenge* disappeared from primetime, with a resulting boost for filmed series from Hollywood. Top executives whose forte was choosing among such series became favored over those adept at live showmanship. Federal legislation was passed making it illegal to pre-arrange the outcomes of televised contests presented as tests of ability. However, the main outcome was to make the networks ascendent over other parties in programming authority and responsibility.

The resulting practice of selling advertising on programming for which the networks are responsible has not rendered advertisers indifferent to content. They remain concerned about audience size (and composition) as well as suitability of the program for their product(s). Sometimes, they exercise their option to withdraw from a program (to the dismay of the networks, since their accounts must be credited). The difference is that advertisers have been shifted from the center to the periphery of the production process.

The second involved no such dramatic sequence of events. Nevertheless, the change is important, and arguably more for what it reflects than for what it constitutes.

In the late 1980s, the three networks essentially dismantled their broadcast standards and practices departments. These were the so-called "network censors." They were notorious, and much maligned by those who made programs and commercials, yet for decades they had been an integral part of network broadcasting. They acted as gatekeepers between the producers of television content and the audience. They reviewed concepts, storybooks, scripts, raw footage, and sometimes even completed productions to make sure that broadcast content was in accord with network codes which sought to avoid either offense or harm to viewers. At their peak, almost 100 people were so engaged. At present, fewer than a third remain—despite a flurry of publicity over the ballooning of questionable language and behavior.

What happened to the standards and practices departments reflects what has been happening to broadcasting itself. With network revenues threatened and audiences declining in the face of competition from other programming sources, and budget cuts underway, such sizable departments could not be justifiably maintained. However, the changes in the electronic environment almost certainly made such a policy shift possible. The new era has ended the near-monopoly of the networks on what the public can see, and with it the necessity of gatekeeping. They can no longer do so effectively, and they no longer are almost solely accountable. Thus, the networks no longer need the protection from criticism and complaint afforded by gatekeeping.

The networks undoubtedly will continue to communicate their expectations to those who produce programs and commercials in matters of taste and judgment. Codes presumably will remain on the books. Assuredly, in some few instances the networks will reject something as unacceptable. However, the transfer of major authority and responsibility for the acceptability of content from the disseminators to the makers of television marks the end of one era and the beginning of another.

Hugh Beville (1989), a pioneer in radio and television audience measurement, traces its beginning to 1928 when a Harvard professor named Daniel Starch was commissioned by NBC to conduct 17,000 personal interviews in 105 cities and towns and in 68 rural counties east of the Rockies. The results indicated that about 35% of these families owned a radio. No data were collected on station or program preferences. Since then, an audience measurement system has evolved from harsh competition among rival firms and the continuing critical assessment of alternative methods that has legitimate claims to accuracy of estimates, comprehensiveness, and utility to television and to advertisers.

At the national level, the preeminent firm is the A. C. Nielsen Company. At the local level, A. C. Nielsen and Arbitron are about equally prominent. Although numerous other means have been used over the years to measure the television audience, and a considerable variety are still employed, the central model has involved a two-stage procedure: (a) information on the channel, and thereby the programming, to which a television set is tuned is obtained electronically and automatically by attachment to the set of an audimeter, a device pioneered by Nielsen in the early 1950s, while concurrently (b) information on those viewing is obtained by reports from the viewers themselves—

by completing diaries about who is present during a particular time segment, a technique pioneered by Arbitron in the early 1950s, until the late 1980s when "people meters," similar in operation to remote control devices, were introduced to collect such information electronically. These data are analyzed so that audience size and characteristics can be reported by the average per minute for the time slot or program in question.

The highly, if imperfectly, representative samples employed to obtain data on set use and audience size and composition lead to very accurate estimates. However, they are only estimates because of the use of sampling, because of imperfect viewer measurement techniques, and because the entire procedure implies a definition of "viewing" with which one could take issue. The system has become comprehensive by providing estimates both for the nation and for the more than 200 geographical entities defined as television markets. The system has served its clients well by providing a mutually acceptable metric for the pricing of television commercial time. It has the further strength of continually being subject to highly critical evaluation by the parties that use it because their interests differ. Those in television have a vested interest in the highest figures possible and those in advertising (at least when purchasing time) in the lowest figures possible.

A major landmark in audience measurement was the introduction between 1959 and 1961 of the four-week "sweeps" periods during which at various times of the year in depth data are collected covering audiences in all of the more than 200 television markets. These data become the basis for the prices charged by the competing stations within each market. They are the foundation of the stations' revenues. As would be expected, there is high competition during these periods to attract audiences, with each station offering what it believes to be the best. Affiliates pressure their networks to put forth the strongest programming possible. There are many expensive specials and unusual presentations. There is an inevitably rather open attempt to "hype" the ratings by presenting atypical programming; these attempts are typically accompanied by denials by television executives that they are underway. Meanwhile, programming during these weeks receives especially heavy promotion, and the entire process receives considerable attention from the media in general—although most viewers surely remain ignorant of what is taking place in accord with the general rule that people have high interests in the celebrities, stars, and products of popular media and a low interest in its procedures and processes, which interest only those connected to them by occupation or profession.

Audience measurement has played a part in the evolution of television far beyond serving the venal needs of the television and advertising businesses. By giving television the information necessary to discard effectively its less popular programming, it has made it possible for the medium to redefine itself continually in the direction of having the broadest appeal. The wide availability of a reliable metric has increased competition between networks and stations. It was only with the development of a sound audience measurement system that shares and ratings could serve as guides to decisionmaking. The system is quick, accurate enough for its purpose, and irrefutable, and while observers may differ on the prognosis for a particular offering, there is never any ambiguity about its current standing. People meters will exacerbate this effect by making more information available more rapidly. Effective audience measurement has shaped the medium as surely as the medium has given rise to its development. Finally, ratings (the proportion of the total possible audience actually in the audience) and shares (the proportion of those in the total audience attending to a particular alternative) have become synonymous with the medium and symbols of its mode of operation.

Television audience measurement has been the subject of much criticism, with such phrases as "the tyranny of ratings" frequently employed. The argument is that the overwhelming emphasis on popularity made possible by the audience measurement system has led to inferior programming. Less popular programs, it is said, are given little chance to change or build an audience, creativity is hampered, and imitation encouraged, and the diversity of programming available is delimited. The villains are the television executives who must choose among programming alternatives in constructing their broadcast schedules.

The typical response of those in the television business is that audience measurement is an efficient means of doing business analogous to practices not only in other media but in all businesses. Beville (1989) is representative when he ruefully asks, "Is it somehow more legitimate to imitate on the basis of dollar or unit sales, box-office attendance, or circulation than for higher ratings, which are the prime broadcasting audience gauge?" (p. 237) Certainly those who focus on the audience measurement system ignore the fact that it is only a tool that permits the paradigm governing the operation of American television to function more effectively. What the defenders of the audience measurement system generally ignore in their rebuttals is that the paradigm inexorably favors one kind of popular programming — that which is massively so.

Transformation

The picture in regard to the transformation of television is a conservative one. Television will clearly change more slowly than had once appeared likely. Broadcasting has proven to be a vigorous medium because it satisfies so much of what people want from television. People who want something different from television will continue to a large degree to have to turn to other media and other sources because there are not enough of them to make the programming to which they would prefer to attend profitable. In the United States, these media and sources are widely available — theater movies, live drama, live music, recorded music, books, and magazines. The sole "television" source that does not fit this model is the use of VCRs for the replay of theater movies, which essentially is the recycling of content from one medium to another.

A crucial factor is what people expect from television. As we saw in the previous chapter, people largely expect popular entertainment designed for mass audiences that is not too demanding, and they allocate their viewing in terms that are compatible with this type of content. Time dictates much viewing, and only when people become available to view does the question of choosing among program options typically become important. This expectation factor is one of the reasons why innovative, less escapist, more demanding programming has difficulties in assembling audiences of sufficient size to make them profitable. They are not what people look to television for, and they are seldom the preferred option of very many people among the alternatives available. Such expectations will not change rapidly in the degree to which they are held by the public because they are so strongly rooted in educational background, basic values and other relatively enduring characteristics associated with tastes and preferences.

There is no likelihood at all that television will change much within the next few years except for slowly increasing use of the competitors to broadcast television, and a modest decline in the audience share for broadcast and for network television. The networks will remain healthy because they will remain able to deliver, at least some of the time, programming that attracts huge audiences of great value to advertisers. The slow shifting of audience attention to other media predicts that they may become somewhat schizophrenic in the quality of their programming — with fewer viewers with desirable socioeconomic characteristics present, average program quality will decline, while special offerings will continue much as before. There certainly is no likelihood that television will become the narrowcast medium once projected, although it certainly will offer greatly increased diversity by more modest criteria through the many alternatives to off-the-air broadcasting sources. The likelihood is slight that there will be any extensive scheduling anywhere of programming that could be described as cultural, educational, serious, or of high quality beyond that which is currently available. Cable will grow as age cohorts who grew up with the programming and the services it provides enter the adult population.

We can expect television to change only when its audiences change in what they expect from and how they use the medium. Technology represents possibility, but audience behavior determines actuality. For these varied reasons, the British students of worldwide audience behavior, Patrick Barwise and Andrew Ehrenberg (1989), have reached a conclusion that would have been considered radical two or even one decade ago — that television 20 years hence is not likely to differ much from what it is today.

That is perhaps too conservative a view. Yet, it is one in behalf of which — allowing for audience shifts among the various means of dissemination, some increases in diversity, occasional offerings of exceptional merit, and innovations occasionally in the conventions and formats employed in entertainment — there is a long history and much evidence.

The Main Source

News is the product of events, decisions by newspeople, and organizational convenience. What transpires — the events covered by the news — sets boundaries for the daily manufacture of news, but by no means dictates the product. Human judgment and caprice, as well as the events themselves, play major roles. These are not circumstances peculiar to television news. They apply to all the news media. What sets television news apart are the numerous circumstances peculiar to the medium. These circumstances result in the news on television being different from the news in other media, even when the same story is being covered. The differences go far beyond the simple addition of film or other visual elements to the oral delivery of a printed account. News is made somewhat differently by each of the media.

Television news is distinct. What makes it so can be conveyed by six topics: The setting in which the medium functions; its rise to prominence; the audience, or who watches; the composition and make-up of the newscast; what the audience comprehends or takes away from the medium; and the public opinion about television news.

The Setting

Television news, whether local or network, conforms to its medium and the economic and regulatory milieus in which that medium functions. Television is a visual medium, and "talking heads" are held in low repute by its practitioners. Television news gives priority to events amenable to film coverage — and having film available is a large step toward inclusion in a newscast. It favors the dramatic, the exciting, and the personal. Nowhere do people so clearly figure in the news as on television. States of mind are not photogenic. In portraying events in visual terms, the image takes over from the cerebral and what was construed as illusion becomes the essence of coverage. We get election campaigns as motorcades and rallies, and crime as a young man talking into a microphone beneath the marquee of the sleazy motel thought to have housed a killer.

These aspects of television news would be mistakenly attributed if the cathode ray tube were held solely responsible. They represent the use of the medium for maximum appeal, and their roots are found in the hunger of those in the television business for popularity and profits. Television news emphasizes the visual because that is thought to be one way of attracting viewers. Television news is what it is for the same reasons that television itself in America is largely entertainment.

Walter Cronkite repeatedly has called network news a headline service. He is right, but with one qualification. The headlines are told as tales of conflict — stories that at their most adroit involve the viewer in drama. The news of the world and the nation is not announced, but recounted as synopses suitable for fiction with a precipitating event, forces arrayed in opposition, and at the end, tentative exegesis, resolution, or denouement. Whether it is man against nature, God, or other men, television news gives structure to events.

Many years ago, two sociologists in Chicago, Kurt Lang and Gladys E. Lang (1953), documented television's tendency to impose its own order on events. The occasion was "MacArthur Day," when the general visited the city following his dismissal as commander of U.S. forces in the Korean War. The Langs stationed observers at the airport, along the parade route, and at Soldiers' Field where MacArthur was to give an evening speech. To many, MacArthur was an abused hero; to others, a military man who was ready to ignore civilian leadership in pursuit of victory. He was spoken of as a presidential candidate, and later would deliver an emotional address to a joint session of Congress. The observers found the crowds desultory and motivated by the possibility of a spectacle. Fascination with MacArthur as a figure of ideology was absent. Television portrayed a different picture — excited, seething crowds; adoration of the hero; attentiveness and awe. Television gave coherence where it was lacking and in accord with the expectations about the event that the mass media had created. Television created its own MacArthur Day in which the general was the center of partisan attention. Television journalists were satisfied with their dramatic coverage. In effect, the general received a hype — motivated not by ideology but by the demands of the medium.

Two political scientists have also recorded a departure by television from the reality experienced by participants. David Paletz and Martha Elson (1976) interviewed Democratic national convention delegates on the congruity between the impressions conveyed by coverage of earlier conventions and their own experiences. The delegates recalled that television had emphasized demonstrations, hoopla, and the excitement of the convention floor; they found their role to be far more business-like, with more time devoted to meetings and serious work than television had led them to expect. Serious work does not lend itself to visual, entrancing coverage.

Tom Patterson and Robert McClure (1976), political scientists, are among those who have critically examined the dedication of television news to visual storytelling. They found that the viewing of national news during a presidential campaign made no contribution to voter knowledge of the issues. Ironically, such knowledge did seem to be increased by exposure to partisan, paid-for telecasts and commercials. These researchers attribute the failure of network news to be informative to the emphasis on the visual and the dramatic within the very limited time allotted to news. Paid-for telecasts sometimes increase knowledge precisely because they occasionally convey something new. Television news seeks to divert as much as to inform, and what serves the first purpose may often be redundant informationally.

It is hardly surprising, then, to find that newspapers appear to be more effective in formulating priorities among their readers than television among its viewers. Most people pay some attention to each, and both often emphasize the same things. But when differences in attention and emphasis have been detectable, newspapers seem to be more influential. This perspective singles out topic instead of partisan influence as an effect of the media — not what people think, but what they come to think about. Donald Shaw and Maxwell McCombs (1977), communications researchers, have labeled it as the "agenda-setting function" of the press. Television may be comparatively weak in this respect not only because it fails to provide much that is new about issues, but also because its visuality, ever-present drama, and brevity may confuse viewers about the varying importance that has been assigned to stories. Conversely, newspapers undoubtedly owe some of their agenda-setting effectiveness to their greater popularity among the better-educated — people who are better able to understand what is reported in depth and somewhat more likely to be attuned to conventions of journalistic emphasis, such as story length, placement, and headline size.

Television news also is what it is because broadcasting has been regulated by the federal government. Until its abandonment in 1987, the FCC's Fairness Doctrine required that a "reasonable" amount of attention be paid to public issues and a "reasonable" parity be offered for opposing viewpoints by television broadcasters. Over the years, the FCC made it clear that news programs were the expected means of fulfillment and that national issues could not be ignored. Thus, the public service obligation that broadcasters had to meet to retain their licenses came to include not only "news" but "national news." The result has been (a) to create a market among stations for news — in particular, national news; (b) to encourage a news style among the networks and other vendors in which stories are translated whenever possible into national news so that "bad news" in Philadelphia or St. Louis becomes a symptom of wider malignance; and (c) in behalf of balance, to make of many stories an account of two opposing parties.

The news market within television, of course, is no more demanding than dictated by the threat of FCC censure and by profits. Thus, by the end of the 1980s, network affiliates were strongly resisting, as they had for decades, the expansion of time devoted to national news. Their rationale: Revenue to the stations would fall if they had to accept what the networks would allocate rather than program and sell the time themselves. Paradoxically, television stations have found that local news can be popular and profitable, and so there has been a widespread increase in the time devoted to local news in the late afternoons and evenings. This would give the impression that there is more of importance and interest happening in San Diego or Atlanta than in the nation as a whole, and sometimes by a ratio of two or three to one. The fact of the matter is that one type of news serves the economic needs of the station better than another. The national headline services have thus remained no more than that. Complex issues and their interpretation receive no relief from the legacy of the Fairness Doctrine, time limitations, and television's urge for popularity. Television news often ignores the subtle diversities that mark public opinion because their recognition is unnecessary — two vivid viewpoints, whatever their merits or representativeness, have been enough to satisfy the reigning deities.

Certain tribulations of television news operation, in conjunction with the imprecation of economizing, similarly shape television news. Transmission can be inconvenient. Camera crews are more available in the cities where there are major television stations. A sizable portion of events must be known about in advance so that reporters, camerapersons, and other personnel can be assigned, or the whole operation would become chaotic and unmanageable. Coverage is cut to fit these circumstances. The ideal newsday is well-planned so that events, reporters, and cameras converge. Film available is not the only factor that enhances the likelihood of coverage. Events that can be scheduled well in advance generally will be preferred — which means nonevents, such as interviews, announcements, and the bestowing of honors. The sociologist Gaye Tuchman (1978) has applied the term "routinization" to the way newspeople go about their work. This invites us to another paradox. The news presumably covers events that are unfolding and therefore which are far from fully predictable, yet the media can manage to do that only by focusing on the predictable and by reacting to the unpredictable in ways that are familiar and that can be invoked whenever the appropriate situation turns up.

The values that guide the decisionmaking of newspeople also contribute to the news product. Journalists like to justify their decisions on the grounds of professional standards and the responsibility of the news to reflect events. They are right that news reporting as an occupation carries with it a set of conventions that lead newspeople to make similar decisions when circumstances are similar. The important point is that these values are as self-serving as they are in the service of the public. News values emphasize the unusual and the bizarre. They give equal weight to what will attract or interest news consumers as to what has social, political, ecological, or other significance. They emphasize outdoing the competition by being first. Journalists, like any group of skilled practitioners, play to each other first, for naturally their peers are assumed to be the best judges of news. Journalists value accuracy and fairness, but they value much else as well.

The concept of news values fails to explain why media differ in their coverage until certain variants are introduced. One is that they are specific to each of the media. This would mean that news values vary with the needs and characteristics of the media and the audience each sees itself as reaching. Another is that a sizable portion of the pool of available news stories is discretionary, so that one will serve as well as another, and many pass the threshold on one or another news value while not doing so on others. This would mean that choices often are arbitrary. Both have a claim to credibility. In any case, where variability exists among the media in coverage, news values cannot be invoked to shield the media from criticism because it becomes self-evident that substantial selectivity is involved in presenting the news. The "news," however we receive it, is not the inevitable tabloid of events, but one of many possible alternatives, and "news values" as they exist today are not criteria to which it is essential for newspeople to subscribe for the sake of an informed public.

Television news is what it is because of the setting in which it is created. The principal elements of television news include the television paradigm that makes attracting as large an audience as possible the first priority, FCC regulations and policies, the visual nature of the medium, various needs and interests of the organization, and the values that people working in each medium come to have about what is newsworthy. Journalists are not everything their rhetoric would claim, but neither are they the proper target of criticism. News is manufactured, and there often are good reasons to be dissatisfied with the product, but the blame does not lie with the newsgatherers. It deservedly belongs to the institution itself which determines how newspeople will behave. When Edward Jay Epstein (1973), journalist and political scientist, concluded his widely-read study of newsgathering at ABC, CBS, and NBC, he decided that the title that would accurately describe the process was *News From Nowhere.* When David Altheide (1977), a sociologist, concluded his examination of newsgathering at a San Diego television station, he chose as a title, *Creating Reality,* with the subtitle, "How TV News Distorts Events." There is an aspect to television news that fits what Gertrude Stein had to say about Oakland, "There is no 'there' there."

Rise of a Medium

One of the biggest stories about the media over the past four decades has been the rise of television as a news source in public imagination.

It has usurped and outdistanced every rival in every conceivable way in respect to public esteem. Newspapers, magazines, and radio, once alone in competition, were variously judged as superior to television for a while. No longer.

Whether we draw on those surveys representing public opinion a decade apart — at the end of the 1950s, 1960s, and 1970s — by Gary Steiner (1963) and by Robert Bower (1973, 1985) or on a series of public opinion polls continuing up to the present by The Roper Organization (1981a, 1985, 1987), we are led to the same conclusion. Television is perceived by the public as the preeminent news medium. It is even accorded superiority at tasks at which it would seem certain to fall second. Here are some of the questions the public has been asked:

- Where do you get *most* of your news about what's going on in the world?
- If accounts were to differ, which of the media would you be most likely *to believe?*
- Which of the media is the *quickest* with the latest news?
- Which of the media is the *fairest* and *least biased?*
- Which of the media is most *complete* and *comprehensive* in its news coverage?

In response to the first question, a majority of the public today will name television. In response to each of the other questions, more people today will name television than any other medium. Two decades ago, the majority named newspapers as the source of most of their news. Newspapers were the leader in credibility when accounts were in conflict and for fairness and lack of bias, while radio was the leader for rapidity of dissemination.

In each of these cases, television's rise in public esteem has been accompanied by a comparable decline in the evaluation of the media providing the most direct competition — newspapers and radio as sources of news; newspapers as most credible, complete, and unbiased; radio as the most rapid disseminator. And it has occurred in part in some contrast to the apparent facts, for radio remains at least in many circumstances arguably the most rapid disseminator, as exemplified in flood and hurricane announcements and presidential assassinations and resignations. Newspapers in few cases could be said to be less complete in coverage than television.

The dominance of television news is both illusion and fact. There is no doubt that "television" is foremost when the public thinks about the "news." And this is where fact becomes appearance. Television has become synonymous with news because the term "news" connotes the national events in which the networks specialize. When asked about "the news," "television" precedes newspapers, radio, and magazines as a symbol. The fact is that television undeniably is first as a symbol, but far from clearly so in the actual delivery of news.

When the public is asked about specific news stories rather than "news," or when it is directed away from national events toward regional, state, and local stories, the status accorded newspapers increases. Often in such circumstances, newspapers receive the greatest public acclaim. Local television news attracts audiences of about the same size or greater than national evening network news, which implies that the public should have much the same thing to say about it as about "television." When the public has been queried in regard to "local television news" or "local news," television does not receive the same degree of acclaim. For the most part, the high ranking hinges on the connotation of the terms "news" and "television." These varied facts reinforce the belief that the standing of "television news" represents more what is in the minds than actually before the eyes of the public.

Sociologist Mark Levy (1978) asked several hundred adults in Albany, New York, to name their sources of news. Television was far less often cited for local than for national or international news; newspapers were first for local news and close to television for national and international news. However, more than a fourth of the sample named both newspapers and television as equally important sources of both kinds of news. Again, a more subtle analysis than simply comparing first choices among the media reduces the significance of television.

The media analyst Leo Bogart (1989) makes it quite clear that what people think about the media depends on what they are thinking about at the time. A representative national sample was asked to name "the best way" of finding out about different topics. His findings:

On domestic news, newspapers win out for such items as "a nationally known politician has been sentenced and fined for contempt of court," and "an aging state senator has been reported to be critically ill." But curiously, a somewhat similar but bigger story, "a world leader is to have a series of operations," is linked with television more often than with newspapers (no doubt, because the public associates this kind of personality story with video illustration).

Television comes up big on stories of fire, snowstorms, tornadoes, and explosions – all vivid in pictorial form. "The Secretary of Defense will confer with the President at his ranch home" immediately suggests the film clip of a man entering a long black limousine. But the message "a bandit gets a 20-year sentence for a $2,000 robbery of a finance company" is associated with newspapers, because it requires explanation.

Television scores well on foreign and national politics, disasters, space, and science. The stories on which television ranks high are not merely those with a highly charged emotional content. On the high-interest item, "the weather tomorrow will be clear and cool," 53 percent regarded TV as the best way to find out, 29 percent radio, and only 13 percent newspapers. Obviously, radio represents the most accessible way of getting up-to-the-minute weather information. Why should television represent the best way to find out about the weather? It must be the personality of the weathercasters who make this mundane subject come to life. (*Press and Public*, p. 247)

We are still dealing with opinions. Behavior now confirms our suspicions. John Robinson (1971), the public opinion analyst, examined the media-use diaries of several thousand Americans. These diaries, collected in advertising research, recorded two phenomena that are astounding in light of what the public says about television news. More than half of the adults did not watch a single national news program in a two-week period. On the average day, three times as many adults read some part of a newspaper than viewed some portion of the evening network news. In the late 1980s, the average daily readership of newspapers was more than 100 million, and the average weekly adult readership of *Time, Newsweek*, and *U.S. News and World Report* combined was about 50 million, but the average nightly audience viewing network news was under 40 million. Thus, all data about media use support the view that television news is not as important as people say it is.

Yet the impression given by superficial measurement of public opinion is not entirely wrong. Television actually does appear to have greater credibility than newspapers or other media. As greater specificity and care are applied to assessing public behavior, the quantitative contribution of television in news delivery becomes less; not so for credibility. Television remains the most credible of the media no matter how public opinion is measured.

This credibility is distinctly of television's own making. The absence of partisan allegiance historically so common to newspapers surely plays a part. The brevity of stories that is so typical precludes detail that might trespass on fact or interpretation that would strain confidence. And at its heart are two features embodied in television — the visual coverage of events and the display of news personnel. These two are the reasons most frequently advanced by those who rate television as first among media in credibility. Those who rate newspapers first cite different reasons, such as completeness of coverage. This discrepancy in rationales hints not at differences on a single standard but the application of two different sets of values. Before television, no one would have attached such notions to credibility. Experience with television thus may be slowly reshaping the public's concept of truthfulness in news.

A simple tale, often mistold. Television is not as dominant a news source as many have too hurriedly concluded. Television enjoys extraordinary preeminence as the symbol of news. It is considered to be the most credible of the media. It is far less important as a news source than the replies of the public, carelessly examined, would lead one to believe.

Who Watches

Evening network news exemplifies the predominance of entertainment in American television. When the ratings for each type of evening network program are averaged, using the program categories employed by A. C. Nielsen Company, the result is a measure of the popularity of the format. When these average ratings are broken down by age and sex for each category of program, the result is a demographic profile of the audience for the format. News, by such criteria, does not fare well.

News is less popular than any entertainment format broadcast in the evening. Drama, suspense and mystery, situation comedy, variety, and feature films on the average attract larger audiences than does the average national news program. More children under the age of 12 are watching throughout Saturday and Sunday mornings than there are adult households paying attention each evening to the national news.

The impression of a delimited audience becomes stronger when the profile for each format is examined. News, of course, is less popular among children and teenagers than any of the entertainment formats. It would be plausible to guess that the greater popularity of entertainment formats among all households is actually attributable, not to adults, but to these younger viewers. Not so.

The entertainment formats are more popular among adults 18-54 years of age than is evening network news. Not one of these entertainment formats attracts, on the average, fewer of these adult viewers than the evening news. In some cases, entertainment formats are half again or even twice as popular among such viewers.

The news audience is also disproportionately older. In some cases, television news is about as popular, and in other cases more popular, than the entertainment formats among viewers 55 years of age and older. This is why the commercials accompanying the news so often are in behalf of the more funereal of drug store and supermarket products — dental adhesives, pain relievers, stomach remedies, and various counteractants to the wear and tear of aging.

It is sometimes argued that the staggering of network news throughout the evening would better serve the public by making news more accessible. The apparently limited appeal of news casts this enlightened-sounding proposal into darkness. Inevitably, some who do not now see the news would do so. Equally certainly, some who now view the news because there is nothing more bearable on television at that hour would neglect it entirely. The proportion of viewers led across the evening hours by the trail of entertainment very likely would exceed those for whom the news was newly accessible, and they probably would be those least likely to use other news sources. Staggered news scheduling is more likely to decrease than increase public exposure to the news.

News Make-Up

Herbert Gans (1979), the sociologist, argues on the basis of comparing *CBS Evening News, NBC Nightly News, Time,* and *Newsweek* that there is a distinctive institution that can be labelled "national news." In his view, eight values are persistently conveyed by news coverage in these media. They are "ethnocentrism," "altruistic democracy," "responsible capitalism," "small-town pastoralism," "individualism," "moderatism," "social order," and "national leadership." In sum, national news places the United States above other societies in regard to liberty, justice, and economic welfare; pays homage to rural and small town experience; supports the notion of the rugged individual; deplores extremism; and emphasizes a white, upper middle class perspective and high elected or appointed officials. This results in a content that largely features well-known personages and gives little space or time to social criticism. Disorder stories, which might concern natural, technological, social, or moral disruptions, are a journalistic tradition, but they typically present a resolution that implies the restoration of order. The resignation of a president under congressional investigation becomes a symbol of how justice applies equally to everyone; a tornado becomes an example of little people and big government repairing the damages of a disaster.

Unimportant people appear almost exclusively in disorder stories or in those extolling small-town pastoralism or rugged individualism. The result is a national television news that essentially is profoundly centrist and conservative despite the frequency with which disorder stories are contrary to administration policies or wishes. It speaks on behalf of the status quo. The preeminence of high status officials, mostly male, and corporate and government entities portrays a world in which important initiatives and undertakings occur only at the highest levels of society. Those who argue that television news is alienating, impersonal, and dismissive of the average citizen have an arguable case.

Television news can be described on numerous dimensions besides its principal themes. In fact, one of the distinguishing characteristics of television news is the extraordinary number of ways in which its combinations of audio and visual, film and narrative, interview and report, can be described. For example, Robert Frank (1973), a political analyst, used 29 different dimensions to describe television coverage of a presidential campaign, including duration of air time, topic or issues, hard vs. soft news, and camera treatment. The principal elements of interest, however, arguably are the scope or range of the news, the depth of coverage, the diversity among network coverage, and the informational value of coverage.

Frederick Schneider (1985), a media researcher, has provided a comprehensive portrait of television news by analyzing content, format, and formal features of the evening news presented by the three networks over a six-month period. His principal findings:

- The news is highly limited in scope, with each newscast averaging about 16 items, and with the majority of newscasts dealing with the United States and its activities.

- Foreign coverage is largely limited to Western Europe and the Middle East, with few reports from Africa or Asia.
- Depth of coverage is severely limited, with each item averaging only one minute and 20 seconds in length, and containing typically between four and five "information segments," or separate bits of fact and commentary.
- The networks are extraordinarily alike in the categories of content presented.
- The networks also strongly resemble one another in the format or organization of the newscast, and newscasts vary only slightly in these regards from one typical newsday to another.
- The first and last stories in the typical newscast are longer, more visually varied, and have a greater number of information segments than the other stories.
- The networks differ considerably in the formal features employed — the television techniques used to convey the news.
- Almost all television news is a reconstruction of the event, with live coverage of an event transpiring accounting for only an extraordinary 1/10th of 1% of all news stories.
- Two out of every three network news stories employ journalistic or reporting techniques beyond the story content that create an impression of credibility and factuality — such as a reporter standing in front of the Supreme Court as he summarizes the day's major decisions.

These varied elements support Tuchman (1978) in her emphasis on the routinization of news practices and the weaving by television of a "web of facticity" to achieve believability, and Epstein (1973) in his assertion that short, simple, stories with strong visual elements are the preferred choice of television newspeople. Two sociologists, David Altheide and Robert Snow (1979), offer some additional limitations to television news:

- The total time allotted to the news is short, the items brief, story selection a minute sample of the possibilities, and the personnel less journalists than television performers.
- Dominant sources of news are institutions, such as governments, and the international wire services, whose accounts the networks follow in planning their own coverage.
- The substantial proportion of time devoted to commercials reduces the scope and depth of coverage, and "the commitment to entertainment" that will attract as large an audience as possible leads to "shallow" reports.

Television news, then, is a construction of reality that serves the interests of its disseminators.

If the overall construction of television newscasts is similar in type of content and format from night to night and across the three networks, there is a remarkable degree of difference among the networks in two respects: The specific stories covered, and the emphases within these stories. And despite the many ways in which the newscasts of the three networks resemble one another, the public to an important degree perceives them as being different.

Diversity in coverage is neither good nor bad. The principle behind having more than one news source is not diversity, but the protection that the possibility of diversity provides. Multiple sources decrease the likelihood that the media can be the instruments of propaganda, or that important news will escape attention. Competition is supposed to spur integrity, not necessarily differences. It would be profoundly disturbing were the three network newscasts to vary so much from one another that they appeared to reflect three different planets, because that would imply that the news is beyond order, events so confused that coherent coverage is impossible, and the nation and world beyond our comprehension — assertions that have a claim to validity but which are highly discomforting. It would also be unsettling were there no discernible differences because such congruity would imply not only a waste of resources devoted to the separate newscasts, but the failure of the protection provided by source diversity to visibly function.

James Lemert (1974), a communications researcher, analyzed the degree of overlap among the networks over a two-month period. He found that about six out of 10 stories were carried by all three networks. Seventy percent were carried by at least two. Most of the overlap occurred for hard news; diversity occurred for background, interpretation, and features. These figures probably fairly represent the commonality of coverage in any year at any time, except when events of overriding importance would increase coverage. What they tell us is that the standards of journalism are authoritative, but not dictatorial; a goodly proportion of news lies with the beholder.

Treatment also offers some degree of discretionary latitude. Several studies have documented that the amount of coverage, and the emphases of coverage, have varied substantially among the networks on such apparently major topics as airline disasters, race relations, the student protest movement of the early 1970s, and the war in Vietnam (Comstock et al. 1978; Lowry, 1971a, 1971b; Pride & Clark, 1973; Pride & Richards, 1974; Robinson & Levy, 1986). In addition, viewers apparently perceive the networks as being different enough to allow for one or another network to be judged by individual viewers as more fair, less biased, and more credible than the other two. This follows from the datum that when asked, viewers will rate their preferred news program as superior on these dimensions to those of the competition (Bower, 1973, 1985).

J. Ronald Milavsky (1988), a sociologist, identifies some of the strengths and weaknesses of information delivery by television news in a comprehensive analysis of trends in AIDS coverage. He argues that news values, organizational values, and beliefs by newspeople about the values of the audience impose constraints on the ability of television to deliver useful information on a health threat. Sources may provide conflicting information that the media find difficult to interpret. Conventions of gentility and the avoidance of offensive words may limit what can be conveyed. Extensive coverage typically must wait upon a breakthrough event, which in the case of AIDS was the death of movie star Rock Hudson; after that, coverage increased sharply. As a result of these factors, television along with the other mass media have not been as effective as they might have been in communicating facts about the disease to their audiences and thereby in helping people avoid contagion.

Variation among the media and in attention to topics calls for continual self-examination by the media. Variation is the product of decisions, some representing definite policies and others occurring happenstance. When the networks concur, there is security in numbers; judgments appear at least to represent the norm for the circumstance. There is the question of whether the norm is valid, but empirically it is fact. The reporter is right to think that he has done no more than any competent person in his place would do. When there is diversity, norms either are ambiguous or being violated. In such cases, standards cannot so easily be invoked as the source of behavior. At the very least, there has been an intervening step in their interpretation that has led to different outcomes. There may be very many points from day to day when individuals will vary in the decisions they reach. If these decisions notably diverge over time, between media or within a particular medium, the news that flows to the public requires intensive scrutiny. These decisions, by the fact of being dissimilar, do not become unjustified. They merely demand explanation. What would be unjustified is that these decisions should occur thoughtlessly, by accident, without acknowledgement, or in indifference to the lack of unanimity about the nature of news. Empirical analyses of news, then, serve two purposes beyond providing the factual basis for judgments of bias: They record the accepted norms of reportage, opening those norms to question, and they document the places where norms have been inadequate or, by accident or design, disregarded — thereby holding up these deviations for inspection.

Comprehension

The television industry in the United States spends enormous amounts of money investigating ways in which to make its news programs more popular. It spends almost nothing on trying to find out what viewers learn from the news, or how the news could be made more informative. Perhaps, one would think, it does not need to. The short, simply-phrased, and visually appealing reports should be readily understood and readily recalled. Unfortunately, that does not seem to be the case. Communications researchers, political scientists, psychologists, and sociologists have converged recently on the question of television's effectiveness in delivering the news.

John Stauffer, Richard Frost, and William Rybolt (1983) found that among a Boston sample of about 600 adults the average number of television news stories that could be recalled was 2.3, only about 17% of the stories reported on four different newscasts. The interviews began immediately after the newscast, all were completed by two-and-a-half hours after the newscast, and the amount of time intervening between the newscast and the interview was unrelated to the degree of recall. This exceedingly low score was achieved by the most generous criterion for recall imaginable — the topic (i.e., "hostages in Iran"). When a subset of about a fourth of the sample was asked to watch the news the next evening carefully and to pay close attention to the stories, the percentage of recall rose — to 25%. These findings are in accord with other broadcast news recall studies in the United States, Europe, and the Middle East.

Political scientist Tom Patterson (1980) in his large-scale study of media coverage of a presidential campaign found that print news was superior to television news in recall. Peter Clarke and Eric Fredin

(1978) found that newspaper reading was associated with offering rational reasons for choosing one political candidate over another while television news viewing was not associated with such responses. Print, then, would seem to be at least equal and probably superior in affecting political cognitions among voters.

The British psychologist Barrie Gunter (1987) has been engaged in a program of research on news comprehension in conjunction with that country's Independent Broadcasting Authority. His major conclusions are summed up in his title, *Poor Reception,* and subtitle, "Misunderstanding and Forgetting of Broadcast News." He makes a compelling case for the application of the theories and concepts of cognitive psychology to broadcast news and identifies the major questions that must be addressed.

These questions include differences among audience segments in comprehension and retention, and the influence on comprehension and retention of several factors: viewer attributes; story attributes; story composition; program format; use of film, photos, or other visual elements; flow (including pace and repetition); and the time of day at which the news is received. Unfortunately, he finds little guidance in the evidence so far collected, except for support for the major conclusion that television news is poorly understood and recalled.

He makes a very telling point, however, when he suggests that even if there were clear-cut answers from research, it is not at all clear that newspeople would be interested in making the necessary changes. Newspeople behave in accord with conventions and values regarding news presentation that for them seem valid. They consistently assert that they do not want to cater to the audience, and that their own values are paramount in decisionmaking. There is almost a superstition that to use research would undermine journalistic values — although research is constantly used in behalf of increasing newscast popularity. Gans (1979) reached much the same conclusions in his study of U.S. national news. Newspeople were uninterested in the audience, did not want feedback from it, and "Instead, they filmed and wrote for their superiors and for themselves, assuming . . . that what interested them would interest the audience" (p. 230). As Gunter (1987) writes:

> [W]hat appears on the news and the way it appears is determined by the codes and practice of a professional subculture whose members believe they have their fingers on the pulse of public tastes and needs for news . . . . [There] is a belief, embodied in journalistic lore, that many audience members are not

particularly interested in the news they now receive, preferring instead gossip about celebrities to those activities, events, and issues deemed to be important by the news editors themselves. Television journalists are also fearful that many viewers would prefer attractive or cheerful "newsreaders" to experienced journalists. In short, they fear that if audience preferences were considered, journalistic news judgment would go by the wayside. Journalistic integrity and standards are best preserved, therefore, by keeping editorial and presentation decision-making processes divorced from the influence of audience research. (*Poor Reception,* p. 319)

The sociologists John Robinson and Mark Levy (1986), at the University of Maryland, go much further. Their title, *The Main Source,* is intended as sharp irony directed at the persistent finding that when asked about the main source of its news, a majority of the public names "television." They document, as we have done, that in terms of audience size, attention to, retention of, and reliance on television in political decisionmaking, this cannot be true; television is not the "main source." They argue that the frequent failure of television news to deliver stories that are understood or remembered implies that the electronic media are not serving the needs of our democracy as well as they could. On the basis of an extensive program of research in the United States and Great Britain, they reach several major conclusions:

- Story treatment, although seemingly stereotypical, differs considerably from story to story and among the television media, and the variations in story treatment affect comprehension and recall. Variations in theme mean that several, instead of one story are being told, and they thereby set boundaries on what is likely to be understood, and variations in other factors affect what in general is recalled.

- Comprehension and recall can be increased by a number of specific reforms (pp. 226-227):

  1) Be explicit about the meaning or interpretation to be placed on events. They write, "Explicit messages are usually far more effective. Stories written 'between the lines' stay 'between the lines'."

  2) Separate stories that are similar. They write, "Otherwise, TV news runs the risk of story 'meltdown,' in which one item blurs into and is confused with a separate but closely following second story."

  3) Use graphics to portray statistics. They write, "We have found considerable audience resistance to statistical data in the news. This aversion to 'statistics' may be detrimental to citizen interests if they do not understand the factors upon which decision makers make or justify

their public policies . . . Visuals are important even if they only convey to audience members the sense that they *can* understand what is happening."

4) Use human interest. They write, "[W]e are by no means suggesting a tabloid approach to television journalism . . . . (N)ews editors often become so preoccupied with getting the story right that they forget to tell their story in human terms. Human interest may involve no more than communicating to the audience a sense of why the news editor felt that story was important."

5) Explain terms that are technical or specialized. They write, "Terms such as 'economic embargo,' 'bilateral agreements,' 'leading indicators,' 'COLAS,' and even 'inflation' are quite technical and unfamiliar to most members of the audience." They cite one researcher who found over 30 examples of such "foreign language" in a single evening's newscast.

Robinson and Levy appear optimistic over the possibility of working with journalists to do research that would improve news delivery. Their final sentence reads, "There is no good reason, after all, why the news, and television news in particular, should be beyond comprehension" (p. 241).

The overall picture, then, is one of many ironies. Millions are spent to achieve popularity, but little to make the product truly informative, although our form of government rests on a presumption of an informed citizenry. Television news is packaged to be undemanding, and its stories are brief, simple, and have visual impact. Yet it is often not comprehended or recalled, and it is inferior in these respects to print media. Television news is said by the public to be its "main source," yet by any measure it falls far short of that mark. Yet it is an important source, important enough for Robinson and Levy to want to reform it, and it has an admittedly awesome power when some preeminent event — an assassination, a coronation, a space shot, a hostage crisis — rivets national attention. In such cases, it is often the imagery of television that forever becomes the key to recalling the event.

Public Opinion

In addition to evaluating the various media, public opinion in regard to the mass media has been examined in several other important ways. They include inquiring about beliefs about bias, secular trends in media credibility, the role of partisanship in perceiving bias, and the rights and responsibilities of the media.

A sizable proportion of the public—although very far from a majority—believes that network news is biased. The precise proportion depends very much on how the question is worded. Generally, between one-fifth and one-third of those polled will agree that network news is colored, slanted, or favors conservatives, liberals, the current administration or its opponents. However, there is not on the whole much agreement over the direction of bias.

This is a pattern that has persisted for years. For example, almost 20 years ago, James Hickey (1972) in *TV Guide* reported that about a third of a national sample of 2,000 adults endorsed the view that television news was "more biased than objective." About a fourth perceived bias favoring the administration, and about a fourth perceived bias against it; 12% perceived bias favoring the Republicans and 12% perceived bias favoring the Democrats; and about 16% perceived bias favoring liberals while about 14% perceived bias favoring conservatives.

Robert Bower, reporting in 1985 on his survey representing the previous decade, found that about a fifth of the public endorsed the view that "the people who report the news on TV . . . let their own opinions color the way they give the news." About 12% agreed that some do, and some don't. That sums to about a third of the public who perceive some bias. About 60% agreed that television reporters "give it straight." There was no significant difference between those who labeled themselves conservative, liberal, or middle-of-the-road in the percentage who agreed that reporters "give it straight," although slightly fewer of those who said they were middle-of-the-road said newscasters color the news than did those who said they were conservative or liberal. When asked about their preferred newscaster, the degree of balance becomes astounding:

- Among the liberals, 34% perceived the newscaster as liberal and 52% as middle-of-the-road.

- Among the conservatives, 32% perceived the newscaster as conservative and 55% as middle-of-the-road.

- Thus, between 86% and 87% of conservatives and liberals perceived the newscaster as in accord with or neutral towards their ideology, while fully 70% of those middle-of-the-road perceived the newscaster as having the same outlook.

The consequence of all this—the lack of consensus about the direction of bias and the large proportion of those critics who can find at least one television reporter who does not distort—is that there is no substantial dissatisfaction with the fairness of television news. The faultfinder who can command the public ear because of his or her prominence can find plenty of people who will agree temporarily, but, as with commercials and with television's effects on children, there are too many crosscurrents in public opinion for it to be effectively marshaled against television.

Over the years there have been many objective, empirical analyses of network news content. These examinations differ from the critical assessments of individuals, no matter how well documented or how specific, by their care in sampling newscasts so as to ensure representativeness, and the use of procedures that minimize the role of subjective factors. Such scrutiny of the news has been immensely aided by the news archives at Vanderbilt University and George Washington University where videotapes of all network coverage are available for review.

Investigations of this kind are invaluable for fairly assessing the performance of television news because they are the sole sources of information that go beyond impressions and partisanship. Nevertheless, the findings do not translate readily into conclusions about bias. Human judgment must first be applied to the objective record.

The difficulty—and it is one that must be understood if foolish conclusions are not to be drawn—lies in the nature of news itself and the expectations we have of it in our society. Bias presumes the distortion of events. News itself as a product of the application of news values and other factors to events cannot help but be selective and interpretive; it is never simply a mirror of reality. News coverage can only infrequently be compared against the events themselves. More commonly, the only standard for assessing the performance of a journalist or a news medium is coverage by another source. There is not often a good reason for assuming that one source is superior to another. News sources can be compared, but the identification of one or another as more truthful, except in simple matters of fact, is always problematical.

Balance is another matter. It is fairly easy to determine whether accounts are balanced with respect to issues, political parties, personages, and groups in conflict. Balance can be examined in terms of time devoted to one or another viewpoint or person, or the proportion of statements that may be said to be favorable, unfavorable, or neutral in describing them. It can be applied to questions of camera treatment. The weight of importance accorded different components of public life — such as international news, domestic crime, health care, defense, and energy — similarly can be evaluated.

Bias, however, cannot readily be inferred from imbalance. News is supposed to emphasize the significant. Disproportionate emphasis does not necessarily mean bias. It may only reflect astute judgment in reportage. It is in recognition of this that the Equal Time requirement of the Federal Communications Act specifically excludes "legitimate news coverage" from its provisions.

For example, incumbent presidents running for reelection often employ surrogates for active campaigning, and thus receive less campaign coverage than their opponents. However, the total coverage they receive during the campaign period is generally at least equal to, and often greater than, that accorded their opponents because of the coverage received in the performance of presidential duties. Similarly, a campaign beset by controversy will receive more coverage than one that is not. The dilemma posed for discerning bias from such imbalance is made clear by the analysis of Richard Pride and Gary Wamsley (1972), political scientists, of ABC and CBS coverage of the invasion of Laos by the United States during the Vietnam War. They classified statements about the United States, South Vietnam, and North Vietnam as favorable or unfavorable in regard to military strength and the morality of behavior. Both networks were much more positive than negative about the military strength of North Vietnam, CBS was somewhat more negative than ABC about U.S. strength, they were roughly balanced in the positive and negative portrayal of U.S. morality, and neither had much to say about the morality of North or South Vietnam.

Altogether, there are at least six instances of imbalance recorded here.[1] Yet, the nature of presidential campaigns and the outcome of the Vietnam War do not encourage the label of bias. Events in these instances seem to be consistent with coverage. The lack of an objective standard of truth, and the expectation that the news should vary with significance, makes the imputing of bias a task for subtlety and care.

Every story, of course, presents new opportunities for journalistic distortion. Empirical analyses pertain only to the past and to the particular coverage analyzed. The empirical record, however, provides no solace to those who would claim that network news has embodied strong liberal or conservative partisanship and the essential sameness of the way television news operates over the years does not imply anything different, since or in the future.

The principal focus of studies concerned with bias has been presidential campaign coverage. Each has made a significant contribution to the understanding of the boundaries and study of bias.

Robert Stevenson, a journalism professor, and colleagues (Stevenson, Eisinger, Feinberg, & Kotok, 1973) analyzed CBS campaign coverage to check on the accuracy of the tabulation by Edith Efron (1971), a journalist, in *The News Twisters* of favorable and unfavorable statements that allegedly overwhelmingly favored the Democratic candidate and liberal positions. He made sure that his analysts agreed on the definitions of favorable and unfavorable, thus ensuring reliable measurement, and unlike the original, Stevenson's study included neutral content. He found that both of the candidates of the two major parties were treated about equally, with both receiving more favorable than unfavorable coverage. He also found that two-thirds of the news coverage was neutral.

There is an important lesson here. Neutral content cannot be ignored in evaluating news performance, for the ratio of favorability toward one or another side depends for its importance on the context in which it appears. Two statements for, one statement against, and 997 neutral tell a different story than 667 statements for, 333 against, and none neutral. If the proportion of coverage that is favorable or unfavorable is comparatively small in the context of overall coverage, the significance of an imbalance between the two becomes greatly diminished.

Frank (1973), employed his 29 different dimensions of television news to compare campaign coverage of the three networks. They varied in attention to major stories, favorability toward candidates, the balance of stories embarrassing to one or the other of the major parties, and the emphasis on soft news during the campaign.

What emerges is a picture of coverage varying from network to network, presumably as a consequence of differing policies, news values, and other factors. The campaign would have evolved differently for a viewer, depending on the network viewed. Again, the fact that the news — on television and elsewhere — is a constructed reality and not the conveying of what took place is inescapable.

The two candidates proved to be different subjects for the medium. One candidate was more often portrayed in facial close-up, before an audience, and declaring his political convictions. The latter two may be explained by the differential opportunities offered by the behavior of the candidates (more speeches, more statements). The first however, leaves us puzzled over why one candidate's face should be disproportionately appealing as a photo opportunity, and reminded of the extraordinary number of ways in which the constructed reality of television news can be adjusted.

Frank reached two conclusions. There had been "wide news reporting diversity, both among and within networks, over different message dimensions and news topics." Despite this diversity, there had been no pronounced or systematic bias. He based the latter conclusion on the inconsistencies of favorability across his 29 message dimensions. Thus, the major lesson of his analysis is that, like neutral coverage, complexity of coverage must be taken into account when assessing bias.

C. Richard Hofstetter (1976), a political scientist, analyzed campaign coverage by the three networks and by major newspapers. He reasoned that the inaccessibility of the events themselves, or what might be called the facts of the case, for comparison with their coverage meant that judgments of bias must rest on inter-media and intra-medium comparisons. Differences between television and print coverage would identify "structural" or technological bias attributable to the different ways in which the two media operate. They would not identify partisanship or the political slanting of the news, because such a conclusion would require the implausible assumption that these were the same within the outlets of a medium and differed between the two media. Differences among the outlets of a medium, or intra-medium comparisons, would identify partisan and ideological bias. That is, diversity within a medium = political bias; diversity between media = structural or technological bias.

Hofstetter reached two conclusions. There was observable structural or technological bias. The two media covered the campaign differently. Television told its own story; newspapers told theirs. However, there were only modest differences among the networks in their coverage of the candidates and their parties. There was no apparent political bias.

It should not be surprising, then, that it is a myth that there has been a secular or long-term decline in the credibility of the news media or that they have been facing a crisis in public confidence. This applies to all the media, but particularly to television. The evidence:

- The "confidence gap" research by sociologist Seymour Martin Lipset, indicates that over the years the degree to which the public expresses confidence in the media has changed in accord with two factors: the ratings given other institutions and the popularity of the president (Lipset & Schneider, 1983).

- Confidence in the media over the past two decades has declined somewhat as has confidence in other institutions, but their ranking among other institutions has remained about the same.

- The ranking of the media among other institutions has never been high, and the percentage expressing confidence in them rises and falls somewhat with the popularity of the president. Because of the adversarial nature of journalism, ratings fall with popular presidents and rise with unpopular ones, and the shifts between the extremes of this continuing oscillation often give a false impression of precipitous declines ("a crisis") — or increases ("a recovery") — in public confidence in the news media.

In regard to television:

- Bower in 1985 not only reported that almost two-thirds of the public believes television reporters are not biased, and that this belief is held equally across the political spectrum, but that the proportion of the public holding such a view had increased somewhat over the preceding decade.

- Four surveys in the mid-1980s — by the American Society of Newspaper Editors, the Times Mirror Corporation, the Gannett Center for Media Studies, and the Los Angeles Times — dispel any notion of a crisis. Some findings can be arranged to imply a negative opinion of the press, but many more and more consistently can be arranged in behalf of the proposition that the public on the whole is favorably disposed toward the news media. Cecile Gaziano (1988), a marketing and opinion researcher, concludes that the four surveys "taken together and compared with earlier results do not portray a crisis in public confidence in the media. In general, the public has a largely favorable impression of the media."

Nevertheless, the media probably cannot escape being occasionally perceived as biased, and particularly by those who hold highly partisan positions on the event or issue covered. Three Stanford psychologists, Robert Vallone, Lee Ross, and Mark Lepper (1985) make this quite clear by their examination of reactions to network coverage of the Arab-Israeli struggle in 1982. Unlike most experiments where groups alike in composition receive different treatments, they gave the same treatment to groups differing sharply in composition. The treatment consisted of six network news segments from ABC, CBS, and NBC covering a series of particularly violent events in Beirut over a 10-day period. The subjects were either pro-Arab or pro-Israeli.

Both of these two partisan groups perceived the accounts as biased, but in opposite directions. The pro-Arabs perceived the bias as anti-Arab, the pro-Israelis as anti-Israeli. Recall indicated that although the stimulus was unchanged, each group experienced something different. The pro-Arabs reported 42% favorable and 26% unfavorable references to Israel, while the pro-Israelis reported 16% favorable and 57% unfavorable references to Israel. Both groups believed that the coverage would sway the public against their side; that is, the media were perceived as "hostile."

Finally, when factual knowledge of the events portrayed was examined, those with greater knowledge were more likely, in both groups, to perceive the media as hostile. This challenges the popular myth among newspersons — that the better informed people are, the more likely they are to judge media performance as fair and balanced.

The remaining topic is public opinion about the rights and responsibilities of the news media. John Immerwahr and John Doble (1982) public policy analysts, polled a nationally representative sample of about 1,000 adults on questions such as these:

- Major party candidates have a right to get as much coverage in newspapers as their opponents get. Agree or disagree?
- Television news has the right to give candidates of one of the major political parties more coverage than it gives to candidates of the other party. Agree or disagree?
- The government has a right to arrest a reporter who constantly is criticizing the president. Agree or disagree?
- The president has a right to close down a newspaper that prints stories that he feels are biased or inaccurate. Agree or disagree?
- (There should be) a law requiring television news to give major party candidates such as Democrats and Republicans the same amount of coverage. Favor or oppose?
- (There should be) a law requiring newspapers to give major party candidates such as Republicans and Democrats the same amount of coverage. Favor or oppose?
- (There should be) a law prohibiting newspaper stories that embarrass the president, the government or the country. Favor or oppose?

• (There should be) a law prohibiting television stories that embarrass the president, the government or the country. Favor or oppose?

The results are startling. About 90% of the public agree that major party candidates have a right to equal coverage. About 80% disagree that television news has a right to give more coverage to one candidate than to another. About one-fifth agree that the government has the right to arrest a reporter and that the president has the right to close down a newspaper. These responses are sharply discordant with the First Amendment, which extends to newspapers, television, and other media, as well as to every American, the right to say what they want short of crossing the legal borders of obscenity, defamation of character, slander, libel, national security restrictions, and the like.

The First Amendment serves as the basis of media policy in the United States by shielding the media from governmental interference. It is on the basis of the First Amendment that the Federal Communications Act specifically excluded legitimate news coverage from its Equal Time requirement. It is precisely the First Amendment that precludes the Federal Communications Commission from entering into the regulation of broadcast content, news or entertainment, by direct, extensive, or specific prescription or proscription. Over the years, the courts consistently have given the First Amendment precedence over numerous other desirable outcomes, including the protection of individual privacy and the reputations of innocent parties. By giving overwhelming accord to statements in clear conflict with principles established by the First Amendment, the public indicates that it has no understanding of the role of the First Amendment in U.S. media policy.

It is hardly surprising that someone should approve of the arresting of reporters and the closing down of newspapers, nor is it surprising that such views are in the minority. What is surprising is the size of the minority. What the reporter and newspaper were said to have already done clearly was protected by the First Amendment, and "prior restraint" — punishing the media for what they might do in the future — consistently has been prohibited by the courts.

About 80% favor a law requiring television and newspapers to give equal coverage to major party candidates. The public wants newspapers held to the same standards as television, and it wants television held to much stricter standards than those imposed by the recently abandoned Fairness Doctrine or by the Equal Time requirement. Slightly more than 25% favor laws that would prohibit newspapers and television news from embarrassing president, government, or country. Again, the size of the minority is surprising.

The means by which these replies were obtained requires comment. They were elicited by presenting "agree or disagree" or "favor or oppose" options. One would not expect such thoughts to figure prominently in the minds of very many Americans except when they explicitly are asked for their opinions. Queries in polls that seek approval of a positive step generally receive greater agreement than the same idea expressed in terms of what should be forbidden, and these queries on the whole fall into the former category, and especially those concerned with new laws. As a result, they may overestimate even elicited opinion on some points. Certainly the findings do not mean that an array of responses supportive of the First Amendment could not be obtained with different phrasing or questions. When opinions are not strongly held or matters not of paramount importance, the views to which people will indicate accord — elicited opinion — can range substantially. These findings, then, should not be taken as the measure of well-formulated, forceful, definitive, or paramount public opinion.

Nevertheless, what we do know is that a huge majority of the public expresses agreement with the view that there should be laws requiring equal treatment, that the media do not have the right to give imbalanced coverage, and that these imprecations should apply to newspapers and television equally. The underlying theme of these elicited views is that the responsibilities of the news media to be fair and evenhanded in coverage far outrank their First Amendment rights in importance. They imply that the public would subjugate the latter to the former, although we cannot so conclude with certainty without knowing much more about public opinion on the media and the First Amendment.

These findings would appear to place the media in jeopardy in regard to their privileges of expression. They do not in fact do so because of the low salience in which the media are held as social issues or problems in themselves, and the almost certain fact that substantial support for First Amendment principles could be elicited by different, or differently phrased, questions. Nevertheless, the findings do indicate certainly some degree of public demand for imposing restrictions on the news media, and they indict both the educational system and the news media for doing a poor job in educating the public about the First Amendment.

So far the many studies of presidential campaign coverage portray television as even-handed ideologically. Perfect balance would never be expected. Emphases and attention inevitably will shift in response to the events of the campaign; efforts at balance will be compromised by the application to events of news values. The best we can hope for is coverage that does not seem uniformly one-sided or thoroughly inconsistent with the way a campaign unfolds.

Note

1. Two instances for the treatment by each network of North Vietnamese military strength; one instance each for the different treatments of U.S. strength; and two instances for differences at each network in the treatment of U.S. versus North or South Vietnamese morality.

5

Political Influence

Television has transformed American politics. It has altered the nominating conventions, changed the organization and style of presidential campaigns, and created a political environment distinct from the days when the major contenders personally would attempt to cross every state by train or plane. Television has helped weaken the influence of party leaders and party mechanisms at every level. It has increased enormously the vicarious participation of the public in politics, yet it has not changed that dictum of many years' standing that the mass media reinforce and crystallize opinion more than they appear to change votes from one party to another. Television's varied influence (and in some instances, non-influence) can be described under six topics: television politics, media roles, election day reporting, the electorate, presidential debates, and media effects.

Television Politics

Harold Mendelsohn and Irving Crespi (1970), astute students of public opinion, have characterized the "new politics" as the conjunction of polls, computers, and television. Politicians now design their campaigns with detailed information on what the public thinks, carefully staking out positions that either take advantage of support or evade disfavor. It is a sorry candidate for the House, Senate, or presidency who does not quantitatively assess public sentiment. These private

123

endeavors take place in a context in which the public polls, often financed by newspapers or by television, inform the world at any given moment of a candidate's likely success.

At the heart of the political use of polls is the computer. A look at a 1950s college text on data analysis reveals an extraordinary object — a machine, chest-high, and about as long as the average person is tall that would be identified by a postal clerk as a mail sorter. What we actually are looking at is an IBM card sorter. Data analysis at that time required physically sorting cards one column at a time and tabulating by hand the results, which registered on mechanical meters. To compare men and women meant sorting first on the column where sex was encoded, and then on the column containing the attribute or opinion in question. This was all very time-consuming, as well as tedious, and effectively precluded the application of poll outcomes to immediate political planning. The evolution of the computer has made it possible to do in minutes or seconds what once would have required days. Data collection techniques have improved, but not much, and the logic of data analysis has hardly changed at all — what has made information about what the public is thinking and how it is responding to campaign events central in politics in the United States is the computer.

Political polling, then, proceeds on two planes, the invisible and the highly visible:

- The invisible plane consists of proprietary polls undertaken in behalf of the candidates and parties at their expense to obtain information that is largely kept secret except in those instances in which the release of data to the press may appear useful for the purpose of achieving a favorable standing in public opinion.
- The highly visible plane consists of the widely publicized polls sponsored by major media such as *The New York Times, The Los Angeles Times, The Washington Post,* or one of the three major networks (often in conjunction with one of the newspaper giants), or undertaken by a major polling organization such as Gallup, Harris, or Roper for later sale to interested media. These polls provide a broad chart of public opinion about the issues and the candidates and become the subject of journalism.

The latter do not substitute for the former because of the difference in their purpose and the consequent difference in the information made available. The purpose of the highly visible polls is to serve the media ith subject matter, and the data are analyzed in crude terms. The urpose of the invisible polls is to guide the political contenders, and ie data are subjected to intensive and detailed analyses by educated nd experienced experts in such craft.

At the same time, television has become the principal means of ppealing to the public. Television commercials carry to the voter ie image thought to be the most acceptable; scholarly, authoritarian, uman, democratic, vital, relaxed, youthful, mature, Polonius at speed. elevision coverage is a principal determinant of campaign planning, ith announcements, speeches, and activities designed to coincide with ie schedule and needs of the medium. Television speeches, debates, nd talkathons are the new centerpieces. Political success has come to epend on skill at manipulating information and on adroitness before ie camera — two circumstances served best by money enough to buy ie expertise that can bring them about. Thus, the media consultant has ecome a prominent figure in campaigns, drawing on information ecialists on the one hand and television specialists on the other to anslate what has been discovered about public opinion into effective olitical television, whether free news coverage or paid-for spots and lecasts. The media consultant in turn becomes a celebrity, at least in ie political realm, being interviewed on talk shows and newscasts for is (few females have become prominent in this occupation) views on ow the campaign is proceeding. It is a mystery, however, why the news edia think that a hired advocate will express a valid opinion since it invariably the opposition that has weaknesses and has made mistakes nd one's own candidate who has strengths and has not erred.

The 1960 campaign initiated the television era in presidential poli- cs. Richard Nixon adhered to the whistle-stop strategy — every state, 38 cities, 150 major speeches, 65,500 miles. About 10 million people w him. He used television for direct appeals only in the final days. hn F. Kennedy focused on the major states thought to be undecided. e turned to television to confront the issue of Catholicism, using in 10 y states a 30-minute videotape of a question-and-answer session fore Protestant ministers in Texas.

Then there were the four televised debates. Nixon, recovering from illness, prepared for them as if they would be won by the kind of guments that had served him as a debate champion at Whittier Col- ge. Kennedy saw them as a chance to make not only his views but his

vitality and magnetism known to the public. About 75 million people
the largest television audience up to that time, saw the first debate.

Sociologists Elihu Katz and Jacob Feldman (1962) pieced together
the impact of these encounters from 31 independent and different
studies of viewer reactions. Only the first debate had a significant
impact. The haggard Nixon was widely perceived as "losing." Kennedy
became more favored by his supporters and less disliked by those
favoring Nixon. Nixon lost comparably in public esteem.

National polls suggest that there may have been a trend toward
Kennedy before the first debate, and the claim by journalists that the
first debate won the election for him is presumptuous — but there is no
doubt it helped, and in precisely the way Kennedy needed. Nixon as
Vice-president was well-known nationally, both within his party and by
the general public. Kennedy was a relatively new face, an Easterner
and a Catholic, for whom arousing support among Democrats nation
wide, the majority in voter registration, was crucial. The first debate
helped him achieve that. The studies also confirmed that Kennedy had
perceived the debates correctly. Voters appeared to absorb more about
the style of the men than about the issues. Kennedy used television
artfully and as a component of a geographically focused campaign
Nixon appended it clumsily to traditional strategy. Practice follows
victory in politics, and presidential campaigns would never be the same
again.

Nixon in 1968 behaved differently. He was televised throughout the
campaign before selected, friendly audiences. Hubert Humphrey, al
ready placed at a disadvantage by the coverage of the rioting an
discord at the Chicago Democratic convention, found his coverage
filled with strident anti-Vietnam War hecklers. It is ironic that Nixon
learned so slowly, since he had used television masterfully in 1952 to
save his vice-presidential spot on the ticket with his "Checkers" speech
in which his dog, his wife Pat's cloth coat, and his mortgage were
invoked before 25 million viewers to dispel public suspicions over a
$18,235 expense fund privately provided him by a small group of
Californians. Eisenhower had weighed dropping him as a running mate
Nixon's performance, by making the effect of rejection on Republican
success ambiguous, apparently left the General, always eager to appear
conscionable, unable to distinguish among right, wrong, or the demands
of his new mission. After Nixon's closing appeal for support brought
thousands of letters, wires, and calls to the Republican National Com

mittee, Dwight D. Eisenhower embraced him with the words, "You're my boy!" Nixon should have realized then that television's strength is its ability to suggest trait, manner, and character, for the success of this program, prepared by an advertising agency, rested on its portrayal of a man of ordinary honesty unfairly rebuked in his pursuit of the American dream — a theme left not to words but to the camera's capturing of Nixon's emotional desertion in mid-speech of the protection of his desk and to the capturing of Pat's devoted expression.

By the late 1960s, the pattern of the television era had become established. The presidential conventions were covered as entertainment as well as news. Among paid-for broadcasts, spots and short programs became more prominent, lengthy speeches less so — for the longer the political broadcast, the greater the drop in audience from what would have been expected for entertainment. Spots showed no more deficit than commercials of any type. Furthermore, as studies were still demonstrating in the 1980s, political spots overcame the selective exposure by which persons disinterested in politics or unfavorable to a candidate will avoid a scheduled appeal. The data are absolutely clear. Televised political spots, because of their brevity and unpredictable (by the viewer's standards) scheduling, are equally as likely to be seen by opponents, supporters, and neutrals. The only significant factor affecting exposure is the number of times and times of day they are on the air. This makes the political spot the ideal means for reaching the public at large.

In 1956, 85% of presidential campaign television expenditures had gone for speeches; three elections later, with total expenditures four times greater, such major presentations occupied only half the budgets. Nevertheless, the speech and other long programs remain important as symbols and as punctuation marks for the campaign. They merely have become recognized as having the more limited purpose of assembling the interested and the loyal, thereby increasing the likelihood that they will remain that way. They are the proper means for reaching the favorable, supportive, and interested public.

Television has changed the nominating conventions from deliberative, if volatile, bodies to orchestrated showcases. This has come about in several ways. By opening the conventions to the television viewer, politicians have become fearful of offending anyone by what transpires. The function of television as entertainment cannot be ignored, as the parties wish to hold as many viewers as possible for the display of the nominee and his running mate. Inoffensive, contrived excitement is packaged. When that is what the parties offer, television cooperates, for the medium shares a goal with the party — a large, attentive audience. When in 1988, the networks began to abandon gavel-to-gavel coverage in favor of selective coverage of major occurrences and the more entertaining ceremonial aspects, the loop had been closed. In the first stage, television altered the conventions. In the second, television coverage changed to fit the alterations. The conventions were now packaged as programs.

The transformation has been hastened by what the parties have done with the primaries, by how television has covered them, and by the journalistic machinery assembled by television for convention coverage. The net result has been to make of the conventions arenas for the acclamation of the nominees rather than for decisionmaking over their choice.

Today, a large majority of delegates to the Democratic and Republican national conventions are elected in primaries and pledged to vote for a specific candidate. Before this reform of several decades ago, only a minority were so selected. In addition, delegates chosen by other means, such as caucuses, typically now become pledged in advance to a candidate. This means that ordinarily one or another candidate arrives at the convention with sufficient delegates to win the presidential nomination.

Television coverage enhances this process of selection in advance of the conventions. It has made early caucuses, primaries, and other nominating procedures the subject of intensive coverage, and thereby has elevated state and regional contests to a high national plane. Television coverage focuses narrowly on who is winning and losing, thereby participating in the winnowing out of candidates. Outcomes confirm or derail frontrunners, and "good showings" or a "win" become "must" achievements for the less fortunate.

Patterson (1980) carefully collected data on media coverage and voter behavior through the presidential primaries, and he presents a convincing picture of media influence. Coverage by the media rises or falls with performance in the preceding contest. The most attention generally goes to the candidate who was the winner or who has emerged, perhaps surprisingly, as a challenger. Knowledge by the public of the contenders varies with amount of media coverage. Consequently, those candidates who falter become progressively less able to compete because, in effect, they have been erased from the agenda of options for many voters.

These processes — the increase in pre-committed delegates and the focus by television on their selection — has sharply reduced the role of negotiation among party leaders in selecting a candidate. For delegates and leaders alike, less remains to be decided or bargained for at the conventions. By the eve of the convention, the field is usually narrowed to two contenders, one of whom almost always is acknowledged as the victor.

Once the convention is underway, saturation coverage occurs that would have been unimaginable in pre-television days when reporters functioned as individuals or small partnerships rather than as immense teams. The literally hundreds of reporters who are arrayed by each network are so thorough in collecting information that little occurs that does not fit television's own prognostications. The 1976 Republican convention exemplifies the conversion of drama to anticlimax. Gerald Ford and Ronald Reagan were each within a few votes of the nomination. It was one of the closest convention contests of the century. Yet no viewer could doubt that Ford would be the nominee because television, long before the vote, had tracked down and verified the choice of every delegate. As the vote approached, the very few delegates who remained undecided became temporary celebrities. Everyone's choice had become a public commitment; a change would require recanting. By the time of the uproarious and emotional Reagan demonstration, his supporters were losers in a charade entertaining the viewers.

Neither convention dazzlement nor seduction by spot, of course, were the main goal of political strategists. The first lost the disinterested and the opposed; the second, as a commercial, could not help but suffer in credibility. From the first primary to election day, what the presidential candidates want most is to be included in regular network news. Favorable or neutral news coverage promises the maximum benefits of media exposure.

Edwin Emery (1976), a journalism professor, succinctly characterizes the trends that had emerged by the 1970s and continued into the 1980s:

> It seemed clear that despite the heavy expenditures to buy time on television and radio, the really desired goal was to obtain exposure on news programs. And the ultimate goal for presidential candidates was to have two or three minutes' coverage on a network evening show anchored by Walter Cronkite,

John Chancellor, or Harry Reasoner. Here, with substantial audiences of mixed political preferences or characteristics, the personality and the message of the candidate might become noticed by people who had not been reached through print media, direct mail, or interpersonal communication. The novelty of the 1976 presidential primaries, financed in part by federal matching funds and flushing out a crowded Democratic party entry list, brought methodical media attention to the "weekly primary vote" not unlike the attention paid to the weekly golf tournament. Daily reports, smash play on election day, analysis the day after, and human interest stories all added up to extensive media exposure for the winners — and rapid elimination for the despairing losers. (p. 93)

Emery also documents a phenomenon that could escape someone without a sense of history and irony. By 1976, the whistle-stop campaign had returned, but in a new guise — and it had been brought back by television. Emery records that in 1976 the primaries were almost uniformly won by the candidate who expended the most effort, time, and money. These were contentious primaries, the Democratic contests narrowing a large field to Jimmy Carter and the Republican contests oscillating between Ford and Reagan. In almost every case the winner spent big, devoted a sizable portion of the budget to brief appeals on radio and television, and trekked from factory to community to news conference in a way that attracted continual television news coverage. Contentious primaries have continued to be the rule rather than the exception, and so too has big spending, use of the electronic media and especially television, and intensive personal campaigning, with winning often contingent on being preeminent on such dimensions. By the prominence it had given the primaries, television had made the handshake and the personal chat again a part of national politics. Now, however, these were associated with the elimination process rather than the final contest, and television became the means by which their occurrence was conveyed to the larger public — and therefore the *raison d'etre* for these "whistle stop" techniques.

The television-dominated campaign derives from the 1960 contest between Kennedy and Nixon. One of Kennedy's innovations was to campaign selectively. He identified states with major blocks of electoral votes that might be won by either candidate. He campaigned intensively in person and through the media in those states, and relied on television to maintain parity in states he seemed certain to lose and the advantage in states he seemed certain to win. The selectivity is not at all as applicable to the primaries and other selective processes because of their sequential scheduling. A candidate can ignore one or another primary, but on the whole, must take them as they come. What has been applied to the primaries is the intensity of effort and the reliance on television.

Media Roles

Nevertheless, television during the primary and presidential campaigns seldom can be identified as *the* factor responsible for a voter's decision. There are very sound and understandable reasons for this. Television is only one source of information, and it must compete with information from friends and family and from other media. Voting itself is a behavior that often follows past practice — those who have voted in the past are far more likely to vote again, and any prior consistency in party loyalty is very likely to be repeated. The candidates in many cases will make equally adept use of television. News coverage gives roughly equal treatment at least to the major candidates and to the two major political parties. The mass media in news, and television in both news and political commercials, undoubtedly have overcome selective exposure to a large degree — the inclination of persons to avoid communication antithetical to their partisanship — because so much simply cannot be avoided if one pays attention at all. Selective perception — the interpretation of what is experienced in accord with predispositions — nevertheless will often operate, and selectivity certainly will preclude immersion in anything extensive or substantial conveying an unwelcome or irrelevant perspective. Thus the media have the power to disseminate a sizable amount of unpleasant, discordant, or unwanted information, while extensive presentations of such information can be and will be avoided by many people.

Television undoubtedly has a larger role as a factor in persuading voters during the primaries than in the presidential election itself, because voters' loyalties among the contenders are generally less strong, if they are present at all. During the presidential campaign, television's role is central and important, but it is seldom that a voter can be said to have switched from one candidate to another simply because of what he or she saw on television. On the one hand, the decisionmaking of individual voters is too complex and relies too much on their past experiences for such instant and simple effects. On the other hand, television along with other media are limited by what can be achieved through exposure, since their messages are seldom consistent, not always understood, and seldom overall favor one or another candidate or party.

The televised coverage of the conventions, following that of the primaries, focuses the nation's attention on the electoral task. Television news coverage and political commercials during the campaign help to maintain voter interest and support. However, the opportunity of television and other media to influence voter choice between the two major parties during the campaign is limited by the fact that in the typical election about 80% of the voters will have made a choice by the end of the conventions, and at least a fifth of those undecided will return to whatever party they have tended to favor in the past. Thus, television's principal role, as it is for all media, is to facilitate and encourage — but not to remake — voter decisions.

Television, newspapers, and other mass media probably have their major influence between campaigns by establishing the framework within which elections are contested. The shaping of political attitudes is cumulative and slow. Campaigns are excitement and drama, building hastily on slowly laid foundations. They are also periods of public discount and skepticism, and the slowing or cessation of governmental and congressional activity. For example, the Watergate break-in of Democratic national campaign headquarters by Republican "plumbers" during the 1972 campaign that eventually led to the resignation of President Richard Nixon had scant impact during the campaign. It only became an issue after the election with new revelations. These revelations were dependent on a Congress back at work that could conduct investigations and on a federal judicial system functioning without inhibitions over interfering in the electoral process, and their perception by the public as having credibility almost certainly depended on the cessation of the election campaign atmosphere of acrimony and contention.

Major events, of course, remain a means by which the media may have great impact, both during and between campaigns. The ordinary flow of news accretes slowly, developing impressions, beliefs, and a general outlook that together constitute for the individual a picture of the world. Big news that everyone comes to talk about is sometimes another matter — a shift in the economy or in foreign relations that seems to justify controversial policies, a bold stroke such as a presidential visit to a foreign capital or a surprise summit meeting, or an achievement such as Jimmy Carter's Camp David success in 1979 in bringing temporary peace to the Middle East. In such circumstances, where the making of news and the manipulation of the media for political advantage converge, an incumbent president, or whoever in a particular contest holds high office, has a decided advantage, for he or she possesses the power to act. Such a person is also better placed to ride the prevailing winds. This advantage of operating from superior terrain is nowhere better exemplified than in the behavior of incumbent presidents campaigning for reelection and incumbent vice-presidents campaigning for the presidency. By acting in their official capacities, incumbents can receive extensive favorable media coverage. Often, these activities will be beyond the boundaries of controversy. By invoking the demands of their official capacities, incumbents can sometimes avoid campaigning themselves and leave the exchange of charge and counter-charge to their representatives. The result is to make such figures extremely difficult to defeat if they begin with a favorable standing among the public. Presidential elections to a substantial degree thus have become referenda on whether or not the voters approve of the person in power.

Big news during a campaign will be limited in influence by the partisanship already aroused and the commitments toward which voters are settled or leaning. The pattern reported by Harold Mendelsohn and Garrett O'Keefe (1976) in their intensive analysis of a sample of voters interviewed repeatedly during the 1972 presidential campaign in Summit County, Ohio, is typical:

- Because of news media coverage, major events quickly become known to almost everyone—few remain ignorant of the alleged gaffes, scandals, or major controversies.

- Only an extremely small proportion of voters—typically fewer than 5%—believe major events have any influence on their voting decisions because they either already have made up their minds or their decisions are based on so many other factors, or both.

- Opinions about such events divide sharply on partisan lines, so that vote switching is rare—the result, no doubt, of the objectivity or ambiguity of coverage which permits the voter to selectively perceive it.

The facilitative function is probably strong for television because it emphasizes the visual and the dramatic so much and is so relatively inept at conveying information about issues. That is, it does not so much teach about the campaign as help maintain voter interest and voter loyalties and funnel the attention of those interested toward unfolding events. Newspapers, because they can cover any topic in greater depth, are generally greater factors in instructing the public about the issues themselves. Yet television often figures importantly in the process by which voters finally confirm their inclinations at the polls. Besides helping to maintain interest and loyalties, and funneling attention, television, by the capacity of its cinematic powers to convey candidates as multidimensional humans, can provide voters with a superior sense of and greater confidence in their evaluation of the candidates.

This capability of television is illustrated by the several thousand Pennsylvania voters studied by William Lucas and William Adams (1978), political scientists, during the Ford-Carter election in 1976. This was an election in which there was extraordinary voter uncertainty, with as much as half of the electorate unclear about its choice a few weeks before election day. Lucas and Adams found that early decision-making by voters was associated with watching network news and with interpersonal conversations about the two candidates. Both of these factors were independently related to the reaching of an early decision, and Lucas and Adams reason that each had the similar function of giving the voters confidence about the correctness of the direction in which they were leaning. Television coverage gave voters a "third dimension" about the candidates that gave them confidence to make a choice. Having talked about the candidates with others, or having seen them on television, supplied something that was otherwise missing or ambiguous.

Television is consistently cited by voters as their major source of campaign information. The findings of Mendelsohn and O'Keefe (1976) during the 1972 Nixon-McGovern contest are typical:

- Throughout the campaign, one-half or more of voters cited television as their principal source of information, with about a third or fewer naming newspapers, and a minute 5% naming other persons.
- Significantly more judged television to be "fair" than judged newspapers to be so, as would be expected from the well-known beliefs of the public about the media.

Opinions like these do not mean that television is actually the foundation for choosing among the candidates, or that in truth it is a more significant or important source than other sources, but only that it is a highly popular means by which people tune in to the political process.

The data from a variety of surveys, however, make it clear that the conclusion that television is the most common means of informing the public about political campaigns is unjustified. Besides the smallness, compared with the average audience for primetime entertainment, of the audience for network news and the greater frequency with which persons are likely to read a newspaper than view a network newscast within any given period of time, television news appears to be embarrassingly ineffectual in informing voters, given the very large sums expended on nightly production.

Election Day Reporting

Those who believe that any new information will upset an established pattern should examine the experience with the presidential election-day coverage reaching voters in the West. Projections of the winner, based on the outcomes of voting in eastern states and on election polls, have long been accused of affecting the result by altering voter behavior in the West. Several studies in the 1960s disconfirmed these fears (Fuchs, 1966; Mendelsohn, 1966; Lang & Lang, 1968; Tuchman & Coffin, 1971). What seems to have happened is this:

• Very few voters in the West were exposed to such projections.
• Of those exposed, most voted as planned, any switching was evenly balanced, and neither switching nor a decision not to vote seemed to be more frequent among late voters than it had been in the East.

Neither turnout nor voter choice was affected.

In both elections in which the issue was examined, however, the eastern results matched voter expectations. Lyndon Johnson in 1964 had been expected to defeat Barry Goldwater easily; the vote for Nixon and Humphrey in 1968 had been expected to be close. Voters already would have taken these likely trends into account in making their decisions about voting and for whom they would vote; thus, projections would have no effect.

Election day reporting that is counter to expectations would have unknown effects. The ostensible underdog might benefit by the arousal of previously discouraged supporters; the perceived winner might benefit by warning complacent supporters that all was not won. Conceivably, turnout would rise without altering the net balance. Conceivably, one or another candidate might benefit disproportionately, but this would depend on marked inequalities among supporters and potential supporters in the proportions that change their minds about voting or not voting.

The governing hand of expectations in diminishing the likelihood of any effect of projections is enhanced by the supportive factor of other contests to be decided. Every presidential election is accompanied by contests for governor, the Senate, and the House, as well as for local offices, and in many states there will be highly controversial initiatives and referenda on the ballot. The belief that projections of presidential winners affects voter turnout rests on the assumption of voter indifference to these contests; this is an assumption difficult to entertain, particularly when many of the initiatives and referenda will directly affect voters personally (i.e., ceilings on property taxes, increased taxes, bans on public cigarette smoking, auto insurance rate regulation, etc.).

The varied circumstances lead to two principles that apply to communication in general and explain why much television political coverage has no or small influence:

- Redundancy of information is essentially null in effect; effects depend upon novelty and the unexpected.
- Novel and unexpected information may be null in effect if thought or behavior are largely a function of other, overriding factors; knowledge of the outcome of one contest will have no effect when there are several others of interest.

The 1980 contest between Ronald Reagan and Jimmy Carter reignited and enlarged the controversy. Percy Tannenbaum and Leslie Kostrich (1983) tell the story in their book, *Turned-on TV/Turned-off Voters*. The use of late- and exit-polls, competition among the network news teams, and the growing obviousness of a huge Reagan victory when at one time a close race had been expected led to projections even before eastern polls had closed, a Presidential concession of defeat by Carter before polls closed in the West, and the widespread belief that many West Coast persons intending to vote had stayed home. Tannenbaum and Kostrich conclude:

- The surprise element of the 1980 election may have led to a decrease in Western voter turn-out, but it is one hard to document, and the effects of projections clearly are small when outcomes are as expected and probably small when they are unexpected.

- The outcome of a presidential race is unlikely to be affected because the trend already is established and off-setting effects among partisans are likely unless extraordinary regional differences exist, but any effect on overall turnout could have important but hard to predict effects on state and local contests.

- Because the media are unlikely to voluntarily curtail their eagerness to report what they think they know, and Congress is unlikely to legislate against a right probably protected under the First Amendment, there is no clear remedy. A partial solution would be uniform closing of polls. A wicked but effective anti-agent would be widespread lying by those interviewed in exit polls, which would render them useless to the media.

The deplorability of any effects of media coverage on voter behavior is open to challenge. Any effects depend upon voluntary decisions by voters, and if they wish to change their minds about voting or for whom they will vote, that is surely within their rights. That they do so in response to media coverage makes the situation in principle no different than at any other time in the campaign. On only one point is there a serious case against the media: Exit polls. Their interpretation depends on the use of such statistical tools as "confidence intervals" and "margins of error." These are ambiguous if not impenetrable concepts to the general public, and their use by the media is unclear even to experts because there are possible variants in their construction that go unannounced. Exit polls are also subject to the vagaries of sampling, which at times means they will be very wrong. What distinguishes them from informal and unscientific assessments of public sentiment is that the probability of error can be stated statistically. This is the equivalent of giving the odds on sports in Las Vegas terms, where those for football, baseball, boxing, tennis, and horse racing each are calculated and expressed differently and have numerous exotic formulations — a circumstance that gives absolutely no hope of public comprehension.

The Electorate

Newspapers and news magazines are disproportionately favored and used as sources of information by the better-educated, by white-collar employees, managers, and members of the professions, and by those more intensely interested in the campaign. Nevertheless, television reaches a huge and diverse public, and no one permanently can escape it the way he or she can a particular newspaper or magazine. Television is the people's medium and the one particularly relied upon by those who, for reasons of education, income, or culture, have limited access to or make little use of other sources—the poor, blacks and other minorities, and the elderly. These groups, voluntarily or involuntarily, are more dependent on television. However, it is a myth that there are two audiences for news in the United States—one that relies on print almost exclusively, and one that relies on television almost exclusively. Patterson (1980) documents very clearly that when people who follow the news regularly are examined, exposure to print and television sources are about equal among all strata. The pattern has three elements:

- There is a large audience for news that follows events in all media to some degree—although print use is more common and television use less common than public opinion polls suggest.
- There is a sizable audience that pays little attention to the news, persons low in education and income are predominant in it, and any news that is received is likely to come from television or radio.
- There is a highly educated minority that consumes print media to a high degree and for whom television is a less important—although not nonexistent—source than for the news audience as a whole.

Thus, there is a bifocal pattern. If the data are approached from audience characteristics, there is the illusion of vast differences between print and television users. If they are approached from the viewpoint of the composition of the news audience, reliance on the various media is much the same for most of the audience.

Viewers undeniably respond to television news in a way that rewards it for being entertaining. Sociologist Mark Levy (1978) found in questioning news viewers that diversion (news is funny, different, satisfied curiosity) and emotional involvement (news is exciting, relaxing) were two major motives for watching. About half of his sample of Albany, New York, adults admitted that they identified so closely with the newscasters that they felt sorry for them when they made a mistake. Other major motives were comprehension of events, mixed with a desire for reassurance about the state of the world and some relief from personal problems, and an interest in intellectual enrichment. These four motives—diversion, emotional involvement, comprehension mixed with reassurance, and enrichment—seemed to describe separate portions of the audience. A fifth set of viewers emphasized things that they thought were wrong with television news (exaggerates, redundant, superficial). Apparently, these viewers watch to criticize. Television is thus well-advised to try to be entertaining with the news, for this approach adds to the audience. Besides whatever value such pleasure has for viewers, being entertaining could be advanced as a public service by attracting those to the news who otherwise might pay no attention—but the price is its trivialization.

The penchant of television for diversion has caused many to think of it as diversionary. The most famous formulation of this view is the "narcoticizing dysfunction" proposed many decades ago in a much-anthologized article by sociologists Paul Lazarsfeld and Robert Merton (1971) as the possible outcome of public absorption in the mass media. They speculated that attention to mass media news and entertainment might substitute for thoughtful and constructive action. A similar view is held by those who blame television for the decline in voter turnout in presidential elections that has continued since 1960. The empirical challenge faced by observations is that again and again it has been demonstrated that attention to the mass media in any given period is positively associated with involvement in and not withdrawal from political participation. Those higher in media attentiveness are more likely to express an interest in politics, more likely to follow a campaign, more likely to vote, and more likely to be active in some way in a political organization.

Does this mean that television could not be contributing to the secular decline in voter turnout? The answer is, no; television could be having an influence. What it is necessary to posit is a long-term influence presumably achieved through the way television covers politics. The proportion willing to vote or otherwise participate declines each year, yet within any given year, those who are more interested and more involved pay particular attention to the media. Such diverging trends, secular and synchronous, have a strong appeal to common sense. People are becoming turned-off, but those who remain interested want to pay attention.

Reinforcement and crystallization — the cultivation of predispositions and the sharpening and elaboration of opinions already held — became the conventional wisdom about the political effects of the mass media as the result of studies of voting following World War II. These studies found that exposure to the mass media — which then meant newspapers, radio, and magazines — seemed to make a difference in the eventual choice of only a few voters. Choice was largely predictable from region, religion, race, socioeconomic status, and party allegiance. Decisions made early in the campaigns left little opportunity for mass media influence. Close elections, then as always, might turn on any one of a myriad of factors, but the media typically did not seem to have a substantial influence.

Television, first present as a source of convention and campaign coverage and a vehicle for partisan appeals in 1952 when about one out of three households had a set, did not appear to alter this pattern. Yet, circumstances, some encouraged by television, have changed the political status of the media. The media are assuming a larger role than seemed plausible three decades ago.

Party allegiance has declined over the years, so that prior voting behavior increasingly becomes an unreliable predictor of future behavior. Issues have increasingly become prominent in voter decisionmaking. Voters increasingly demand that candidates are acceptable to them in regard to their stated positions. A party label for many will not suffice. Ticket-splitting is becoming more and more common. Voters have become progressively dissatisfied with both of the major parties, making it easier for them to shift between parties and for third party challenges, at least transiently, to gain observable support. Early decisionmaking is becoming less common. For example, in 1976 and 1980, about a fourth of the voters reached a decision in the final two weeks. This compares with about 10% doing so in the 1950s and about 12% in the early 1960s. Since the 1950s, each generation that has matured into the ranks of voters has equaled or exceeded preceding generations in the proportions who declare themselves "independents"; thus, nonaligned voters are becoming more common.

These varied trends are not only signs that traditional strong predictors of voting behavior are becoming weaker and less reliable, they also constitute conditions for the furtherance of that trend. Children reared in families where these trends flourish will not receive the socialization into one or another of the major parties as was so common a part of childrearing in the 1950s and earlier. At the same time, as adults they less often will find their friends, colleagues, and spouses offering a consensus and in accord with them. The overall result is a highly volatile electorate, and one that is more dependent than before on information about the issues and the candidates in order to reach a decision.

Television has contributed to these trends by weakening the role of party leaders and the party mechanism. It permits a candidate to appeal directly to voters both through newscasts and paid political advertisements. The endorsements of party leaders or a party convention, and the use of party personnel in campaigning and getting out the vote become less important. As a result, candidates are less reliant on party support and—because of the important role of paid advertisements—more dependent on campaign funding. This phenomenon is visible at the Presidential level in the television coverage of the primaries, and in every phase of races for the House and Senate. In addition, members of the House and Senate today are freer to ignore party positions in their voting and their stands on issues for the same reason—their reelection is less dependent on party support and more dependent on their ability to communicate to the electorate, which in turn depends on the access to television that derives from money and cleverness.

Presidential Debates

Television also provides a commanding stage for media events, such as televised debates between presidential candidates. Such presentations have overcome the normal barriers that many people erect against political communication. The measure of their notoriety is that they become the substance for extensive coverage by other media—a trick none of *them* have been able to pull on television. The huge audiences drawn by these spectaculars approximate in size and diversity those for the Super Bowl. Their prowess lies not only in the status they achieve by being extraordinary, but in the fact that by simultaneously preempting all three networks they leave the television audience with comparatively little else to watch. Such presentations can expose the public to information that in any other form would be avoided. Television is different not simply because it presents talking pictures, but because of the audience only it can assemble.

It is not surprising that these debates have become the focus of extensive commentary, conjecture, and study. A special issue of *Speaker and Gavel* (Ritter, 1981), the journal of the National Forensic Honorary Society, estimates that by the time of the 1980 encounters (Jimmy Carter vs. Gerald Ford) at least seven books and about 100 articles of a scholarly nature had been published. There have been more since, and they are all in addition to the countless journalistic commentaries. Of the scholarly works, *The Great Debates* compendiums of Sidney Kraus (1977, 1979, 1988), a political communication specialist at the University of Indiana, have been preeminent in assembling empirical studies and conducting a "survey" of the surveys (in 1960, by Elihu Katz and Jacob Feldman; in 1976, by David Sears and Steven Chaffee). Evidence collected on the 1980 (Jimmy Carter vs. Ronald Reagan), 1984 (Walter Mondale vs. Ronald Reagan), and 1988 (George Bush vs. Michael Dukakis) debates largely has confirmed patterns that emerged in the investigation of their forerunners.

The 1960 debates between Jack Kennedy and Richard Nixon are a landmark because they represent the first of what has become an institution, and because they have mythic status as "the means by which Kennedy won the election." However, the 1976 debates between Jimmy Carter and Gerald Ford lay claim to equal historical importance because the conditions for them were also responsible for making such confrontations a recurring part of presidential politics.

The question that must be addressed is why there were no debates in 1964, 1968, or 1972. The answer can be found in the 1960 debates. Nixon was an incumbent vice-president in a popular administration, and Kennedy was a senator from Massachusetts not well-known nationally, and a Catholic besides. Nixon was ostensibly highly experienced in foreign policy, as well as having been a congressional representative and a senator. Kennedy's experience was limited to the Congress. Nixon had greater recognition and stature, and at the outset appeared to be favored by the public in the polls. He was widely thought to have "lost" the first debate. That at least was public and journalistic opinion. He subsequently lost the election. Journalists continue to credit Kennedy's election victory to his debate performance.

The implications were not lost on politicians and their advisers. The person who holds the higher terrain has the most to lose and the least to gain by the exposure of a televised debate. In 1964, 1968, and 1972, there was always a candidate in that position who was able to avoid a debate — an incumbent president. Ostensibly, a major factor was the disinclination of Congress to suspend section 315 of the Federal Communications Act (the Equal Time requirement) so that the debate could be confined to major party candidates. In 1976, it was decided that sponsorship by an organization independent of the networks would make such encounters a "legitimate news event" that could be covered by all media rather than a television presentation. It requires only a little realism and not much cynicism to think that one or another comparable resolution would have been possible in the three preceding elections if an incumbent president had so desired.

The incentive to engage in a televised debate in any election is greatest for the candidate who is least known, has not established an image, is trailing in the polls, or has not fully gained the commitment of those likely to support him. Debates provide hope if not always the means for rectifying such deficits. In 1976, both candidates for the first time in 16 years had equally strong incentives to engage in a debate. Ford was the incumbent, an unconvincing advantage because he had inherited the presidency after Nixon's forced resignation, and he initially trailed badly in the polls. Carter had pledged early to debate to prove his mettle, and had reason to think that his being a newcomer to national Democratic politics made his superiority in the polls suspect or unreliable.

The precedent set by an incumbent president agreeing to a debate has made it almost impossible for a future incumbent or any future candidate not to do so. President Carter, having been the non-incumbent in 1976, could hardly refuse do so in 1980 — although he tried until it appeared that his refusal was hurting his popularity. Neither could President Reagan in 1984, nor could George Bush in 1988 — although in each of these instances these gentlemen appeared to hold the higher terrain at the outset of the campaign.

There are three myths about televised debates between presidential candidates that need to be put to rest. The first is that Jack Kennedy won the election with his debate performance. The second is that such debates typically have a clear and resounding influence on the election outcome. The third is that there is typically a clear "winner" of such confrontations. Let us take these in order:

- *Kennedy the winner.* There was the beginning of a trend toward Kennedy in the polls before the first debate, and the difference in his standing before and after the first debate was a small gain of three percentage points. The trend over the entire campaign suggests that this probably overestimates any gain over this period, and certainly of any effect of the debate. Nixon's standing, however, was unambiguously lower at the time of the first debate than his peak a few weeks before. This pattern favors the view that Kennedy secured his advantage and avoided losing support by a good performance over the view that the election was won or lost that night.

- *Resounding influence.* It has proved impossible to trace decisions registered on election day to exposure to a debate so that one or another candidate clearly can be said to have benefited from his or her performance. The situation with Kennedy is typical. He increased the degree of support among supporters, and degree of acceptance among opponents; Nixon did neither. Few if any votes appeared to have been switched. Thus, Kennedy emerged in a superior position to continue the campaign, but not with more votes. Sixteen years later, Ford had much the same experience. He was credited by the public and by journalists with winning the first debate, and he was beginning to attract support from voters with Republican inclinations who had been uncertain about him. However, that trend was clearly visible in the polls before the debate. Like Kennedy, Ford fortified his position and strengthened his campaign without converting any noticeable number of voters. In 1984, Walter Mondale was credited by journalists with winning the first debate, yet the sizable margin by which he trailed President Reagan did not diminish after the debate. Again, the trend in place (in this case, no trend) persisted.

- *A clear winner.* Debate "winners" are determined by two sources — journalistic commentators and public opinion surveys. The latter quickly become incorporated in the former. Typically, the percentage point difference between those being said to have won or lost is quite small — typically about eight points. The basis for declaring one or another a winner is often a score of about 35% vs. 27%, with the rest saying "neither" (a tie) or "no opinion." The score emerging from the polls in the 1988 vice-presidential debate favoring Lloyd Bentsen over Dan Quayle by about 50% versus about 25% is an anomaly — the 25 percentage point difference is two to three times greater than ever before recorded in these events. Debate performances are always more favorably judged by supporters of the candidate; selective exposure and perception, and especially the latter, are at work. The differences recorded in the public opinion polls largely come from people who are independents, undecided, or at least less than maximally certain about their choice. The judgments of journalistic commentators may sway public opinion when they precede the collection of poll data, as happens when commentary immediately follows the debates. In any case, the public's initial judgment over the winner soon becomes incorporated in conventional knowledge, like a sports outcome, so that there tends to be a progressively rising number naming the person initially scoring better as

the winner. Thus, small differences become defined as clear winning
margins.

Because their novelty inspired so much research and examination,
the 1960 and 1976 debates in particular provide examples of the complexities behind these generalizations. In both cases, about two-thirds
of those leaning toward a candidate perceived him to be the winner.
Slight shifts upward and downward in these partisan sentiments and a
slightly unequal division among the uncommitted made up the small
margin by which one candidate exceeded the other in being named the
winner. This implies that when support is reasonably firm, the advantage in this respect lies with the candidate with the most supporters in
the audience. Ordinarily that would be the candidate leading in the
polls, although the tendency for better-educated persons to pay more
attention to events of this kind would build in a slight advantage for the
Republican candidate because, on the average, Republican voters are
better educated.

In 1960, the approximate parity that the candidates enjoyed in the
polls on the eve of the first debate permitted Kennedy to be named the
winner by achieving a modestly superior ranking of his performance.
In 1976, Ford performed well enough in the first debate to be named
the winner over Carter by more persons. Over the three debates, Carter
performed well enough to achieve near-parity with Ford in debate
performance, although the preeminent role of the first debate in a series
in shifting attitudes probably gave Ford a small overall advantage. In
1976, there was already a trend in the polls in Ford's favor, as there was
with Kennedy in 1960; in both cases, these candidates' performances
in the first debate were supportive of this trend. In Ford's case, persons
who ordinarily voted Republican but had not clearly decided because
of Watergate and Ford's status as an unelected incumbent began to
declare their intentions to vote for Ford.

In both 1960 and 1976, by election time most voters recalled little
of the debates and most voted in accord with their predebate choices or
the choices that would have been predicated from the voters' backgrounds, although for a very, very few, the debates themselves presumably played a decisive role. In 1960, Kennedy won because the trend in
his favor went unhampered by a poor debate performance. In 1976, Ford
made it an extremely close race — victory was not certain until the polls
closed in California — by the same means.

If it cannot be said that televised debates have clear and resounding effects on the partisan support registered on election day, what can be said about them? They have been examined extensively by communications researchers, political scientists, sociologists, and experts in forensics, as well as by journalists, and a fairly consistent pattern has become visible — one that is clear enough that not much new can be expected to be learned from future such events, although every campaign will surely deliver some novel aspects. The pattern can be described in terms of four elements: Audience size, popular evaluation, opinion formation, and format and scheduling.

Audience size invariably has been huge. In 1960, it was estimated that four out of five adults viewed some portion of the series. Figures of the same magnitude have continued to apply. The debates vie in attendance with great sporting events, which they can be said to resemble in producing winners and occasionally disappointing confrontations. However, such figures vastly overestimate actual audience attention. Probably no more than a fourth of the public follows any one debate closely, and no more than a fourth follows a series with any degree of consistent attention. The public's orientation toward television as a medium of entertainment and episodic attention would favor tuning in and tuning out.

The degree of divided attention and inattention directed toward the screen at any time is well known. Audience size typically declines with subsequent debates; any metric based on the first of a series is probably exaggerated. Although the debates certainly reached many who ordinarily ignore political communication, attention to them is greatest among those who are best informed and least in need of additional information — those with a greater degree of education, greater interest in politics, and a greater level of participation in politically related activities. Thus, in regard to audience size and composition, we are left with statistics impressive in size but much less so in regard to the quality of the experience reflected.

The public has decidedly favorable views about televised debates. Sizable majorities believe they are worthwhile and should be a regular feature of presidential elections. A majority report taking them into account in the decisionmaking over whom to vote for. About nine out of 10 adults typically indicate that learning about the issues was their principal motive for viewing. About three-fourths typically assert that they wish to evaluate the candidates as individuals. Although one might be skeptical of whether issues, in fact, figure as strongly in motives as voters say they do, the performance of the press in covering the debates has been a sorry one from the perspective of issues. Journalism-ization describes their treatment. Newspaper and television coverage give only a moderate degree of attention to what was said; instead, they concentrate on identifying a "winner" and on the drama associated with the two candidates meeting on the same stage. Newspapers and television tend to remake the debates on the patterns of sports and entertainment.

The debates appear to play a subtle rather than commanding role in opinion formation. People who attend to them also report more frequently changing their leanings toward one or another of the candidates. This implies purposeful information-seeking in viewing the debates by a substantial proportion of the audience, which would mitigate somewhat the expected factors of divided attention and inattention. No net effect is observable on election day presumably because shifts in degree of support and certainty over choice do not often become switches between candidates, and the occasional switches largely balance each other out, so that there is no sharp debate-based swing in either direction. The post-debate coverage provided by newspapers and television limits effects on public opinion by largely ignoring the substance of the encounters. The apparent assumption that having experienced a debate the public will have cognitively stored what transpired in an accurate, comprehensive, or retrievable form is unwarranted, but conforms to the dictum of the news business that news is what happens next. Finally, with occasional exceptions, debates seem to increase at least temporarily the acceptability of both contenders, presumably because both perform fairly well in setting forth their views. This is to be expected, and can be considered part of the pattern because, after all, they have merited becoming the finalists.

The debates have varied in scheduling and have become progressively more rigid in format in regard to the asking of questions, the time allotted for reply and counter-commentary, and the latitude allowed moderators. Typically, there have been a series of debates for the presidential candidates, and a fewer number for the candidates for vice-president. Newspeople address questions in turn, with the candidate not addressed given a chance to comment or reply. The series usually ends four or more weeks in advance of the election. Format and scheduling are invariably the subject of harsh negotiation between the sponsoring organization and the candidates because the former is interested in public information and the latter in survival or victory. The encounters resemble joint press conferences more than debates because of their rigidity of format, restrictions on time, minimization of confrontation, and favoring of simple statements over developed arguments. In regard to the effects of format and scheduling on outcomes:

- The first debate typically is the most important in regard to affecting public opinion. Swings in degree of support are widest then or occur most frequently. This makes good sense. The audience is at its maximum. Less that is new will be learned from succeeding encounters. A candidate disadvantaged early may not be able to overcome his or her mistakes. Thus, the impact on voters of a series of debates typically declines progressively.

- The less time that elapses between a debate and the election, the greater the likelihood that debate performance will have some clear influence on the outcome of the election. The degree to which shifts in degree of support are more frequent than vote shifts between the candidates, the tendency for shifts among voters to off-set or balance each other, and the amount and frequency of campaign-relevant information that reaches voters each passing day after a debate suggest that any clear effect on opinion would be time-limited.

- Rigidity of format and restrictions on what may transpire are a function of degree of risk to the candidates, with debate formats less rigid and restrictive when participants are of the same party and contending for the nomination than when debates are between the candidates of the major parties contending for the presidency.

On the whole, presidential nominees are highly risk aversive. They would avoid debates when they already have an advantage, they prefer debates scheduled well in advance of the election day so that they can recover from mistakes over those close to election day with their "sudden-death" implications, and they prefer formats that allow them to present their views with a minimum of challenge even if such formats grant the same opportunity to their opponent.

The 1980 debate between Carter and Reagan is a case study exemplifying several of these factors. Carter had refused to debate throughout the primaries (where his opponent was Ted Kennedy) and the presidential campaign. Early in September, he had refused to take part in a debate with Reagan that would include the third party candidate, John Anderson. It was widely believed that Anderson would take more votes from Carter than from Reagan; Carter was protecting his position as Nixon had failed to do. Reagan had engaged in five debates, including four with his primary adversaries and the one post-convention encounter with Anderson. As the campaign entered its final stages, Carter appeared to be gaining in the polls. This was a turn of events expected by many analysts because of a larger overall Democratic registration, a recession, and a sizable number of ordinarily Democratic voters among Reagan supporters — all circumstances favorable to a shift toward a Democratic candidate. As an incumbent gaining advantage, Carter tried to avoid a debate with Reagan. He acceded only when it appeared that his refusal might cost him support, and when the likelihood of Anderson being eligible to participate was sharply decreasing with the decline of his standing in the polls. The debate was held October 28, only seven days before the election. Carter became perceived as the "loser," although it was the usual case of the differences in the proportion of the public saying that one or another candidate had won being modest until journalistic coverage and commentaries established Reagan as the recognized winner. Carter subsequently lost the election.

The timing of the debate, and the perception of an inferior performance by Carter, were hardly the sole factors responsible for Carter's defeat. In fact, they were not even the totality of late campaign factors. However, the circumstances surrounding the 1980 debate made the stakes unusually high for both candidates, and especially so for Carter. Myles Martel (1981), a professor of speech communication and adviser to Reagan on debate strategy, would later write:

> It would be no exaggeration to compare the 1980 presidential debate preparation process with an advanced game of chess. Nearly every move regarding the decision to debate, format, strategies and tactics, and the execution of the debates themselves, was fraught with political implications. One mismove — one untoward statement or look — and the election could have been lost. (p. 46)

Martel accurately describes the importance attached to the debates, whatever their number or timing. He almost certainly exaggerates their importance, even when it is a late debate and the only one. Nevertheless, in this instance history had forced Carter to the least wanted of options — the big gamble.

The influence of presidential debates goes far beyond the contests for that office. The example of 1976, which reintroduced the campaign centerpiece of 1960, placed televised debates generally on the political campaign agenda. This effect has been strongly reinforced by the presidential debates of 1980, 1984, and 1988. Televised debates, as a result, have become a central part of campaigns at every level, and along with them, as with the presidential debates, have come disputes about whether and under what conditions, format and scheduling such encounters should be held and disputes about who was the winner and on what basis. Today, televised debates have become established element of campaigns not only for president and vice-president, but for governor, the Senate, the House, and even for local offices.

Debates have come to play an important and occasionally, perhaps crucial role in elections. Although largely reinforcing predispositions and crystallizing opinions, they also offer to a few new information that contributes to making rather than reaffirming a choice.

They are extraordinarily poor specimens for surgically identifying the varying roles of "images" and "issues" in campaigns. The reason is quite simple. Historically, issues clearly have come to play an increasingly important role in determining voter choice compared to party loyalty or identification, past voting, and such voter attributes as socio economic status, geographical area, or urban versus rural place of residence. However, the combination of television and subsequent news coverage in the case of debates places the candidate at the forefront. Television focuses attention on the individual, and the news media deemphasize the coverage of issues in favor of the performance of the participants. The consequence is that the images projected by the candidates are translated in this context into issues. Is this the kind of man or woman who should hold important office? That becomes the issue around which disputes over the debates revolve.

Debates are seldom decisive on this or any other issue because of their format, their scheduling, and the capabilities of the participants – which minimize the likelihood of one or another of the participants being severely disadvantaged. Nevertheless, because of their presence on television, sizable audiences, and extensive media coverage, debates arguably remain the single most important opportunity for a candidate to lose the election through ineptness and the consequent halting or slowing of a trend in the candidate's favor. These factors, which apply to some degree to debates in contests at all levels, particularly are pronounced in regard to contests for the presidency, and that is perhaps nowhere more apparent than in the degree to which they make central the question, Is he or she fit for the office?

The 1988 election largely reinforced earlier impressions. The standings in the polls after the first of the two major party conventions proved, as they had in the past, to be highly unreliable. In this instance, Governor Michael Dukakis held a lead of well over 10 percentage points after the Democratic convention. By the end of the Republican convention, the candidates appeared to be about equal or George Bush had gained a slight advantage. The news media early ceded to Dukakis a strong advantage; the phraseology by some television commentators implied that his lead was insurmountable. Apparently they forgot that the same pattern of early Democratic advantage had occurred in the Carter-Ford campaign in which the actual election was one of the closest in history. There, too, television commentators gave credence to Carter's enormous early lead; apparently, the memory of television news organizations is brief indeed.

Debate performance again did not translate significantly into votes. The extraordinary degree to which, in the public's opinion, Lloyd Bentsen outperformed Daniel Quayle in the vice presidential debate did not appear to help the Dukakis-Bentsen ticket. Apparently, the public at the time of the debate did not accord the question of the vice-presidency much importance. The fact that at the time the public expressed much greater doubts about and less confidence in the qualifications of Quayle than in those of Bentsen implies that rather than increasing the vulnerability of the Bush-Quayle ticket the question of Quayle had long ago been taken into account in voter decisionmaking and subsequent events had become irrelevant. Similarly, the perception by the public and the press of Dukakis as performing somewhat better in the first debate was reflected only scantily, if at all, in his standings in the polls, with the maximum estimated gain two percentage points or less. The perception by the public and the press that Dukakis performed comparatively poorly in the second debate thus hardly cost him the election, but it did not make it easier for him to win new support.

The 1988 election, then, adds to the evidence assembled on the limited although important political influence of television. The events of 1988 also enhance the conviction that elections can be understood at least as well in terms of patterns as of historical events, and perhaps better.

Media Effects

Ordinarily, it is difficult to attribute effects on public opinion and voter behavior to the media, although the media are crucial elements in the construction of both. The reasons are numerous. Among the more important:

- The media taken together or singly are seldom identifiable as sole sources, and thus it is difficult to identify exposure as surely the cause of knowledge, opinion, or behavior.
- The frameworks, values, and perceptions of reality by which people evaluate the news are constructed over long periods of time, from years of elementary and high school socialization through old age, and to identify the contribution of the media is difficult.

However, there is evidence that television and other mass media can directly affect the cognitive processing of political events, and thereby political behavior such as voting. Shanto Iyengar and Donald Kinder (1987) call the effect "priming." In effect, it links the process of agenda-setting (by which the emphases of the news media influence the priority that the public attaches to major issues) to the evaluation of political candidates and political parties.

Iyengar and Kinder focus exclusively on television. They first examined the influence of the attention given by network television news to such subject issues as energy and inflation on the public's ranking them as important problems. They consistently found an agenda-setting effect. That is, the frequency of stories devoted to a topic affects the importance the public accords to the topic. They further confirmed this agenda-setting effect by a series of experiments in which subjects saw newscasts otherwise alike except for the emphasis on a particular topic. Whatever the topic, the subjects who saw the version emphasizing it rated the topic as more important than those who saw the contrary version. Because the emphases of television news change over time and from day to day, so too will the public's priorities. These are important findings because earlier research had indicated that newspapers are usually more influential in setting the public's agenda than television. That probably remains more often the case, but Iyengar and Kinder make it clear that television cannot be ignored:

All told our evidence implies an American public with a limited memory for last month's news and a recurrent vulnerability to today's. When television news focuses on a problem, the public's priorities are altered, and altered again as television news moves to something new. (*News That Matters*, p. 33)

The most important contribution by Iyengar and Kinder, however, does not concern agenda-setting but priming. They have conducted an extensive series of experiments using either recreations of newscasts that appear authentic or actual newscasts. These newscasts differ between experimental conditions in the event, issue, or topic emphasized. To increase the validity of the findings, Iyengar and Kinder use subjects who are voting adults, and the newscasts are viewed in ordinary, informal surroundings so that attention and interest match home viewing.

After seeing the newscasts, the subjects are asked to evaluate a political figure to whose performance the emphasized elements of the newscasts are highly relevant. Typical figures have included Presidents Carter and Reagan. For example, one newscast might emphasize the Camp David accords for a Middle East truce, considered the major achievement of the Carter administration. Another newscast might emphasize the Iranian hostage crisis, considered the major failure or the most unpopular aspect of the Carter administration. The evaluations have consistently risen or fallen in accord with the topic emphasized by the newscasts. For example, the evaluation of Carter rose when Camp David was emphasized and fell when the hostage crisis was emphasized.

Iyengar and Kinder have also found that the specific introduction of the name of a political figure as responsible for the problem or its solution increases the frequency or degree of such evaluations, and that they are more common in regard to the figure's competence than integrity. Television not only influences the public's priorities, but the priorities influence the public's evaluation of political figures. By making a figure more clearly relevant to a problem, television can increase such evaluation.

The extent to which it is the evaluation of competency that is affected depends on the political figure. Ordinarily, evaluation rises and falls with whether or not the figure is perceived as being able to do the job, but in some instances integrity may be more affected because the figure's standing rests on that quality. That was the case with Reagan. "Priming" affected Carter's competency far more than his integrity ratings, and Reagan's integrity more than his competency ratings. This illustrates the considerable degree to which treatment by the media may interact with the perceived attributes of major figures in constructing public opinion, with deviations from the typical not uncommon.

These varied findings imply that the decisions reached by some voters on election day may be strongly influenced by the play given events by television news as election day approaches. Effects on the election itself would require a sufficient number of undecided or sway-able voters to alter the result. Priming effects on election outcomes, then, are dependent not only on the content of the news but also on the composition of the polity. Iyengar and Kinder have focused on television news, and by so doing they make a good case for its importance in the political process, but what holds for television almost certainly holds to some degree for other media. In any case, this body of research strongly suggests that a late campaign factor adversely affecting Carter in 1980 was his decision to cancel campaigning and return to the White House for last-minute hostage negotiations a few days before the election. By becoming a major story of television and in the newspapers, it placed the weakest element of his administration on the public agenda as the public was preparing to go to the polls.

Whatever aspect of the role of the media is under scrutiny, it is important to distinguish between close and not-so-close elections, and between stable and unstable electorates. The role of the media is particularly important in close elections and when the electorate is unstable. In earlier decades, the struggle between the parties ordinarily has been for the uncommitted or uncertain because the large majority has been stable in support of one or another of the candidates. Their importance becomes enhanced when an election is close, and their number is grossly enlarged with an unstable electorate. As party loyal-ties decline, more people become susceptible to persuasion at any given point in the campaign. As issues become more important, voters turn more to knowledge about the stands of candidates than to their party labels. In the most volatile circumstance of all, large numbers of voters will be unstable in their choices in what appears to be a close race. The actual result may be a landslide, as occurred in 1980 when Reagan defeated Carter. These three circumstances — close elections, unstable electorates, and close elections with unstable electorates — are becoming more common because the decline of party loyalty and the increasing importance of issues sum to voter uncertainty and volatility.

The implication of these varied changes in the political environment is that the influence of the mass media is increasing, for the foundation on which reinforcement must rest — loyalty — is not so clearly present. Even the basis for crystallization — opinion — may not be so often present because it no longer derives so directly from the position taken by a party. The position of television in this picture is problematical. Television news is not good at covering the issues: a headline service, actually entertainment, too visual, dramatic, but not informative medium — whatever the precise phrase, the message is the same. Television presents picturebook history. It does reach people who may disdain newspapers, even though newspapers on the whole may reach more people in the average day. Television has the best chance of reaching those who ignore politics; but such persons, low in interest, untouched by events, and generally indifferent to the news in any form, are the least likely to vote.

Why, then, is everyone so willing to acknowledge television as a powerful political medium? Because it has engaged so visibly and in such a theatrical manner in the function that mass media always have served — the monitoring of politics — and because its status in public opinion as the preeminent news medium bestows a status on coverage that holds regardless of actual audience size.

Politicians are well advised to seek television coverage, partly because nationally it is a medium with three major voices (compared with the many more that make up newspapering), so that the audience assembled for a single message is beyond the capability of other media to assemble. For example, Chaim Eyal (1979), a communications researcher, examined the emphasis given to various topics by the three networks and by newspapers in New Hampshire, Chicago, and Indianapolis, and found that the networks were almost identical but that newspapers differed so much that one could not fairly speak of a newspaper portrayal of the world but only of the portrayal presented by a newspaper.

Media events such as presidential debates dramatize this prowess, but it is continually at work. There is something more: Television is not simply quantitatively important, but qualitatively different. The Checkers speech, the first Nixon-Kennedy debate, the readiness of those Pennsylvania news viewers to decide between Ford and Carter — these exemplify that capability of television to convey something about people beyond what they say or the acts which are attributed to them. Yet television's pronounced devotion to entertainment, which enhances rather than conflicts with this contribution to image, also precludes the medium's domination of politics, for the trends have included a shift toward rationalism. For, contrary and paradoxical though it may seem, the weakening of party ties has been accompanied by the rise in importance of issues — the very matter that most eludes television.

The media are not inert or ineffectual in political influence. That influence simply does not occur in any simplistic way within the campaign for the presidency by the two major party nominees. The media play a continuing, important role in creating the political attitudes, loyalties, and impressions between campaigns that become the context in which campaigns are fought. They influence the process by which candidates are selected by leaving scant ambiguity over the viability of a candidate, the front-runner, and the consequences of whatever contests are impending. They draw attention to the major party nominees by their coverage of the conventions, and create and maintain public attention on the electoral process. Continuously, the media dig into, follow up on, and pursue possibly controversial or damaging questions about the backgrounds of the various candidates. They cover the successes and failures of the two major party candidates, and with an unceasing emphasis on how well each is doing in winning the election. In the primaries, this emphasis on what has come to be known as the "horse race" aspect of the campaign presents the front-runner with "must win" situations and favors the select few leading candidates by giving them the most attention. The range of voter choice thus is delimited. In the campaign itself, this emphasis forecloses the ability of either of the candidates to establish one or another issue, or a set of issues, as paramount. This almost certainly means that the media to some degree, are self-fulfilling in their limited role by excluding coverage of topics that might make a difference in whom a voter will support while emphasizing who is likely to win.

The 1988 campaign provides the most recent documentation that a principal emphasis of media coverage is the "horse race." The American Enterprise Institute (*Broadcasting*, Nov. 14, 1988) analyzed 1,338 election stories carried by ABC, CBS, and NBC during the primaries. More than 500 dealt with who appeared to be winning, and another 300 dealt with campaign strategies, for a total of more than 60% that were horse race stories. There were 215 stories, or 16%, that covered issues. So sensitive is television on this question that the magazine, *Broadcasting* ("TV's Political Coverage," 1988, Nov. 14), concluded that the data on horse race and issue stories "suggests that much of the conventional wisdom concerning television coverage of politics is just plain wrong" (p. 76). Better enroll in a remedial arithmetic course, fellows!

Television was certainly as prominent and in some ways more so than ever before in 1988. Electronic news gathering techniques forced one contender out of the Democratic primaries by documenting that his speeches were plagiaristic of those by a well-known British politician, while investigative newspaper journalism ended the campaign of the Democratic front-runner by documenting sexual liaisons with a photogenic woman not his wife. Sound bites, often supplied by campaign staffs, were ever-present in television news. Negative commercials— that is, those attempting to discredit the opposition candidate—were more prominent than ever before, and were often the topic of television news stories. In these instances, what has transpired in entertainment has also come to be the case in politics, with the media covering themselves and becoming their own subject.

The 1988 campaign also provided a fine example of the search by the media for dramatic themes. In mid-campaign, Dukakis was accurately portrayed as trailing in the polls by a good margin. He was widely said to be conducting an inept campaign. His performance in the second debate with Bush may not have cost him votes, but it certainly did not enhance his chances to gain them. Then Dukakis artfully changed his stance. He ceased to argue that he should not be judged by the label "liberal," which Bush repeatedly had applied to him, but by his accomplishments as governor of Massachusetts and by his proposed policies. Dukakis embraced the label as representing a continuation of the traditions of Franklin D. Roosevelt, Harry S. Truman, and John F. Kennedy. His portrayal changed. He became the fighting underdog exhorting cheering masses by passionate avowals. Television needs themes to make its stories coherent and interesting, and it gave extensive filmed coverage and commentary to the reborn candidate. The theme became "the return of Harry Truman." Nostalgic footage of Truman holding up the *Chicago Tribune* issue that declared his opponent Dewey the winner was segued into Dukakis coverage. Could it happen again? Suspense had been restored to a seeming walkover. The answer was no, for Bush won the popular vote by about eight percentage points. There was some truth to a newly inspired candidacy, however, for Dukakis did better than his opponent among late deciding voters and perhaps among those switching from one candidate to another in the closing days. The unanswerable but intriguing question that remains is whether Dukakis became a changed candidate in response to what he and his advisers perceived as deficits among the electorate and the media, or did his portrayal by the media, and particularly by television, change in response to what the media perceived as the best, most dramatic story for those closing days — the apparently beaten fighter rising from the canvas to fulfill his initial promise. Probably both.

6

Entertainment as Information

The imperfections of television as a news source do not exempt it from being a medium of information, and the news is far from the sole type of programming to disseminate information. Television is predominantly entertainment, and this means by which it diverts its audience inevitably also informs them. The tales of urban crime and police procedure, the mini-series and docudramas, and the antic confrontations with the vicissitudes of job and sex that make up situation comedy make of primetime a continual screening of experiences often unfamiliar and sometimes all too familiar for viewers. Television thereby brings them news about the unknown and confirmation of the known. The sagas of marital discord, moral lapse, and everyday evil that make up daytime soap operas, and the noisy game shows that generally precede them, similarly function as pages from the book of life — while nevertheless, like all of television to some degree, including the news, being taken in as entertainment.

Made in California

Television has two capitals in America. One is Los Angeles. Burbank, one of the seemingly endless municipalities that make up the balkan state of Los Angeles, is as crowded with production companies and studios as the surrounding hillsides are dotted with houses of optimistic hues anomalously set among brave evergeens and palms. Next door in Studio City, in the lobby of the Sheraton-Universal, children wait impatiently for their parents to escort them to the repetitious mock disasters of derailing trains and snapping sharks just over the hill. Deals big and small are ventured, examined, put aside, and reopened and sometimes closed in venues that stretch from the Beverly Hills Hotel's Polo Lounge to La Serre (*the* French restaurant), Art's (*the* deli), and Dupar's (*the* breakfast place) in the San Fernando Valley. This is the new Hollywood, which signifies not an incorporated entity with an architectural novelty as a landmark (the Capital Records tower) and extensive sleaziness, but the community responsible for television and film production.

Los Angeles is the factory of vicarious experience in the United States, a specialization in manufacture that began decades ago with silent movies and the Jewish merchants who found their star in the assembly of ideas and capital in pursuit of public adoration. They applied the principles of the garment business to entertainment, and found the fit good. These were men who made their money by expertly betting on public taste. Jeremy Tunstall, a sociologist, and David Walker (1981), a journalist, both British, quote literary critic and social historian Irving Howe (1976) to describe them:

Samuel Goldwyn, Louis B. Mayer, William Fox, the Warner Brothers, the Schenks, the Selznicks, Harry Cohn, Jesse Lasky, Adolph Zukor—all followed pretty much in Laemmle's footsteps . . . they were on the lookout .. . for a key to wealth and power.

They found it . . . . It was a business that appealed to them: strictly cash, a minimum of goods and apparatus, and brand new. A bright young Jew could get in at the start without having to trip over established gentiles along the way . . . .

The Moguls were mostly semiliterate men, ill at ease with English, but enormously powerful in their intuitive grasp of what American—indeed international—audiences wanted. They were soon dining with heads of state, traveling among the international set, winning and losing fantastic sums at Monte Carlo, realizing their wildest personal fantasies, satisfying their every whim, amiable or sadistic . . . .

Often vulgar, crude, and overbearing, they were brilliantly attuned to the needs of their business . . . . Trusting their own minds and hearts, shrewd enough not to pay too much attention to the talented or cultivated men they hired, the Moguls knew which appeal to sentiment, which twirl of fantasy, which touch of violence, which innuendo of sexuality, would grasp native American audiences. (*World of Our Fathers*, pp. 164-165)

These are the roots of movie and television production today, and certain prominent aspects of the original remain in place — the heavy reliance on intuition, the recruitment of the talented and cultivated to the business of attracting mass audiences, and the manipulation of sentiment, fantasy, violence, and sex in that behalf.

New York, the second city by far in television and film production, is the business office and news headquarters of the medium. Within a few square blocks there are, at 54th Street and the Avenue of the Americas, that symbol of hemispheric congeniality referred to by taxi drivers as Sixth Avenue, the American Broadcasting Company in a bronze-sheathed tower across from the New York Hilton; a block away, at 53rd Street, the Columbia Broadcasting System in a black granite-encased tour de force designed by Eero Saarinen for William S. Paley, where corporate autocracy is manifested in the barring of paintings, prints, and office decor unless they have official sanction; and, down the street and around the corner across from the skating rink, the National Broadcasting Company in the art deco Rockerfeller Center beneath the magnificently refurbished Rainbow Room. Here are the three networks, their presidents, their hundreds of vice-presidents, multitudinous staffs, and the endless luncheons, drinks, scheming, and planning that dictate the listings in *TV Guide*. What is thought in New York is what happens on the West Coast, and eventually on the television screens across America.

These are our two greatest cities, rivaled only weakly by Chicago as a center of commerce and Washington as a center of government. Television, like our great newspapers and national magazines, is the work of urban men and women. This is the worldwide feature of television and other major mass media. They are invariably the products of large, and very often, a nation's most important city or cities, and they are created by people who by education, interests, and talents as well as by place of residence and line of work, differ considerably from most of the huge audiences whose attention they govern. In the United States, the television industry parlance for those audiences is, "the fly-overs."

The mass media by their nature require people enamored of the powers of the word, the image, and the idea. They typically are highly competitive, bright, and clever; they are experts at using language as a weapon to get their way; like the actors and personalities that appear on the screen, for whom "my face for the world to see" is an abiding motive, they often are driven toward the justification of their beings by the public acceptance of their ideas. Like horseplayers, they live and die by the adequacy of their prognostications.

They abide in a world where talent is a commodity whose value depends only in small part on brilliance and in large part on the revenues associated with popularity. They are likely to have a taste for shock, flamboyance, and the rupturing of complaisance, because audience attention and titillated dismay are the ventricles of show business, and for the manipulation of emotion, which is equally at its heart. They nevertheless sometimes harbor the values of literature, which cares absolutely for expression and purpose and not at all for popularity, and of public service, which holds up goals of social justice and edification. As a consequence, some of them are also likely to find themselves often severely conflicted. For such ambitions, like those for the realization of their personal vision and the capturing of public fantasy by outrage, cannot generally be achieved in a mass medium operated principally as a vehicle for advertising.

The powerful role of the values of show business is illustrated in the interviews conducted with members of the Hollywood television community by sociologist Muriel Cantor (1980) and by two journalism professors, Thomas Baldwin and Colby Lewis (1972). Cantor interviewed about 60 producers of primetime television and 24 producers of children's television, focusing on their beliefs about their craft. Baldwin and Lewis interviewed about 40 producers, directors, and writers of primetime action series about the use of violence in television drama. What these people had to say about drama and cartoons is strikingly similar to what news personnel, in television and elsewhere, generally have to say about the news — the principal sources for their decisions are three-fold:

- the conventions of the genre in which they work,
- the expectations of colleagues as to what will succeed and what is worthy, and
- the demands of the organizations (in this case, primarily the networks) which are their clients.

As news personnel prefer to think of themselves as servants to the rules set by the deity news, the Hollywood people see themselves as servants to the god entertainment. The children's producers applied simple principles of distraction and fast action acquired from their experiences in theater cartooning. What was acceptable was whatever would hold a child's transient attention. The younger producers of general audience programming, who had had little or no experience with other media, saw their audience as unsophisticated and, by comparison to themselves, rural; they had few compunctions about conforming to creative limitations imposed by the networks. They did not see themselves as conveyers of ideas, but as assemblers of skills and talents. Many of the older producers, who had had more varied media experience, saw themselves as creators of entertainment and chafed at network-imposed restrictions that affected stories and casting because they believed such interference hampered their pursuit of popularity. What differentiated these two groups was not adherence to show business, but the acceptance by one and the rejection by the other of the conditions of its manufacture. A third group of older producers, many of whom also did considerable writing, opposed interference not because of its effects on popularity but because of its assumed threat to their ability to treat social and political issues.

When questioned about the use of violence, the Hollywood people explained that man against man is the most convenient conflict for resolution within the television format. Show business here requires a fast-moving story that peaks and recedes among the commercials before achieving a crescendo; physical combat, threat, weaponry fit. Television, whether it is Saturday morning or after school, primetime or daytime, comedy or action, game show or soap opera, is dedicated to the principle that gaining attention by whatever means is good. Social and political motives may create conflicts, and important ones, but they are comparatively minor as factors affecting the everyday business of making television.

The producer is the central figure in television production. Horace Newcomb and Robert Alley (1983), who bring to television the perspective of the English Department, make this clear by their interviews with such well-known producers as Norman Lear, Quinn Martin, Garry Marshall and Grant Tinker. These people uniformly seek to put their stamp on what they produce, and to have maximum independence to do so. Newcomb and Alley quote Lear:

> When I was asked whether I had a *right* to say the things that were said in the shows, in the early days I would avoid admitting that we did more than entertain. Then I began to realize that I was 50 years old, a grown man, with

responsibilities and attitudes, and why wouldn't my work express them? (*The Producer's Medium*, p. 192)

And also Richard Levinson and William Link, whose *Columbo* has claim to being a television classic:

> On all our television movies, we do *everything* . . . There are many producers who don't choose to exercise control. They have line producers, executive producers, and all they do is handle stories. But we — and the more we've been doing television the more we like it — out of a compulsion for better work, make every decision. (*The Producer's Medium*, p. 145)

Newcomb and Alley argue that there are a set of producers who exercise extensive authority, impose their vision and values on their work, and create television of which they clearly can be said to be the authors, and others who function simply as part of the entertainment assembly line. The former produce television that is distinctive, complex and, they argue, that has a claim to being artistic. In any case, producing successful television, whether artistic or assembly-line, is lucrative because after two showings on a network all rights for syndication or resale to cable revert to the producer.

This portrait of an elite cadre of creative producers is reinforced by the analysis of innovativeness in programming by Joseph Turow (1984), a Purdue University communications researcher. He found that network behavior followed the acknowledged principle for large organizations in general. The networks only became innovative when threatened by declining ratings and competition. It was a desperation maneuver. When producers were innovative, however, it was because they valued such behavior and had the freedom to engage in it — by having sources of income independent of innovative television programming, such as making movies for theater release or an established series. For the networks, innovation is defensive; for the creative producers, it is an enduring style of operation.

The business offices and the production factories, centered 3,000 miles apart, both give their allegiance to popularity, but to a degree and in manner sufficiently different that often they are pitted against each other. At root, it is the inevitable fray between the distributor and the craftsman.

In careers in the mass media, there are forks at which one must choose between managing and making, judging and shaping. Those who choose the former route cannot help but sacrifice their creative urges to business judgments. What others create become in their hands products to be priced and peddled. Those who choose the second route cannot help but acknowledge, and in many cases become uncanny practitioners of, the business side of television; yet business for them is constrained by, not always at peace with, and sometimes subservient to, art and craft.

Thus, newspaper and magazine publishers and advertising departments have separate interests from editors and writers, as to a lesser degree do the editors from the writers. In television, as in other media, these different interests are a matter of survival. The network president, the programming chief, the analysts of audience fealty and fickleness, seek to fill a schedule whose popularity will justify peak advertising rates. The producer, the director, and the writer are in accord that popularity is not irrelevant, but they often differ with those in command of distribution on its substance and the means of its achievement.

The motives that directed some members of the creative community into the making of television levy a concern for the quality as well as the quantity of audience response. They see their work cheapened when it cannot emerge as they believe the principles of storytelling demand. They often are ready to settle for a smaller audience of many rather than maximum millions in behalf of the integrity of their work. In other instances, even those without such concerns may see the judgments of the business offices as simply wrongheaded in regard to the gross popularity sought. In both cases, both groups are quite correct to see their careers as contingent on the most perfect expression possible of their ideas.

The television production community is led by its distinctly different self-interest to challenge continually the mandate assumed by the networks. What varies is not the basis of the conflict, but its focus. At one moment, it is the advance time allowed for the production of new programming, which the entertainment makers may believe is insufficient to achieve quality. At another, it is the budgetary allowance for a particular project, which again may seem insufficient. At other times, it will be restrictions on violence or on the depictions of characters whose ethnic or religious identity may involve a risk of public objection from some organization, or on a plot or treatment that may arouse controversy unredeemed by enhanced ratings. At still another, it may be the treatment, the cast, the resolution or denouement, or some other translation of a particular theme.

The networks adhere to the motto of most businesses: Make no enemies. When an animated version of *Flash Gordon* was in preparation for NBC, one anxious network employee looked at Ming the Merciless who rules the Planet Mongo on which Flash and his party are trapped, a figure symbolically more in tune with the days when China was thought of as the source of the yellow peril than as a market for Coca Cola, and said, "Can't you make him a little less yellow?"

These tensions and conflicts are inherent in the business. The suspension of television production between art and commerce makes frustration inevitable for many in the creative community, and yet for any particular job, project, or time period, misgivings generally will be set aside because the alternative often is to find another line of work. Paradoxically, those who govern television cannot so easily escape temporarily the duality of their situation. This is because they are engaged in making policy decisions, and the two goals of profitable, popular television and television that represents the best of the medium and could be said without embarrassment to serve the "public interest, convenience, and necessity" seldom suggest the same decision.

What the business people and the creative people — to put the distinction in the terms employed by the two groups themselves — share is participation in a heated, tumultuous enterprise centered in two great cities. Broadcasting as a whole is spread across the land, and its diverse elements come together annually, like those of many American institutions, at trade meetings in such centers of planned conviviality as Las Vegas. Nevertheless, manufacture and dissemination of the production, as contrasted with its mostly local relay to the home, are the province of New York and Los Angeles. Television people are not simply intelligent, educated, literate, verbal, and middle or upper-middle class. They are not simply cosmopolitan in looking toward colleagues for guidance and taking their cues and attaching importance to what happens thousands of miles away. They are undeniably an elite, but in particular an elite that itself is part of the two cultural capitals toward which the rest of the country occasionally stares and to which members of other elites elsewhere continually give their attention.

Los Angeles, along with San Francisco, is where people travel to see if desperation is justified — the last chance. Its abysmal flatlands in summer, stretching endlessly under yellow skies, its cheery hills and canyons bearing houses precarious before fire and landslide, the blue Pacific whose beaches are both the site of bonfires of dropouts and the homes of the professionally superordinate, are tied together by the freeways and the automobile. The English architectural writer, Reyner Banham (1971), depicts the authentic L.A. in defining it as three natural ecologies — hills, seashore, and basin — united by the manmade ecology of concrete freeways and Detroit or foreign (Japanese for the masses, German or English for the elites) sheet metal. Los Angeles is a city of distances, and the constant movement in the isolation of private vehicles from dwelling to shopping center to workplace turns people inward just as it inevitably isolates them from others.

Los Angeles, as filled with as competitive, ruthless, hardworking a citizenry as any modern city in the world, nevertheless stands for the belief that there must be more to life, or at least an alternative. It is all right to cast aside values in behalf of feeling better in L.A. The offbeat, the odd, the deviant in Los Angeles are likely to become marketed as a religion, a lifestyle, a therapy, or a path of greater conformity to human potential. Los Angeles is the capital of the conversion of personal vision to commerce. Pleasure and profit there, as in the rest of California, supposedly are easily joined. This is the homeland, the backdrop, the reference, the milieu, for the making of American television.

Fiction is always a source of insight about a milieu or place. Los Angeles can be grasped, if ever so uneasily, in the barrenness of Joan Didion's *Play It As It Lays*, the defeated aspirations in the novels of Raymond Chandler, the doomed grasping paradise in James M. Cain's *The Postman Always Rings Twice*, and the temptation to shun the obligations of the past on which turn the works of Ross MacDonald. The message of the L.A. novel is that there is something about the place that seduces and betrays. Its most perfect expression is Allison Lurie's *The Nowhere City* in which L.A. functions as a character paring a visiting couple to their true selves, leaving the woman, initially cloistered and priggish, smugly sensual, and the husband, at first in pursuit of self-indulgence, unable to hide from his need for protective conventions. L.A. fiction centers on the psyche and its inability out West, despite the illusion to the contrary, to escape itself or control what it will become.

Los Angeles in our national consciousness is both myth and promise — of excitement, the big time, success, and personal fulfillment. Yet its place in our cosmology is far from one of easy acceptance. Depictions of Los Angeles often pass quickly from realism to caricature, and its natural end becomes a conflagration such as concludes Nathaniel

West's *The Day of the Locust:* The great earthquake whose destructiveness is foreshadowed in the present day mural on an L.A. wall of an elevated freeway crumbling into a dead end in midair. Thus there is also more than a hint in our national consciousness of an ambivalence over the reward for flight, self-indulgence, and the pursuit of pleasure.

Fiction can also tell us about the media. It is written by people intensely close to their subject, and the Hollywood novel, the Madison Avenue novel, and the television novel are reports from the field by combatants. What they tell us is what the media mean to those who work in them. What happens in mass media novels, typically, is that good intentions have unsatisfying consequences, and the causes of unrealized aspirations are the values that the media exemplify. The consuming necessity of popularity checkmates subtlety while the filtering of decisions through a bureaucracy works against originality. What is lost is the capacity of work to reflect individuality. The persistent theme is corrupting influence. One apt phrase is, "the conversion of art to employment."

Because the point at issue is the integrity of communication, the values that mass media are principally said to corrupt are those about communication itself. There is almost invariably a loss of innocence, sometimes over ideals, but more often over the inability to maintain established standards against new criteria seemingly imposed by the marketplace. The artistic impulse, and its necessary discipline, are made secondary to the narrower but less demanding norms of professionalism; professionalism that values individual creativity gives way before the mechanistic application of audience research and committee decisionmaking.

The television novel naturally gives particular emphasis to a second theme — the consequences of the power that accompanies prominence in the media. Naturally, because television is the medium that most quickly and assuredly can elevate a performer or public figure. The message here is that of Lord Acton: Such power is so great that it defies being used well.

A third common theme is that of chicanery. The media are not only portrayed as manipulative of the public, but rising with them as dependent on deceiving others. What sets the media novels apart from those about any big organization is the cynicism. Sammy Glick of Budd Schulberg's *What Makes Sammy Run* was never a happy man, and living by the lie cost him much, but certainly not success. The fact that the fictional portrayal is closely modeled on one of those early Hollywood moguls merely makes the point more convincing.

The fourth frequent theme is the capacity of the media to alter what people might otherwise perceive. Gavin Lambert delicately acknowledges this power in *Slide Area* in an episode in which sound effects and sensory stimuli are enough to make a woman, blind and dying in a Hollywood mansion, believe that her last days are being expended on an international tour of the sites of youthful triumph. We have seen how news on television may convey something different from the events themselves; the medium of most perfect observation is no less distorting than any other. In *The Origin of the Brunists*, Robert Coover depicts reportage of a religious cult as responsible for heightened proselytization about doomsday, and ensuing coverage as responsible for transforming the cult into a worldwide religion. When the failure of the initial prophecy is reported in the press, the members seek to vindicate themselves by gaining new adherents, and the story the media then concoct achieves social legitimacy for the cult's theorems. In both these instances, reality has been reconstrued by the media.

What is one to make of such a portrait? A stranger to our culture might conclude that it is the antithesis of the mass media. The truth on the whole is much more paradoxical. What these novels express is recognition of the power of the economic and social machinery of the media to govern the lives of those who work within them, coupled with acknowledgment of the power of the media to influence events and public behavior, and unabashed fascination with both.

And there is the answer. This is not an antithetical portrait but one of grudging and anxious admiration. The media for many are irresistible as places of employment precisely because they are so powerful in those two ways. The governance that the media exerts over the ambitions, ideals, and fulfillment of those who work in them tests talent, worth, vision, and true grit. The power that the media exert in society makes access to them enormously rewarding—a reward that is particularly gratifying when one has survived the tests of the first kind.

Two cities. Individuals in conflict. The division of labor between selling and making. One centered in New York, the other in Los Angeles. A professional class, as are other professional classes, distinctly set apart from the mainstream in ways particular to itself. Ambivalence over the institution and the work that it demands. These

constitute the milieu of television and the context in which its entertain
ment is manufactured. The strains show continually in the product in
the compromises between and occasional victories of institution and
individual.

Television entertainment is marked by its emergence from New York
and Los Angeles. These two cities, in their different ways, exemplify
urban culture in the United States. They constitute a frontier of though
and behavior. Media people not only constitute a distinct professiona
class, but the places from which they perceive the world constitute an
experience distinct from that of the rest of America. Television enter
tainment consistently and inevitably treats topics central to life — sexua
mores; crime and justice; retribution; achievement; and the use o'
authority men and women hold by virtue of wealth, education, and
position. Although television unmistakably operates within the var
ious confines of mass entertainment, by its very nature as a creature o
these two cities for many it is invariably occasionally disturbing, a
variance with values, offensive, and novel. It is a force for what sometimes
may be progress and for what most certainly is change. The conten
is specifically American, but this urbanization of culture through the
mass media is a phenomenon common to all societies because the media
invariably emanate principally from cultural and political capitals. It is
a phenomenon greatly escalated by television, for television is the
medium that most closely approximates one or a few voices rather than
many in addressing a country. In these respects, Los Angeles becomes
superordinate. Except for national network news, it is the site for the
making of television, and in the mass media as elsewhere, those who
translate general orders into concrete products have the decided advan
tage in determining their shape.

Programming

The content of television programming has fascinated social scien
tists, scholars, and critics since the introduction of the medium. Aca
demic, as opposed to journalistic, scrutiny typically has followed one
of two lines. In one, the focus has been on the commonalities and
consistencies across programs. In the other, it has been on the differ
ences and diversity among programs. Empirical and qualitative analy
ses have had some place in both lines of inquiry, but the empirical has
been preeminent in the first instance and the qualitative in the second

Empirical studies quantify elements of programming that can be identified and tabulated, and typically result in broad statistical descriptions of the content of various program categories. They ignore differences within these categories in favor of accurate description of the genres as a whole. Qualitative analyses employ various concepts and theories to lay out the various meanings that might be attached to, conventions and mechanisms employed by, and specific features of programming, often focusing on individual series or even episodes. They often forego any claim that what they describe is typical, although they will almost invariably assert that it has import in understanding American culture. In fact, both approaches must bear the same two burdens:

• Description that is accurate, whether quantitative or qualitative.

• Interpretation that casts light on the way television functions in America.

Empirical and qualitative analyses both will receive attention, because the characteristics that define television programming can be depicted only by taking into account both the commonalities and consistencies across programs and the differences and diversity among programs.

The first empirical studies focused on violence. Later studies have examined such varied topics as the portrayal of ethnic minorities, women, social class, means of personal achievement, and environmental issues. Violence, because of concern over possible influence on the behavior of viewers, has remained a focus. These empirical examinations document the generalities of television entertainment, yet they never tell us the whole story, for exception, nuance, and subtleties escape them.

These examinations have often been motivated by the belief that television departs from some ideal standard of balance, equity, fairness, or impartiality, and that such beliefs would have increased credibility if thoroughly documented. Here, the interest is in what typifies television programming. Two especially important sets of data are the continuing examinations over the past two decades by George Gerbner, Larry Gross, and their colleagues at the University of Pennsylvania (Gerbner, Gross, Morgan, & Signorielli, 1986) and by Bradley Greenberg (1980) and his colleagues at Michigan State University, all communications researchers.

A pervasive theme of television entertainment is the satisfaction to be achieved from consumption. This theme applies to both material possessions and substances to be eaten or drunk. It applies equally to commercials and to the programs that accompany them. Television commercials almost invariably emphasize the enjoyment that will ensue from use of the product. This applies alike to buying a new car, employing a detergent, or eating a candy. Among television programs, the most obtrusive in their emphasis on consumption are the game shows, in which competition for sometimes sizable rewards varies from the straightforward and intellectually challenging to volunteering to varying degrees of condescension as the price of participation. Primetime drama and daytime and primetime soap operas are hardly far behind. Key elements are the affluence in which so many characters luxuriate, the frequency with which wealth is the motive for dishonest scheming and crime, and the houses and apartments in which events take place. It is not solely that so many stories revolve around the rich, but that in so many instances dwellings and their furnishings are beyond the means of those portrayed as occupying them.

Not all of this portrayed consumption is necessarily harmless, and that which is potentially harmful is not at all beyond the means of average viewers. Commercials promote beer and wine, but so does primetime drama. Greenberg (1980) and colleagues concluded that there were at least two acts of alcohol consumption during the average hour of programming. They speculate:

> To the extent that social behaviors on television, such as acts of drinking, are performed by liked characters, in a positive context, without negative consequences, or with positive rewards, social learning is likely to occur .... It can affect the viewer's aspirations and expectations . . . it can impinge on the viewer's beliefs with regard to . . . acceptability or appropriateness . . . and it can induce either imitation or a desire for imitation. (*Life on Television*, p. 146)

It is left to the reader to judge whether the portrayals of alcohol consumption in drama conform to these requirements.

Another theme is that the world is a mean and risky place. The compatibility of violence and crime with the need to tell exciting stories succinctly in visual terms has made physical transgression a continuing component of television. The continuing analysis of television violence over the past two decades by Gerbner, Gross, and colleagues (Gerbner

Gross, 1976; Gerbner, Gross, Morgan, & Signorielli, 1986; Gerbner, Gross, Signorielli, & Morgan, 1986) has led them to calculate that the likelihood of a television character falling victim to violence is about 10 times greater than the probability for the average American adult. Because television tries to avoid unnecessary offense, the physical consequences for the victim, the unpleasantness for onlookers, and the emotional suffering of relatives and friends of this violence are seldom portrayed; it is quick and antiseptic.

Television is duplicitous in its treatment of the social hierarchy. Since the 1950s, it has depicted a world in which the social pyramid is reversed, with more people in the professional and educated middle and upper-middle classes than in the working, blue collar, or poverty classes. Truly poor people almost never appear on television except rarely as minor symbols of social dissolution in the background of urban crime shows. Hispanics have hardly been visible at all, with Greenberg remarking about television at the beginning of the 1980s, "They're hard to find. If you watched 300 different television characters, say, you'd find less than a handful of Hispanics" (p. 11). The proliferation of urban crime shows during the decade probably increased their presence slightly, but as a proportion of all characters, they account at best for a very, very, very few percentage points. Blacks were seen infrequently before an explicit change in network policy in the late 1960s in response to the civil rights movement, and since then have constituted about 10% of all characters with minor variation from year to year for a figure that annually has approximated or fallen somewhat below their proportion in the population. However, blacks receive the same inversion of the pyramid as occurs for television characters in general, with far more in the professional and educated middle and upper-middle classes than below.

Television is arguably in agreement with social norms in its depiction of women. There have been decidedly more major male characters in primetime since the beginning of television, and equality has not yet been achieved in this respect. Typically, women defer to men, and are unlikely to give orders to men while highly likely to receive orders from them. They are typically portrayed as subsidiary helpmates, as mothers, as creatures seeking status, advantageous marriage, or sexual liaison, or as objects of sexual conquest. In commercials, during the first two decades of television females were typically portrayed as product users and men as product experts, and especially so for products used in housekeeping. Since then, women have had somewhat stronger roles particularly in a few prominent commercials of the mid-1980s mocking these earlier conventions, but even today it seems unlikely that they have achieved equal treatment. Females have fared somewhat better in daytime soap operas in frequency of appearance, and more often give orders although (it's true) mostly to women. However, Mary Cassata and Thomas Skill, University of Buffalo communications research ers, reported in 1983 that the 1972 conclusion by Natan Katzman in *Public Opinion Quarterly* that a strong soap opera theme is male dominance of females remained true if slightly diminished.

This theme of male preeminence is reinforced by the strong role assigned to males and by the portrayed degree of participation in the work force of women. Males, usually white, almost invariably youthful or in the prime of life, sometimes prosperous members of a profession such as law or medicine but often ambiguous as to the source of their very apparent real means, are typically the fulcrums of decision and action. That very ambiguousness of income becomes central, because it implies the capacity to live above and beyond the constraints imposed on ordinary mortals. The committing of violent acts arguably could be said to symbolize force and power (although certainly in specific instances it may stand for fear, desperation, and weakness), and Gerbner, Gross, and colleagues (Gerbner & Gross, 1976; Gerbner, Gross, Morgan, & Signorielli, 1986; Gerbner, Gross, Signorielli, & Morgan, 1986) have documented that on television males have been decidedly preeminent in that capacity over the past two decades. At the same time, women have entered the labor force more slowly on television than in real life.

Television continually reiterates the theme of shady business practice. In primetime drama, legitimate businesses not only are often fronts for crime, but businessmen cheat, embezzle, and murder to advance themselves; and torching their own premises becomes a means of raising capital. Behavior in conflict with the public good as well as against the law, such as illegal disposal of toxic waste, indifference to pollution, and taking advantage of a gullible public is common — so much so, that in the mid-1980s *PBS* presented a documentary entitled *Hollywood's Favorite Heavy: Businessmen on Primetime TV.* On the other hand, television comparatively infrequently portrays crime as committed by those low in socioeconomic status, and while white collar crime is hardly unknown, it cannot be fairly said that in real life more crime — especially of the kind depicted on television — is committed by the upper than the lower social orders.

An exception to this portrayal of men and women of high social stature as conniving and dishonest are doctors of all kinds, dentists, and others in the so-called helping professions. They not only escape calumny, but are typically portrayed as extraordinarily effective and certainly almost always as goodwilled and wise. These are groups with professional organizations quick to flare at mistreatment in the media. More importantly, an entertainment medium such as television would not dare to portray such persons in a way that might damage their effectiveness or the willingness of people to make use of their services. No one seriously believes that the negative portrayal of businessmen has any near-term effect on the conduct of business or the state of the economy, although it might well help to establish skepticism and even hostile public opinion that might have long-range effects on the relations of business with the government and the public.

Television is schizophrenic in its treatment of law enforcement. Police and private detectives solve crimes with a success rate matched in actual practice only by the ticketing of parking violators by meter maids. Private eyes in real life seldom are central to a criminal investigation, but in television drama the miscarriage of justice is often only averted by their intervention. It is one of the ironies of television that while real life criminals sometimes in press accounts admit to having learned useful techniques and dodges from television or to have borrowed the crime *in toto* from some program, police officials invariably find television drama at sharp variance with real police work. Television certainly does insist that crime does not pay, but it often implies that the law must be broken in order to bring criminals to justice. The abrogation of Constitutional guarantees in television drama in arrest and conviction is commonplace; *Dirty Harry* is a stock figure. The sociologist Otto Larsen many years ago found that antisocial means frequently were employed in television drama to attain socially-approved goals (Larsen, Gray, & Fortis, 1963). That often remains the case. On television, justice and law are not synonymous and the end quite often appears to justify the means.

Belief in the occult, life on other planets, life after death, and hidden and possibly malevolent purpose behind the inexplicable, subjects so relentlessly exploited by the supermarket check-out counter tabloids

("Two-Headed Woman in Topless Bar") have not been ignored by television. In comedy and drama, for general audiences as well as for children, humans with supernatural powers, extraterrestrials, witches, ghosts, and vampires have been frequent. In documentaries, cameras have focused on the empty field where some strange residue was said to have marked the landing of a flying saucer. The theme is that there is another perhaps more powerful life.

The soap opera has received extensive attention as a distinctive and intriguing category of programming. The classical soap opera of radio days and earlier television is the *Grand Hotel* (MGM, 1932) formula at the community level. In these daytime sagas, a handful of characters, each pursuing an independent destiny, variously become entangled in each others' lives. Each lifeline is a series of trials and mishaps — illness, an unhappy marriage, unrequited love, bigamy, a failing business, a dishonored promise, and as taboos about what could be portrayed began to tumble, adultery, alcoholism, drug abuse, and rape. Life is portrayed as a succession of crises carrying people first closer to, then drawing them away from, a stylish liaison, an object of ardor, wealth, calamity, or dire harm. The troubles keep on coming, but driven by ambition, hope, greed, or naivete, the characters struggle ceaselessly against the tide.

These tribulations are distinct from the conflicts long central to primetime drama by representing nothing more than the dark underside of humdrum life, as if the pathetic trivia from the inside local pages of newspapers must also find its place on television. The audience looks upward much of the time in these stories, for they are tales heavily populated by the middle and upper-middle classes, and particularly professionals. If the problems are unusual in quantity and regularity, they are less so in degree and not at all in category — marriage, money worries, sex, booze, drugs. The stories illustrate modes of coping, and emphasize the seeking of professional help. The soap operas thus provide some solace by depicting the troubles of others as more oppressive if similar, with help or resolution possible. The largely female audience has been able to identify with little or no discomfort.

The primetime soap operas have introduced additional elements. The events are played out on a grander scale by actors better known to the general public. They differ from the classic daytime soap operas by incorporating elements long common to primetime drama. Conflicts are not over businesses, but huge fortunes; jobs and positions are not only at risk, but high office; business dealings are not only dishonest, but ruthless and vicious; the lifelines not only intersect, but do so through false identities, kidnap plots, and extortion attempts; and the troubles not only include personal trials and mishaps, but serious crime, physical violence, and murder. In accord with the recombinant principle, these elements soon began to appear on daytime soap operas, so that prime-time and daytime soap operas have become progressively more like one another. By so doing, both have become more like primetime drama, yet they remain distinctly apart because of their ever-continuing stories without the resolution of an ordinary series episode, the emphasis on emotional responses and entanglements, and the focus on day-to-day traumas.

Robert Allen (1985), a professor of communications at the University of North Carolina, in his excellent examination of the evolution of daytime soap operas, argues that these new elements have made them "malleable" in viewer interpretation, and therefore more attractive to viewers other than housewives — "women in the paid labor force, college students, adolescents, retired men and women" (p. 179). As part of the increase in the consumption of television, the soap opera audience has grown larger over the past decade, and as a consequence somewhat more varied in makeup. The new elements, then, represent not only the influence of the emergence of primetime soap operas, but a response by daytime soap operas to changes in the audience.

The concepts Allen uses to analyze the soap opera are drawn from semiotics and the intensive scrutiny of literature, and such terms as "codes," "poetics," and "text" are common. He sees the soap opera as a highly open system of symbols amenable to a variety of "negotiated meanings" for different sectors of the audience; in this respect, they can be contrasted with television commercials which typically permit few or even a sole interpretation. In this view, Allen is in accord with the sociologist Elihu Katz and his colleague (Katz & Liebes, 1985) who have found substantial cross-cultural differences in the understanding of such an apparently straightforward, if melodramatic, show as *Dallas* — which implies that such differences may occur between many categories of viewers, such as males versus females, older versus younger, black versus white, and richer versus poorer. Allen makes the legitimate point that empirical investigations of all kinds, including content analyses, experiments on media effects, and surveys of audience behavior, cannot fully, and in some cases even tolerably, encapsulate the process represented by the consumption of symbols. He makes an important point when he argues that the use of the kind of concepts he employs enriches the understanding of soap operas and of other kinds of television programming. One must be wary, however, of the "fallacy of application": Because a schema or set of concepts can be applied effectively to different subjects of inquiry does not make those subjects equivalent in quality, importance, or significance.

Allen's viewpoint represents what Newcomb and Alley (1983) call the "ritualistic" as opposed to the "transportation" model of communication. In the former, the emphasis is on the meaning derived by the viewer from the content and process of media consumption; in the latter, it is on the effects on the viewer of the content delivered by the media. Both are important and so one can only endorse Allen's view that:

> the point here is not to deny that many working-class women enjoy soap operas (they obviously do) or to rule out the possibility of "learning" as occurring as a result of watching soaps (it almost certainly does) or to regard as aesthetically deficient anyone who does not enjoy watching soap operas (that would merely be to invert the aesthetic canon). Rather it is to remind us that the term "soap opera" carries with it a set of deeply embedded attitudes toward it, that it has come to "mean" because of its position within and across discourses — a position relative to notions of art, mass media, social stature, gender, and culture. (*Speaking of Soap Operas*, p. 29)

A view which, with appropriate substitutions, could be as well applied profitably to the rest of television.

Self-interest is what gives shape to what is broadcast, and the way conventionality is the invariable framework in soap opera and prime-time programming for selective deviation exemplifies this principle. In soap operas, abortion seldom is treated as acceptable. Premarital cohabitation, divorce, and illegitimacy are portrayed as facts of life. The distinction is between behavior that would arouse the partisanship of viewers and religious orders, and statuses that have come to be accepted as perhaps problematic or to some regrettable but are essentially beyond condemnation. During primetime, homosexuality and racial antagonism can be placed in comedy more easily than in drama because the former permits ambiguity in regard to approval. Black characters enjoy the same inverse social structure as have whites, with more in the middle and upper-middle classes than in lower strata — although in real

life the pyramid is more sharply exaggerated among blacks. The caution
with which television enters new territory is illustrated by the tendency
for blacks, when they began to appear more frequently in commercials
two decades ago, to be placed in larger-than-ordinary crowds of whites
to ensure that they would be unobtrusive.

Nowhere is this invisible hand of prudence more strikingly displayed
than in the analysis of the treatment of the environment in comedy and
drama by Rutgers historian Richard Heffner and his colleague Esther
Kramer (1972). They found that during a week of network programming, topics were treated in accord with their potential for disrupting
television's ordinary conduct of business. Conservation and nature
were treated approvingly and pollution was condemned, in line with
public sympathies. Population control, although opportunities occurred
for favorable or unfavorable treatment, was dealt with obliquely and
ambiguously. Where television had a direct interest through advertising
revenues, in transportation, private means were strongly favored over
public means. Television dramas and comedies take their risks with
calculation.

There is also the pervasive theme best described as California-
ization. Television is mostly made in California because that is where
the movies are made, and the movies came to be made there in large
part because of the climate and the opportunity for outdoor filming.
Thus, the stories told by television, as well as by the movies, are not
only frequently set in California, but because of that fact, they also deal
with California topics, and what is depicted has a decidedly California
cast. Tunstall and Walker (1981) make the point:

> The imaginative traveller through the state of California is constantly re-
> minded of somewhere else, of places real and fictional, their names half-
> forgotten as movie and television titles . . . slip and slide in the space of
> memory. California looks like everywhere for a simple reason. The state's
> landscapes have doubled for all regions of the world. Like an infinitely
> versatile extra, California's topography has had a walk-on role in countless
> productions. The Ojai Valley played Shangri-La in the movie *Lost Horizon;*
> the Mohave Desert has been the Sahara; Camp Pendleton, on the coast
> between Los Angeles and San Diego, was once Iwo Jima; the Santa Monica
> Mountains, Korea. China Lake, its expanse fittingly lunar, was once the moon.
> California's landscape is a universal backdrop against which many a story can
> play . . . . (*Media Made in California*, p. 13)

As Tunstall and Walker describe it, Los Angeles began to become the capital of television production, replacing New York, in the early 1950s. The studios were in dire straits because of the sharp decline in theater revenues brought about by television and the break-up of their ownership of large motion picture theaters (on which each owning studio could force its product) under federal antitrust statutes. The preeminent pioneers were two set-in-California series, *I Love Lucy* with Lucille Ball and Desi Arnez, and Jack Webb's *Dragnet.*

At this point in time, a sizable number of films were made in Italy, Great Britain or Spain. In the 1960s, location shooting in California again became predominant because of cost advantages. The movies joined what had become the convention for television. As Tunstall and Walker write, "The techniques of modern television production favor outdoors action, and audiences like action-adventure series: California with its roads and hills and its supply of movie-trained professional stuntmen was the obvious place to make such programming" (p. 16).

These factors established the foundation for all of television to shift westward. Game shows became clearly made in California. Talk shows became centered in California because hosts could recruit better guests than almost anywhere else and could pursue their careers off-television in Las Vegas or Hollywood. Situation comedies similarly became made in California, although often set elsewhere. Nevertheless, *Three's Company* makes the case that even here there has been a California presence.

The many and varied themes of the programs are interspersed with continuing illustrations of exemplary behavior. Daring rescues, self-lessness, loyalty to others, and the struggle against difficult odds have accompanied the conflict and violence in nighttime drama. Persistence, immunity to temptation, bravery, and inventiveness have been regularly portrayed. *Gunsmoke,* the longest-running series in television history when finally cancelled after 20 years in 1975, featured Matt Dillon as a lawman who was intelligent, concerned as much for the welfare of his townsfolk as for the letter of the law, and, while iron in resolve and unflinching before danger, never one to resort to violence except when it was his only recourse. That model has reappeared in countless series. Television regularly portrays human endeavor at its peak or at its best; its conventions and the conventionality of treatment these foster simply do not lead to its full portrayal.

The writer and newspaper columnist Ben Stein (1979) created a stir in the Hollywood community with his *The View From Sunset Boulevard,* and his name today still evokes a certain rueful appreciation for his iconoclasm. He argued that television producers were much alike in their thinking, that these thoughts were reflected in the programs they produced, and that the outlooks embodied in these programs were antithetical with, hostile to, and discordant from both reality and mainstream America. The television programs and their producers were depicted as seeing the military as self-serving and unnecessary to the security of the country; small towns as idyllic in appearance but filled with greed, hate, intolerance, and viciousness beneath their tranquil surfaces; businessmen as dishonest; the rich and wealthy as among the enemies of the general good; and crime as usually committed by the well-off, and when not so committed, as attributable to the society rather than the criminal. These complaints are widely taken as asserting that political liberals dominate television production, and construct in the programs they produce a reality that conforms pointedly and persistently to their ideological viewpoint.

There are a number of reasons why it is difficult to wholly subscribe to such complaints. Any predominance of liberal political ideology is unlikely to be so strong as to constitute hegemony. Even if such views are preponderant, there is no guarantee that they are strongly enough held by enough people, or that enough people who do hold them strongly perceive what they produce as the proper vehicle for their expression, for alleged homogeneity of programming to occur. One major criticism is that these complaints ignore the tendency of professionals in the media to strongly favor professional over ideological values as a guide to workplace performance. For example, a newscaster may vote Democratic (or Republican), but he or she is not likely to ignore a big story that is unfavorable to that party because career success is defined by covering big stories. Another is that they ignore market factors. Thus, Todd Gitlin (1983) records in his account of the making of television programs that with the election of Ronald Reagan in 1980 there was a decided shift in action-adventure series toward "law and order" shows with tough cops and clearly heinous criminals. The hope was to cash in on the ostensible conservative swing of the country, but these shows failed one after another. One interpretation, of course, is that the comparatively liberal creative community was not adept at such programs; the other is that support for Reagan did not extend to preferences in entertainment. The important point is that the television community had no difficulty in producing programs more or less counter in theme to the liberal sentiments that are said to dominate their productions. The perception of public mood and sentiment, or market factors, took precedence over these alleged opinions, even if accurately recorded. The creative community cannot evade the tests of popularity, and what it produces must be acceptable to a sizable proportion of the public. That said, within those parameters television programming by necessity reflects the outlook of those who produce it, and that outlook is that of an urban elite, college-educated in the liberal arts, middle and upper-middle class, and liberal on the whole in disposition if not ideologically extreme.

Television is in the business of attracting attention, and sexual and moral titillation are means that are reliable. Much of what is on television today would not have been considered acceptable by broadcasters or the public 20 or even 10 years ago. Public tastes and social standards have changed, and television has made some contribution to these changes by probing the borders of convention accompanying each season. An image of American life flows out from Los Angeles and New York that is compatible with the urban experience peculiar to them, but for much of the country this image gently readjusts norms. For a large segment of the public, television is a follower and not a leader of social experience, but for another large segment, it is a leader. It was once possible for a child to grow up unaware of homosexuality. Television has made that impossible, and has removed much of the power of the family, church, and community as guardians of knowledge. At the same time, television cannot transgress public standards to a degree that would turn audiences away, stimulate demands for increased governmental interference, or conflict with the mercenary goals of advertisers, for that would interfere with the orderly and profitable conduct of business. Thus, television viewing weaves its occasional flirtation with nonconformity into a continuing romance with conventionality.

These conventions of popular entertainment provide television, as they do other media, with rules that minimize the possibility of public offense. Explicit violence is acceptable; explicit sex, not at all. People perceive a great deal of sex occurring because, as Cassata and Skill (1983) report, the public apparently readily translates the innuendos, suggestiveness, and narrative devices by which actual intercourse is avoided into physical if unobserved reality. Sexual behavior is most acceptable when treated as a device to facilitate narrative or comedy. That is, it is almost never itself the subject. Crime cannot pay, but justice vindicates violence and violation of the law. By adhering to such rules — which, of course, are often violated in the cause of artistic or mercenary motives — the media attempt to escape criticism. Television enters the home and seeks to satisfy at every moment a large and heterogenous audience. On television, the idealized escapades of solitary men and, less frequently, women, and the elevated social milieus provide objects of admiration and a vicarious upward mobility. Retribution, so often inadvisable in real life, can be enjoyed indirectly. The trappings of a better life so continually displayed do not become oppressive because they are mitigated by demonstrations that affluence does not bring happiness. Such entertainment is escapist in the sense of partially evading reality, but it is not without its positive contributions.

Television programming can be said to have three boundaries. On one side, there is the necessity for popularity, and all it implies — adherence to conventions of the various genres, the avoidance of serious offense, the distortion of social reality in behalf of telling a good story, and the occasional pursuit of attention by a foray beyond the threshold of what had up to that time been considered acceptable. On another, there is the boundary of the geographical, educational, social, and political factors that define the elites who run television, and through whose interpretations these factors come to pass. Finally, there is the third frontier of creativity, diversity, and departures from the commonplace — uncommon but not unknown.

Viewer Psychology

The psychology of how the messages inevitably a part of entertainment instruct viewers has not been exhaustively explored, but a number of principles have been established by empirical investigation. Two leaders in this endeavor have been the well-known psychologists Albert Bandura at Stanford and Leonard Berkowitz at the University of Wisconsin. The means they and their followers have employed have been a series of intriguing laboratory-type experiments that meet rigorous scientific standards.

These investigations have focused largely, but not exclusively, on the influence of violent film and television portrayals on the subsequent behavior of viewers, and there are many important differences that set apart the studies associated with each of these two men. What they have in common is a concern for the underlying mental processes on which any learning that transpires from viewing television is contingent.

The experiments conducted by Bandura have used children of nursery school age as subjects. Obviously, the results apply most clearly at this age, but they also have relevance in regard to adults and older children. There are two reasons for their broad generalizability, both related to the way science proceeds. Young children in this case were simply the best subjects for testing propositions about the influence of television because their relatively undeveloped repertoires of behavior made it more likely that some link could be readily demonstrated between what the viewer saw and what the viewer subsequently did, and the purpose of the scientific experiment is to examine relationships between cause and effect under optimally sensitive conditions. The experiments also have a claim to wide applicability because they are derived from a formulation called social learning theory that offers a very convincing explanation for much of human behavior. Thus, children in this case are not the limit on but the means to general knowledge.

The framework for these experiments has continued to the present day to be much the same as that of the first one published in the *Journal of Abnormal and Social Psychology* in 1963 (Bandura, Ross, & Ross, 1963a). The subjects were about 100 nursery school boys and girls divided into four groups, each of which then had a very different experience. Each child in one group individually saw an adult attack a Bobo doll — a large, inflated balloon figure — in a number of highly specific ways, such as with a mallet, accompanied by such declarations of wrath as, "Sock him in the nose! Kick him!" In a second group, they saw the identical attack in a color film portrayal shown on a television receiver. In a third, they saw an identical attack via color television carried out by a woman dressed as a Cat Lady, a type of fantasy personage like that which appears in children's programming. And in a fourth, the control condition, they saw no attacks. Afterward, each child was given the opportunity to play for 20 minutes while being observed through one-way mirrors. To enhance their inclination to behave aggressively, the children were mildly frustrated by being led away from a room full of attractive toys to a relatively more barren second play area. In this new situation, there was a Bobo doll; a mallet such as the one employed in the assault; other items conducive to aggressive play, such as dart guns and a tether ball with a painted face hanging from the ceiling; and an assortment of toys unassociated with aggression, such as a tea set, cars and trucks, and coloring paper.

The children who had seen examples of violence were themselves more aggressive in their play. In each of the three conditions in which there had been a display of aggression, between 80% and 90% of the children duplicated one or more acts they had seen performed. The children exposed to violence also exceeded those in the control condition in quantity of aggressive play different from what had been seen. Those who had seen the live demonstration displayed more aggressive behavior than those who had seen the Cat Lady television sequence, but both those who saw the Cat Lady and the adults portrayed on television as behaving aggressively behaved more aggressively than those in the control condition.

The increase in aggressiveness different from the demonstrations could have resulted from the excitement produced by the experience, but the greater quantity of duplicative behavior means that the varied exposures to violent behavior provided examples, or lessons, that were followed. Observing what adults in real life and on television did changed what the children chose to do when confronted with stimuli from the adult environment (in this case, the Bobo doll and the mallet). Observation can be thought of as:

- adding to the repertoire of behavior of which the children were capable, or
- changing the meaning of the stimuli and thereby the behavior that was displayed when the stimuli were encountered.

The fact that the Cat Lady television sequence had less effect than the live demonstration suggests that cues encouraging the interpretation of observed behavior as make-believe or fantasy reduce its instructional efficacy, but the fact that both television versions had some effect implies that experiencing something through an audiovisual medium has an impact similar in kind to direct, real-life experience. This is precisely what those imbued with the power of television have been saying for years: It duplicates distant reality in the living room.

This experiment followed one published two years earlier that had demonstrated that children would learn simply by observing others, without practice or direct reinforcement of the act in question (Bandura, 1973). It extended this principle to vicarious, televised, or filmed experience. The first step was the demonstration of the basic psychological process. The second, of its process applicability to television and film. Soon after, there began to appear in scientific journals experiments exploring the conditions upon which such instructional effects are contingent. They continue to this very day.

The next experiment by Bandura (Bandura, Ross, & Ross, 1963b) belongs to this strand. In the control condition, no televised films were seen. In the three other conditions, nursery school boys and girls saw color television sequences in which:

- Two adults named Rocky and Johnny merely play vigorously with several balls, a Bobo doll, a hula hoop, a lasso, dart guns, a baton, cars, and plastic farm animals.
- Rocky attacks Johnny, gains control of the toys, and receives 7-Up and cookies.
- Rocky attacks Johnny, but is successfully repulsed by Johnny.

In each case, Rocky displayed a number of discrete, identifiable aggressive acts while playing with the toys. In the version in which Rocky is victorious, Rocky attacks after he is refused access to the toys, stumbles, and is pounced on by Johnny but thoroughly defeats him, and after eating the cookies and drinking the 7-Up, leaves the scene with the toys packed in a bag singing, "Hi ho, hi ho, its off to play I go" while Johnny cowers in a corner. Events are the same in the sequence in which Rocky is defeated, except the roles are reversed and it is Rocky who at the end is shown cowering in the corner.

Subsequently, in the playroom, the emulation of Rocky's aggressive play was much greater among those who saw him rewarded or not punished than among those who saw him punished. In later interviews, those who saw Rocky as victorious were highly critical of him but expressed the desire to behave like him — an inclination that they had fulfilled in their actual behavior — and made derogatory remarks about his victim. Those who saw Rocky punished were also critical of him, but did not make derogatory remarks about Johnny. The results validate the intuitive judgment that children do not think much of a loser and will emulate a successful bully. The larger implication is that television portrayals are most efficacious as instruction when behavior is depicted as successful or rewarded.

The experiments of Berkowitz and his followers, the first of which also appeared in the same *Journal of Abnormal and Social Psychology*

(Berkowitz & Rawlings, 1963), further elaborate some of the means by which television instructs its audience. In these experiments, the subjects were of college age, so the results are most clearly relevant to young adults. However, they also elucidate general principles that would appear to apply much more widely.

The paradigm is the same for a number of experiments. Subjects are first frustrated, subsequently undergo vicarious experience by seeing one or another film sequence, and then have the opportunity to behave aggressively against their frustrator. What varies principally among them is the content of the films, and what they have in common is that differences in the behavior of the subjects appear to be the consequence of the instruction the films have conveyed.

The first experiment is typical. It addressed the question of whether vicarious exposure to violence by film or television reduces aggressive drive, thereby lessening the likelihood of aggressive behavior. This is the catharsis hypothesis which holds that exposure to a violent portrayal purges viewers of aggressive drive or inclination. Earlier, another psychologist, Seymour Feshbach (1961), had published an experiment in which angered subjects had displayed less subsequent aggressive imagery on a psychological test after viewing a violent film, which seemed to support such a proposition. Berkowitz thought otherwise. He acknowledged the legitimacy of the results, but not the validity of the interpretation. He argued that the psychological dynamic involved was not catharsis, but inhibition. He reasoned that the film had sensitized the subjects to their aggressive impulses, much as a pornographic film might sensitize viewers to double entendre or sexual motives, and that as a consequence they had been inhibited in their display of hostility.

In order to test his interpretation, Berkowitz designed an experiment in which exposure to portrayed violence and other factors would be equal but the degree of inhibition would differ. The subjects were first insulted and harassed during an I.Q. test by the experimenter's assistant. After viewing the films, the subjects' tasks included rating the professional proficiency of the assistant in a manner that implied the ratings could affect his career. Inhibitory tendencies were thus reduced for all subjects by providing a target who could be thought of as deserving retribution. The film sequence was the brutal prize fight from the Kirk Douglas movie *Champion* (United Artists, 1949). The principal comparison involved a condition in which the beating administered to

Douglas was described as the just reward of a scoundrel and another in which Douglas was said to be a good man beginning to show remorse for his misdeeds. In the jargon of psychology, this pitted a portrayal of justified aggression against a portrayal of unjustified aggression. The former presumably would further reduce inhibitions; the latter would not.

The catharsis hypothesis would predict similarly reduced hostility in both conditions as the consequence of the vicarious experience of violence. In fact, the subjects displayed greater unfavorability (or more hostility) in their ratings after viewing the justified aggression. This outcome strongly supported Berkowitz's interpretation. The combination of a deserving target and filmed illustration of revenge overcame inhibitions about aggressive impulses aroused by the vicarious experience. The implication is that these subjects took what they had seen as an example of appropriate behavior and applied it to their own circumstances.

In later experiments following the paradigms introduced by Bandura and by Berkowitz, other ways in which film and television portrayals can alter behavior have been explored. Among the factors examined have been the role of cues in the portrayal, the meaning given the portrayal by the viewer, the identification of the viewer with persons in the portrayal, the accompaniment of the portrayal with critical remarks, and the physiological arousal or excitement induced in the viewer by a portrayal.

In one experiment (Berkowitz & Geen, 1966), for example, the name of the experimental target of aggression was varied. In one condition, he was identified as Bob. In another, as Kirk, the same name as the film victim. In this and in many later experiments, pre-manipulation provocation of the subjects was achieved by administering a mild electric shock — often somewhat stronger than necessary — as feedback during a puzzle-solving task. Post-manipulation aggression was measured by reversing the roles, with the subjects now delivering shocks to the person who had previously shocked them. This aversive experience was necessary to ensure some degree of aggressive drive directed toward the target that could be subject to media influence. In this instance, aggression was greater when the name of the target matched that of the film victim. The implication is that the film altered the meaning to the viewer of the cue represented by the target's name — either inhibitions were reduced or aggression stimulated.

In several experiments, the meaning that is attributed by a viewer to a portrayal has been demonstrated to affect subsequent aggressive behavior. In one instance (Berkowitz & Alioto, 1973), college-age subjects who saw a film of a football game whose participants were described as intent on injuring each other subsequently delivered a greater degree of electric shock than those who saw the same athletic encounter described as athletes engaging in their profession. In two other instances, college-age subjects who viewed the fight sequence from *Champion* displayed greater aggressiveness, again measured by electric shock delivery, when the boxers were described as vengeful than when they were said to be cool professionals (Berkowitz & Alioto, 1973; Geen & Stonner, 1972). In television entertainment, the plot guides viewer interpretation. What these experiments suggest is that an example of malicious or retributive behavior in television drama at least temporarily alters the viewer's judgment about how to act and about what is or is not permissible.

In several other experiments, the behavior of subjects has been affected by the description of a television or film portrayal as accurately representing real events instead of being a fictional account. In one, a war sequence was described as a real life film for some college-age subjects and a fictional account for others (Berkowitz & Alioto, 1973). In another, college-age subjects were either told that a videotape of men fighting in a parking lot was real or a staged affray (Geen, 1975). In a third, children of elementary school age were either told that a film of college rioting was newsreel footage or clips from a Hollywood drama (Feshbach, 1972). In the first two, the subjects delivered a greater degree of electric shock when the portrayals were depicted as representing real life; in the third, the children delivered a higher level of aversive noise when told the rioting had actually occurred. Television drama by definition is fictional, but like all fiction, it often claims public attention by its ostensible reflection of reality. In these experiments, the belief that the behavior observed was true to life apparently enhanced the likelihood of it having an effect on the viewer's own behavior. The implication is that the greater the degree that television entertainment is perceived as realistic, the greater the likelihood that it will influence behavior.

When viewers identify with the character, they are more likely to experience a portrayal as instructive. Male subjects of elementary school age saw a film of a boy playing a war strategy game. Some were told that, according to a questionnaire they had completed, the boy in the film was very similar to themselves in interests and abilities, and others were told that he was not at all like themselves. When given an opportunity to play the same war strategy game after viewing the film, the boys who had been told they were similar to the boy in the portrayal more frequently aped his strategy (Rosekrans, 1967). The implication is that television entertainment is particularly likely to function as instruction when persons portrayed are perceived by viewers as somehow similar to themselves — a circumstance certainly achieved at many points in television drama.

A variant on this is the hedonic or pleasure principle which holds that viewers are more likely to be influenced by portrayals that please them. In one experiment, children imitated characters they liked more than they did those they did not so strongly favor (Slife & Rychiak, 1982). In another, children behaved more aggressively if they had expressed pleasure rather than distaste over the violent portrayals they had seen (Ekman et al., 1972). The implication of these experiments on liking for characters and enjoyment, as well as the preceding experiment on perceived similarity between the viewer and the portrayed character (which presumably would heighten identification) is that involvement in film and television portrayals heightens the likelihood of their influencing behavior.

The interpretation that viewers give to what they see on the screen is obviously governed not only by the plot and other attributes of the television stimulus but by their own experience. The experiments provide many examples. Identification, liking, and enjoyment as responses to a portrayal obviously depend on characteristics of the viewer as well as on what television portrays. Another example is an experiment in which college-age subjects delivered a lesser degree of electric shock after hearing censorious remarks about the behavior portrayed in a violent sequence of the James Dean movie *Rebel Without a Cause* (Warner Brothers, 1955) than when they did not hear such remarks (Lefcourt, Barnes, Parke, & Schwartz, 1966). The instructive capacity of entertainment in this instance was partly dependent on the exposure of the viewer to critical remarks about the portrayed behavior. When present, these presumably affected the viewer's own judgment about the acceptability or desirability of that behavior. The implication is that television entertainment to some degree governs such judgments about the behavior it portrays by the reactions and comments of its characters.

There is a formulation in psychology developed by Percy Tannenbaum and Dolf Zillmann (1975) which holds that behavioral effects
attributable to the viewing of a film or television episode may result
from the excitement induced by the experience. This is the arousal
hypothesis. The technical term for the process is "excitation transfer."
The hypothesis holds that any stirring exposure to these media, or for
that matter any stirring experience, may alter subsequent behavior
by increasing its intensity or propelling some particular mode of behavior across the threshold of restraint. Its validity is demonstrated by an
experiment conducted by Zillmann (1971) in which college-age subjects were exposed to either a violent film, an erotic film, or an
uncompelling and bland film. As in the Berkowitz experiments, the
subjects first received mild electric shocks, saw one or another of the
films, and then had the opportunity to deliver shocks to the person
from whom they had earlier received shocks. Subjects who had seen the
violent and erotic films delivered a greater degree of shock; those who
had seen the erotic film delivered a greater degree of shock than those
who had seen the violent film. Other experiments have confirmed that
exciting portrayals can alter the viewer's state of arousal. Blood pressure, sweating, skin resistance, and other measures of physiological
arousal have been demonstrably affected by exposure to such portrayals. The psychologist Russell Geen (1975) provides an example. His
college-age male subjects either were strongly provoked or not provoked by the degree of electric shock administered by a confederate of
the experimenter, then saw a videotape of a fistfight between two men
described as real or staged or no videotape. Blood pressure was increased by provocation, and that heightened arousal was maintained
when the fight was said to be real but declined sharply to near normal
when it was said to be fictional or no videotape was seen. Sweating also
was greater when the fight was said to be real. Subsequent aggression —
as measured by the delivery of electric shock to the confederate — was
in accord with the arousal formulation. It was greater among those
provoked regardless of other circumstances, and among those provoked
it was greater when the fight was said to be real and heightened
physiological arousal was maintained.

Emotional arousal probably plays a role in the varied experimental
results that have been attributed to the instructional influence of television and film. The arousal hypothesis gains credence from the fact that
in many of these and other experiments, provoking subjects by the

administration of electric shock by itself has been enough to increase the degree of aggressiveness displayed, for such an experience can be interpreted as another means of emotional arousal. However, there are a number of reasons why the arousal hypothesis at best is a partial explanation and instruction merits the status of a major contributor.

First, arousal does not explain the imitative influence of portrayals. It might explain heightened levels of behavior, such as increased non-imitative aggression when it occurs in the Bandura experiments, but not behavior identical to what has been viewed. Second, arousal fails to account for certain of the observed effects, unless one is willing to engage in the nonscientific expedient of blindly inferring arousal and only arousal whenever there is a demonstrated influence on behavior. There is no sound reason for believing that rewarded, justified, or malicious violence; a portrayal in which the victim's name matches that of the real life target; the perception of a portrayal as representing reality; or the belief that someone in a portrayal is like oneself intrinsically are more arousing than a television or film sequence conveying the identical behavior under a different label or circumstances. Some of the following factors arguably might heighten arousal somewhat, such as malicious violence, matching cues, the perception of realism, and identification, yet it is difficult to believe that any such heightening could wholly account for the effects that have been observed. It certainly would be hard to build a case in behalf of arousal for rewarded over punished, and justified over unjustified, violence.

In the Geen example, the labelling of the fight as real increased aggression only among provoked subjects. Yet, there was also increased aggression among provoked subjects who either saw no videotape or for whom the fight was labelled as staged and whose blood pressure had returned to normal. The implication is that the effect was not entirely a matter of heightened arousal but also of angered subjects given an opportunity at retribution. Provocation or frustration, as is emphasized later (Chapter 7), is a facilitating but not a necessary condition for violent portrayals to increase aggression. For arousal to be a satisfactory, complete explanation it would be necessary for it to explain not only imitative aggression but differences in aggression recorded after exposure to portrayals that are identical but differ only in their labelling or the circumstances in which they are viewed. This would place an extraordinary burden on the prowess of the variants that prove superior in this respect to induce heightened excitation.

The most plausible interpretation is that arousal is complementary to content factors and to the cumulative effects of exposure to such factors. It may account almost wholly or play a major role in some short-term effects; it almost certainly adds to or heightens effects primarily attributable to content factors and to their cumulative influence, and it surely plays a particularly important role in effects on young children because of their greater vulnerability (as a consequence of their comparative inexperience) to arousal by media exposure. It is far from the whole story.

One of the important properties of experiments is that they permit the empirical testing of factors on which an effect may be contingent which would be hard to isolate in everyday life. The varied experiments on the behavioral influence of film and television violence have performed well in that respect, and they lead to a catalogue of factors demonstrated to play a part in such media effects (Comstock, 1986b):

- Reward of lack of punishment in the portrayal for the perpetrator of violence.

- Depiction of the portrayed violence as justified.

- Cues associated with the violence in the portrayal that are likely to be encountered in real life (such as a likely target resembling a target in the portrayal).

- Portrayal of the perpetrator of violence as similar to the viewer.

- Depiction of behavior as intended to inflict harm or injury (such as a sports contest in which the participants are said to want to seriously hurt each other).

- Violence portrayed so that its consequences do not stir distaste or arouse inhibitions over such behavior.

- Violence portrayed as representing reality as contrasted with concocted fiction.

- Portrayed violence that is not the subject of critical or disparaging commentary.

- Portrayals of violence whose commission particularly pleases the viewer.

- Portrayals, violent or otherwise, that leave the viewer in a state of unresolved excitement.

- States of anger, frustration, or provocation on the part of viewers.

Television is instructive because it provides examples that people can apply to their own circumstances. These examples are particularly likely to be followed when the behavior is portrayed as efficacious or rewarding. They are also likely to be followed when the behavior is endowed with social approval — a notion that best seems to incorporate the findings about justified and malicious violence, for the common element is the message that retribution is conventional. Instruction similarly becomes more likely when what is portrayed is made particularly relevant to the viewer — for this appears to be the element uniting the findings about a cue in a portrayal that matches one in real life, the depiction of a portrayal as representing real-life events, and perceived similarity with a character in a portrayal. Instruction also becomes more likely when television presents information not otherwise available from the environment, and particularly so when that information represents something about which the viewer wants to know. What remains unclear, and what probably never will be fully untangled, is the degree to which television serves as a source of information compared with other influences. However, it so frequently exemplifies in its programming the principles on which instruction by entertainment rest that it is probable that television often instructs at least a few in the audience, and in some instances, instructs many.

These factors can be encapsulated by four underlying dimensions. With the identification of such comprehensive or transcendent meta-factors, it becomes possible to formulate expectations about the influence of innumerable specific factors not themselves as yet experimentally tested. These meta-factors are:

- *Efficacy* — the portrayal of behavior as leading to reward or the avoidance of punishment, particularly in regard to achievement of material and social goals, such as money and friends.

- *Normativeness* — the portrayal of behavior as accepted or widely engaged in, within the boundaries of the commonplace, and not leading to ostracism, criticism, or loss of social standing.

- *Pertinence* — the portrayal of behavior as particularly relevant to the circumstances being experienced by the viewer, through overlaps between the portrayal and real world cues, participants, and motives.

- *Susceptibility* — the degree to which viewers are in a state in which the media may exercise influence, such as anger or a need for the solution to a problem.

These four meta-factors encourage broad and creative thinking about how the media may influence behavior. By doing so, they also form the foundation for two final, very important points. They concern the wide applicability of these principles, and the complexity that sometimes enters into the effects of portrayals on any one individual or group.

These principles were developed in the study of the effects of film and television violence on aggressive behavior, but they have a solid claim to extremely wide application. All that is necessary is to adapt the four meta-factors to a different topic. It has been demonstrated repeatedly that by manipulating the same three meta-factors (efficacy, normativeness, and pertinence) in portrayals and taking advantage of the fourth meta-factor (susceptibility), all sorts of behavior can be affected—from dental hygiene to the extending of help to a person in need. They converge on a single stellar principle, and an accompanying fact—human beings are guided by their expectations about their behavior, the behavior of others, and the likely outcome of events, and these expectations are formed from the vicarious experience obtained through the mass media as well as from direct, personal experience.

Sometimes, the effects attributable to the media appear to be simple or unidirectional. That is, only one of the meta-factors appears to be present, or if more than one are present, they converge in the same direction. In those instances, the likelihood of effects is greatly increased. In many cases, the media do not present any such coherent or clearly interpretable set of characteristics. Behavior that is aggressive or antisocial at various times may be both rewarded and punished; behavior that is positive, constructive, or "prosocial" will similarly receive inconsistent treatment. For example, in the typical crime drama, antisocial, criminal, and violent behavior often are rewarded early to establish a challenge to law enforcement, and then detection, pursuit, arrest, and other accoutrements of law enforcement will be rewarded, and antisocial and criminal behavior will be punished, while violence will continue to be rewarded, but now as part of law enforcement. The reward for violent behavior is consistent, but not for its perpetrators and not for some other categories of behavior. In some instances, behavior will be rewarded precisely because it is non-normative, and the portrayal will emphasize that aspect; thus, two meta-factors work in opposite directions. Punishment may be so distant from the portrayed behavior that it is irrelevant. The same film and television stimuli will not be perceived alike by all viewers; effects depend on the fit between such stimuli and viewer perceptions. Portrayals that are identified with, liked, or enjoyed are more likely to affect behavior than those that do not engender such responses. However, intensely disliked portrayals may sharply heighten arousal. Whether the positive or the negative response would have the most influence is moot, and depends upon the interplay of the various meta-factors in each of these cases. Experimental effects are straightforward. Real life effects are not because the elements so carefully disengaged in the experiments are commingled in real life. What we have, then, is an empirically tested theory, a valid theory, a theory with wide applicability, but nevertheless a theory requiring subtle and thoughtful application that takes into account the portrayal, the real life setting and circumstances, and the state and characteristics of the viewer.

7

Growing Up

Few would quarrel with the applicability to much of television of
Groucho Marx's judgment in *Duck Soup* (Paramount, 1933), "A five-
year-old child would understand this. Send someone to fetch a five-
year-old child." Television, of course, does not require anyone to fetch
the child. Children typically are quickly captivated by television, and
view it regularly throughout their young lives. They apparently find
something of interest, and they do so at almost all hours of the broadcast
schedule, for there are sizable numbers of children viewing every day
from morning until as late as 10 p.m. Viewing, of course, is at a peak
on Saturday mornings, but almost as many children are in the audience
daily from midafternoon through early primetime, and much of what
children view is intended for general audiences. How much children
understand of what they see is a question not answerable by inquiries
directed to adults, for children cannot understand the subtleties of plot,
the motives of characters, and the consequences of action to the same
degree as can adults. Yet, episodic though their appreciation may be, it
is undeniably real enough at the youngest of ages and it never apprecia-
bly diminishes, although viewing in terms of hours per week changes
as children grow older.

Children have been the focus of numerous studies concerned with
the social effects of television, and the issues addressed include the
medium's influence on behavior, the impact of its unremitting mercan-
tile emphasis, and its role in their development toward adulthood. The

197

findings of these studies divide into seven topics: expert opinion; time use; viewing; beliefs, knowledge, and perceptions; scholastic achievement; advertising; and, behavior.

Expert Opinion

One way of creating knowledge is to survey experts. The results may be interpreted in two different ways. They may be taken as valid advice — as the synthesis of the benefits of training, experience, and recognized knowledgeability. Or, they may be taken as the documentation of informed conventional wisdom. In either case, they give us something we didn't have before — knowledge about what the experts think.

There are two surveys of experts on television and children available. John Murray (1983), a psychologist, queried more than 100 social scientists who had published articles, books, or reports on the topic about a statement in the 1982 report of the National Institute of Mental Health, *Television and Behavior: Ten Years of Scientific Inquiry and Implications for the Eighties* (Pearl, Bouthilet, & Lazar, 1982a). The statement read:

> the consensus among most of the research community is that violence on television does lead to aggressive behavior by children and teenagers who watch the programs. This conclusion is based on laboratory experiments and on field studies. Not all children become aggressive, of course, but the correlations between violence and aggression are positive. In magnitude, television violence is as strongly correlated with aggressive behavior as any other behavioral variable that has been measured. The research question has moved from asking whether or not there is an effect to seeking explanations for the effect. (p. 6)

Sixty-eight of the experts returned his questionnaire. More than 80% strongly or moderately agreed with the statement.

A more wide-ranging survey of experts was conducted by three communications researchers, Carl Bybee, Danny Robinson, and Joseph Turow (1982). About 500 college-level teachers and scholars of communications rated 18 possible effects as to whether television was "the cause," "an important cause," "a somewhat important cause," or "not at all the cause." A majority thought television was "a somewhat important cause" or better for 15 of the effects, and the remaining three did not lag very far behind. Here are the top 10, along with the percent designating television (to some degree) as a cause:

- Increased world knowledge – 91%.
- Increased buying behavior – 84%.
- Decreased physical activity – 80%.
- Increased social value reinforcement – 80%.
- Decreased reading – 80%.
- Increased desire for immediate gratification – 76%.
- Increased curiosity – 70%.
- Increased aggressive behavior – 66%.
- Increased ethnic stereotyping – 66%.
- Increased verbal ability – 66%.

And the others:

- Decreased attention span – 58%.
- Increased interest in sex – 58%.
- Decreased creativity – 58%.
- Increased distortion of political perceptions – 58%.
- Increased prosocial behavior – 52%.
- Increased alienation – 47%.
- Increased sex stereotyping – 45%.
- Decreased social values – 42%.

Although precisely how one should interpret some of these phrases is ambiguous, it is clear that a majority attribute substantial effects to television. Negative effects include abilities and activities involved in academic achievement: reading, immediate gratification, attention span, and creativity. Positive effects include world knowledge, which scored highest of all. The experts, then, think television harms formal scholastic achievement while providing general knowledge. They also believe television has contributed to misperceptions about sex roles, ethnic groups, and politics. There is substantial agreement that television has increased consumer behavior among children. There is also confirmation of Murray's finding that most experts think television contributes to aggressive behavior.

Time Use

The most quoted statistic about children and television is that by the time the average child graduates from high school, he or she will have spent more hours viewing television than in the classroom. However, there is a great deal more to be learned and understood about children's use of time and their viewing of television other than that they view a lot of it.

During the fall and winter television season in the late-1980s, the A. C. Nielsen Company estimated that children 2-11 years of age viewed almost 28 hours per week. The estimate for teenagers was about 23½ hours. These compare with estimates of about 34 hours for adult women and about 29 hours for adult men 35-54 in age. Older adults (ages 55 and over) were estimated to view considerably more (for women, about eight hours more; for men, about nine hours more), and younger adults were estimated to view slightly less (about an hour and a half less). These figures establish children as substantial, but not the heaviest of television viewers, and teenagers as comparatively light viewers.

The prominence of television in children's lives is made clearer by data that place viewing in the context of other activities. Here, we find that television occupies more time than any other out-of-school activity, accounts for half or more of all leisure time, and is only proportionately less prominent as a leisure activity for children than for adults because of children's engaging in "free play."

The amount of time children and teenagers in the United States spend with television has increased steadily since the medium was introduced in the late 1940s and early 1950s. This parallels a general increase in daily television viewing by all demographic categories. A second major trend has been toward the equalization of television consumption across social strata. In the case of children, inverse relationships between amount of viewing and intelligence, as well as family socioeconomic status, have declined, although they are still observable. These two trends mean (a) that there has been increasing acceptance of experiencing popular culture through television by all strata, and (b) that television has come to occupy an increasingly prominent place in the lives of children and teenagers.

Albert Hollenbeck and Ronald Slaby (1979), two child development specialists, have recorded that viewing, in the sense of giving attentive interest to the screen, begins as early as six months of age, and Aletha Huston and colleagues (Huston et al, 1983), also child development specialists, have reported that viewing on a regular basis begins at about the age of three, with average daily viewing estimated at one-and-one-half hours. Average hours spent viewing increase during elementary school, decline during high school, remain suppressed by college and/or early involvement in child-rearing and marriage, and then return to a level similar to that for the late elementary school years until increasing again among those 55-plus in age. This cyclical pattern reflects the major role of available time, or opportunity to view, in determining the amount of television that a person will view.

In their study of time use by several hundred children in Berkeley, California, Elliott Medrich and colleagues (Medrich, Roizen, Rubin,& Buckley, 1982) not only identified television as one of the five major "domains" of time use among children (the others were: alone or with friends; with parents; jobs, chores and shopping; and in organized activities), but proposed that families can be located on a dimension reflecting the centrality of television within the home. Centrality was said to increase when "the television was on during dinner; children said they could watch as much as they wanted; children reported watching often with friends; and when the mother watched a lot of television herself" (p. 216). The greater the centrality of television, the greater the viewing by children. Television centrality increased as household socioeconomic level declined. In effect, parents to a large degree determine whether the child will be a light, moderate, or heavy viewer of television, and at the extremes of the centrality dimension are households where television is at the center of life and those where it is peripheral or muted.

The Berkeley data indicate that black and white families differ in regard to children and television in many ways congruent with findings discussed earlier — that at every social stratum blacks view more television than whites, and that the inverse relationships between socioeconomic status and amount of television viewed and attitudes favorable toward television that exist among whites do not hold for blacks. Although permissiveness and the centrality of television were inversely related to socioeconomic status among both black and white families, among black families at every stratum there were far more children who were heavy viewers and far more families in which the centrality of television was high. Television thus occupies an especially prominent place in the lives of black children and within black households with children.

The introduction of television changed the world in which children grow up not only by its own presence but by the changes it imposed on other activities and media. Among those directly affecting children are the large decline in comic book circulation, the significant reduction of theater movies as family entertainment, the emergence of teenagers as an important audience for theater movies and arbiters to an important degree of the kinds of movies that will be made, and the transformation of radio to a medium to a large degree devoted to music aimed at teenagers.

Certainly, one profound change of which television is a central component is the great increase in entertainment in the lives of children and teenagers. Television increased overall mass media consumption by the general public by an average of about an hour a day, with television accounting for about three-fourths of all mass media consumption. Television is primarily an entertainment medium, and even its news and public affairs programming must present its information in a way that is highly attractive, diverting, and not too demanding. Television covers the other entertainment media, such as movies and records, and newspapers and magazines cover the entertainment media, including television. The result is that growing up occurs in an environment in which the symbols of popular culture are present to a degree unimagined before the introduction of television.

No similarly forceful statement can be made about the likelihood that greater amounts of television viewing take the young person away from other activities. On the whole, children and teenagers who are lighter or heavier viewers do not seem to differ much in the other activities in which they engage. If there is a principal exception, it is probably reading. Learning to read is difficult, and television offers an escape. Later, even for competent readers, television is usually easier, and because both viewing and reading are at-home activities, television is often a successful competitor. Amount of television viewed appears to have no relationship with time spent on or frequency of play, sports, music lessons, visits to zoos, theaters, or museums, and the like. This seeming implausibility makes sense when it is recalled that (a) television is viewed when other compelling opportunities are absent, and (b) the providing of those opportunities has everything to do with parents, the schools, and the community and nothing to do with television. It is not the attractiveness of television that leads some children who engage in few other activities to spend far more than the average amount of time viewing television, but the absence of the opportunities to engage in those activities. Even so, the admonition of Medrich and colleagues (1982) merits serious consideration:

> Even if television viewing had no measurable effects on children . . . it would still be argued that it is an inadequate agent of socialization and a poor use of time relative to other alternatives. Furthermore, while television may have few measurable negative consequences, it has few measurable benefits for children either . . . . Most children watch too much television given the time-use options. Their time might be better spent, in the sense that doing other things might teach them more about their world and foster development of talents, intellect, and physical abilities. (*The Serious Business of Growing Up*, p. 227)

For many years, it was predicted that by the mid-1980s at the latest, the majority (and some would have said "almost all") of homes would be wired for cable, and various specialized services would abound, including much programming of a cultural and educational nature for young people. Among the benefits were to have been programming designed for specific ages from which children and teenagers might benefit more and which they might enjoy more than the programming aimed at heterogeneous young audiences on which broadcasters depend in their search for audiences of maximum size. However, cable diffusion has been much slower than predicted, and specialized channels increasingly have turned to more general programming as the audiences for specialized fare have proven to be too small for economic viability. As a result, the promise of universally or at least widely available superior programming for children and teenagers has not been realized.

On the other hand, the VCR has exceeded expectations about diffusion (a phenomenon largely attributable to sharply falling prices for VCRs and fees for rental or purchase of VCR programming, as well as the American passion for gear, exemplified in the diffusion of high fidelity and stereo equipment). Its ascent of adoption has been far sharper than that for cable, and a majority of households own a VCR. For children and teenagers (as well as for everyone else), this means that (a) there will be the opportunity to view programming previously unavailable because its sexual, violent, cultural, or educational content barred it from other means of dissemination; (b) the viewer can "narrow-tune" by topic and content; and (c) young people may become more accustomed to viewing on the basis of topic and content, and thus demand more from, or use less, non-VCR program sources. These trends are apparently well underway, with children and teenagers in VCR households spending substantially more time using television.

Viewing

Children and teenagers are no different from adults in their relative indifference to content, as can be seen from their viewing of programs made for general audiences before they can understand much of the content. Of course, about 60% of all children 2-11 in age are in the Saturday morning television audience at its peak between 9:00 a.m. and 10:30 a.m. because they have nothing that takes them away from the programming designed for them, and the afternoon lies ahead for other activities. However, the fact that about 20% are in the audience at any given time throughout the afternoon exemplifies the principle of content indifference. The major qualification, of course, is the same that holds for adults. Once television has been selected as the preferred activity, program options will be carefully reviewed for the most satisfying.

By the time children become teenagers, they undoubtedly are much like adults in their response to television. Before that, however, their attention is probably even more discontinuous than that of adults when watching general audience programming which they do not fully comprehend, and close to maximum recorded levels when watching a program that is novel to them and designed for them. This leads us to a principle governing attention to the screen: Attention rises with the ability and need to assemble a narrative successfully, as is the case generally with movies, and for children, with children's programming, and falls for content that is redundant and episodic, as is the case generally for news, commercials, and sports.

There is good reason to think that the prevailing definition of television viewing, which is based on the needs of the television business to measure audience size, gives a somewhat false impression of children's use of television. Alison Alexander, Ellen Wartella, and Dan Brown (1981), communications researchers, compared reports by parents and children and found that parents often categorized their children as watching television while the children thought of themselves as playing with their toys. Daniel Anderson and colleagues (Anderson, Field, Collins, Lorch, Pugzles & Nathan, 1985), also communications researchers, compared estimates of the viewing of five year olds based on parental diaries and actual eye contact with the screen. The maximum diary estimates were about 40 hours a week. The maximum eye contact estimates were about three-and-a-half hours a week. Neither can substitute for the other to discriminate among or identify lighter or heavier viewers, because time spent with television was uncorrelated with attention to the screen.

As with adults, "viewing" does not describe what transpires in the experiencing of television by children and teenagers as accurately as does the term "monitoring." This monitoring depends on continual mental processing. Aletha Huston and John Wright (1989) of the University of Kansas describe this processing in terms of stimulus features, viewer attributes, and situational factors.

Stimulus features divide into those representing content and those representing form. Form (sometimes called "formal") features include auditory, visual, and structural elements by which content is conveyed. In the abstract, the two are independent. In practice, within a cultural context or a genre of programming, content and form features are often related (as in the case of music that signals a suspenseful episode in which the protagonist is at risk). Children and teenagers, and presumably older viewers as well, use both types of stimulus features in choosing among programs, in deciding whether to attend to a particular portion of a program, and in understanding what is happening. For example, music may serve as a cue, telling the viewer whether a sequence is more likely to please girls or boys, when something important or interesting is going to happen, and how to interpret what has been shown (such as comprehending an event as menacing).

The principal viewer attributes of interest are age, and to a significantly lesser degree, sex, with chronological age understood as an imperfect proxy for the level of cognitive development. Cognitive level indexes the ability of a young viewer to understand the content and accurately interpret the form features of television, and along with age, identifies differences in program preference and satisfaction. Principal findings are:

- The ability to understand content and form features increases with cognitive level.
- The implicit recognition and response to form features precedes any explicit ability to identify them.

- Comprehension predicts attention to the screen, which increases with cognitive level.
- Congruencies between content and form features (i.e., regularly employed conventions of program construction) help young people learn from and understand television by making interpretation easier, as do interpretive comments and explanations from adults.

Situational circumstances include competing stimuli such as toys or reading matter, and the presence and behavior of other viewers. The opportunity to engage in some other activity suppresses attention to the screen, and the more so the more attractive the alternative. Many will recall that the original *Sesame Street* was evaluated on the basis of whether an attractive plaything could divert children from the screen, with sequences discarded when such was the case; thus, it ensured one of the processes supposedly necessary for learning, attention. Children also follow the cues of others, attending to the screen when one or another other person present attends.

These findings disabuse us of the model of children and teenagers viewing television with the medium entirely in control, and with television's visual elements almost exclusively guiding attention. However, on the whole, young people (and probably adults as well) selectively attend to the screen as a function of numerous content and form features, viewer characteristics, and situational circumstances. As cognitive level increases, children become more effective in monitoring television because they recognize the form features on which enjoyment and understanding depend; the technique of viewing is acquired. Viewing constitutes a transaction in which time and attention are constantly being shifted between the screen and other activities. In this sense, all viewers—children, teenagers, and adults—are active and not passive in their consumption of television. However, it remains important to distinguish between the more common circumstance when this activity occurs on an almost autonomic level and the less frequent instances in which viewer involvement is high and cognitive activity highly focused and intense.

The Israeli psychologist Gavriel Salomon (1981b, 1983) further extended the role of mental processing in regard to television by his concept of the "amount of invested mental effort in nonautomatic elaboration of material." He argues that amount of invested mental effort while viewing (often referred to by the acronym, AIME), a voluntary matter, governs some effects of television. For example,

expectations about appropriateness for exposure to a given experience —
such as reading a book, attending a lecture, or watching television —
conceivably govern the degree of effort that is actually expended; that
is, effort is governed by expectations about the stimulus as well as by
the stimulus properties. In addition, invested mental effort is proposed
as a major factor influencing whether or not media or some other
communicatory stimuli will result in comprehension, learning, or later
recall. The greater the mental effort expended, the more likely such
outcomes.

Compared to print, television is said to elicit low expectations about
the appropriateness of invested mental effort, and therefore not much
informationally is learned from its entertainment by children and teenagers. This expectation, to some degree, may be carried over to other
types of programming, such as news, debates between political candidates, and informational, cultural, and educational fare. Thus, they may
be less effective as educational experiences than they otherwise might
be; this is probably an effect that holds for adults as well as for children
and teenagers. A final implication is that the educational effectiveness
of television and other media can be enhanced by increasing the amount
of invested mental effort that is expended.

Knowledge, Beliefs, and Perceptions

The phrase "knowledge, beliefs, and perceptions" is intended to
encompass the wide range of cognitions that television may influence
among children and teenagers. In the abstract, it is easy enough to
distinguish among the three, with "knowledge" representing assumed
facts; "beliefs," expectations and inferences about behavior and events,
their motivations, and their consequences and the assignment of some
value to these phenomena; and, "perceptions," the evaluation of magnitude and relationship among physical and social stimuli. In practice,
obviously, matters are not so simple. For example, the labeling of a film
as "violent" or "pornographic" reflects some assumed knowledge about
the definition of violence or pornography, beliefs about what would
qualify, and the perception of a particular stimulus as having exceeded
the threshold. Thus, no sharp distinctions among them will be attempted, although in some cases it will be clear enough to which domain
a particular finding applies.

Two large-scale investigations, each composed of many studies involving thousands of children, parents, and teachers, examined the effects of the introduction of television on children in the United States and Great Britain. The late Wilbur Schramm, Jack Lyle, and Edwin Parker (1961), all then of Stanford, conducted the U.S. version, *Television in the Lives of Our Children,* and Hilde Himmelweit, A.N. Oppenheim, and Pamela Vince (1958), of the London School of Economics, conducted the British, *Television and the Child.* They were extremely wide-ranging, remain justly well-known today, and still have validity, either because what they found is still true or because they are the criterion for identifying changes and trends.

In regard to television's effects on knowledge, both found only limited effects. Schramm and colleagues concluded that most effects involved knowledge about entertainment. An expected increase in vocabulary did not occur except for names and phrases referring to entertainment figures and products. Himmelweit and colleagues found increases in knowledge about geography, science, sports, music, handicrafts, and household chores, but none for English literature, history, nature or rural studies, art and architecture, current affairs, or religion. Both groups concurred that the positive effects were confined to less intellectually able children whose access to and ability to use alternative sources of information was limited, and Schramm's group concluded that the more intelligent might suffer in knowledge from a great deal of television viewing because of the greater intellectual value of displaced activities. These outcomes lead to several conclusions:

- Television viewing is most likely to increase knowledge about what it specializes in — entertainment.
- Television's contribution, if any, to scholastic achievement is thereby likely to be limited.
- Effects are limited not only by what is broadcast but by what is viewed, as exemplified by the lack of increased current events knowledge in Great Britain.
- Effects are dependent on television providing something not available from other sources, as it presumably did for the less capable children.
- When television diverts attention from or displaces engaging in more informative and stimulating activities, the effects of viewing on knowledge may be negative.

Certainly, there is ample evidence that children and teenagers will acquire and retain information disseminated by television from commercial programming when the format is designed to teach. This was made clear two decades ago by the evaluations of the "CBS National Citizenship Tests" by S. William Alper and Thomas Leidy (1970), two opinion researchers, and remains true today. This series was intended to teach its audience facts about U.S. government institutions. For a program covering Constitutional rights and obligations, three comparable groups of about 1,000 teenagers were tested representing (a) a pre-program sample, (b) a post-program nonviewer sample, and (c) a post-program viewer sample; six months later, a national sample of 9,000 teenagers divided into viewers and nonviewers was again tested. The tests covered topics included and not included in the program, and both factual knowledge and beliefs or attitudes. There were no shifts in knowledge or beliefs representing uncovered material among either viewers or nonviewers. However, for covered material there were definite gains recorded among viewers for both knowledge and beliefs. These gains appeared to persist after the passage of six months. The reason commercial television viewing has such limited effects on the knowledge of young people is the entertainment programming in which it specializes.

There have been a number of studies of the use of television news by children and teenagers (Comstock et al., 1978), and they indicate that:

- A large majority of children and teenagers believe they get most of their information about public events from television, ranking it far above teachers, parents, peers, or other media.

- Exposure to news programs increases factual knowledge, as does exposure to newspapers and other print media, but children and teenagers are far more likely to see news than to read news, so television is the primary information provider.

- Children and teenagers typically are not much exposed to the news by any means.

- Exposure to news programs is increased when parents have a high interest in the topics currently being covered or when parents strongly encourage their offspring to express their opinions about events and issues.

- The opinions of children and teenagers correlate positively with the perceived opinions of parents and not with those of favored newspersons, indicating that while television may supply information, parents influence opinions.

- Learning from news increases when information is repeated and when a story has a high emotional content.

The resulting model would hold that:

- Media use is influenced by parental opinion and behavior.
- Learning occurs from media use.
- Opinion formation is largely shaped by parents and not media.
- Stimulus characteristics can enhance the learning that occurs.

Several studies have reported relationships between television viewing and beliefs about violent behavior that are suggestive, if not demonstrative, of some influence by the medium. For example, S. H. Lovibond (1967) found ideas, attitudes, and values favorable to force and violence among adolescents correlated with comic book use before the introduction of television, and correlated with television exposure after its introduction, with comic book reading drastically reduced (and the earlier recorded correlation no longer present). Among about 800 fourth, fifth, and sixth grade boys and girls, Joseph Dominick and Bradley Greenberg (1972) found attitudes favoring the use of violence to settle interpersonal conflicts positively correlated with exposure to television crime and violence and inversely related to perceived parental opinion. Jerry Singer, Dorothy Singer, and Wanda Rapaczynski (1984), in a sample of about 60 children whose average age was four, found amount of television viewing, and especially viewing of violent programs, associated with a belief in a frightening, mean, and risky world.

There is also evidence suggestive of some influence of television on expectations about sex roles. Terry Freuh and Paul E. McGhee (1975), child psychologists, found that heavy television viewing was associated with stronger convictions in favor of traditional sex roles among both boys and girls of elementary school age. Based on the children's stated intentions about whether they would engage in 10 activities, the authors conclude that television-influenced behavior will be a product of the consequences for television characters of traditional and nontraditional behavior, the similarities between one or another parent and television characters, general beliefs, and expectations about the likely consequences for them of the behavior in question.

Jerome Johnston and James Ettema (1982) give support to these views. They evaluated the effectiveness of the 13-episode *Freestyle* public television series which was designed to change beliefs and attitudes about sex roles among boys and girls ages 9-12. They collected data from about 5,000 children in seven different communities who were variously divided into nonviewers; those who viewed at home as they would ordinarily view television; those who viewed in classrooms where organized, supportive discussions of the programs took place; and those who viewed in classrooms without such discussions. In the classroom, with the organized discussion, they found that the programs changed beliefs and attitudes in the sought-for direction. Most clearly affected were beliefs and attitudes about the appropriateness of such activities as mechanics, nurturing, and athletics for boys or girls; thus, attitudes toward the participation of girls in athletics became markedly more favorable. Many such shifts still were measurable several months later. In regard to the viewers' own interests, there were few changes, although girls appeared to increase their interest in mechanics. Beliefs and attitudes about more abstract skills such as leadership, risk-taking, and independence appeared unaffected. Viewing at home or in the classroom without discussion had more limited effects, although there were a few shifts in the sought-for direction.

The findings of Johnston and Ettema lead to some intriguing conjectures. Television perhaps can alter expectations in the short- and long-term when it deviates from the normative (or stereotyped), and when it is designed to have such effects. This supposition leads to the expectation that television on the whole would have negligible or no effects on the sex-role expectations of children and teenagers because, for the most part, its portrayals are normative and in accord with the everyday experiences of young viewers, and are not designed to alter expectations.

Several studies have linked prior experience to perceptions of violence and aggression in television and film entertainment. In a sample of about 600 fifth- and sixth-grade boys, Bradley Greenberg and Thomas Gordon (1972) found that children who were black or socioeconomically disadvantaged, or both, variously perceived violent television scenes as less violent, more acceptable, more lifelike, more likeable, and more humorous than the racial or socioeconomic strata with which they were compared. Victor Cline and colleagues (Cline, Croft, & Courrier, 1973) found less physiological arousal to violent television among boys who were heavy viewers of television than among light viewers. Robert Drabman and Margaret Hanratty Thomas (1974) found that children asked to scrutinize the play of other children in a distant room via a television monitor waited longer to seek adult help when the playing children became violent and destructive if they had seen a violent television episode a few minutes earlier. Dolf Zillmann and Jennings Bryant (1982) found that after extensive exposure to explicit erotica, male and female undergraduates judged an erotic portrayal as less pornographic and less offensive, and as more suitable for use on broadcast television or unrestricted availability to children. They also assigned shorter sentences to a rape perpetrator they read about in a newspaper article. Daniel Linz and colleagues (Linz, Donnerstein, & Penrod, 1984) found that after extensive exposure to "slasher" films featuring violence against women in a sexual context male undergraduates judged such films as less violent and less degrading to women, and judged a female rape victim observed in a law school documentary as less injured and less worthy.

These varied findings support two broad propositions. They are:

- The perception of television portrayals is a function of the values and criteria brought to the screen by the viewer.
- Television portrayals of deviant or extreme behavior, or behavior otherwise foreign to viewers' everyday experience, may somewhat desensitize viewers to similar future stimuli and experiences, and especially so when these stimuli and experiences themselves are media portrayals.

These propositions imply a circularity. Prior experiences and the criteria and values they impose affect perception of the media as well as judgments about the real world. In turn, criteria and values are shaped by media exposure, which is one type of prior experience.

Scholastic Achievement

The influence of television on grades earned in school and on the acquisition of skills such as mathematical, reading, and writing ability has been a question persistently and widely raised about the medium since its introduction. The available evidence is clearcut on some points and inconclusive on others.

There is no doubt that the amount of time typically spent viewing television and scholastic achievement are inversely related for both children and teenagers. This conclusion does not rest on the pattern discernible in a set of findings in which some might appear to be in conflict with one another, as is so often the case, but on results that are compelling because of (a) the quality of measurement, (b) the size and comprehensiveness of the sample, and (c) the consistency of results.

During the 1980 school year, the state-run California Assessment Program (1981) obtained data on mathematical, reading, and writing ability and television exposure for everyone present in the sixth and twelfth grades throughout the state on the day of testing. The sixth grade sample size was 280,000 and the twelfth grade sample size was 230,000; this represented 99% of the enrolled population. By the very nature of such a government endeavor, the instruments represent state-of-the-art acceptability.

With certain important qualifications, the results on the whole are highly consistent. For both grade levels, for each of the three skills, and for every level of family socioeconomic status, there was a negative correlation between amount of television viewing and scores.

There are six important qualifications or amendments: (a) family socioeconomic status is much more strongly associated with achievement than amount of television viewed, with achievement declining as socioeconomic status falls; (b) the inverse association between amount of television viewed and achievement increases as family socioeconomic status rises, with the strongest relationship occurring for pupils from the highest recorded socioeconomic status category; (c) the inverse relationship between amount of television viewed and achievement is stronger at the twelfth grade than at the sixth grade level; (d) for the lowest family socioeconomic status level, the inverse relationship is barely observable, and occasionally there is a rise in achievement with increases in amount of television viewed before a decline in achievement appears; (e) among students whose English was limited in fluency, amount of television viewed was positively related to achievement, and even a downturn at the highest level of viewing did not produce scores below the average for the lightest category of viewers; and (f) the number of pupils recorded in the highest viewing categories is not trivial, with 20% watching four or more hours a day and another 11% watching between three and four hours a day in the sixth grade, and about 16% watching four or more hours a day and about another

13% watching three to four hours a day in the twelfth grade. Time spent on homework and reading outside of the class assignments were also inversely related to amount of television viewing at both grade levels.

The pattern of these findings is reminiscent of data reported by Schramm, Lyle, and Parker (1961). Among children scoring high on tests of intellectual ability, they found an inverse relationship between amount of television viewed and scholastic achievement. Among children scoring low on such tests, they found a positive relationship between amount of television viewed and scholastic achievement. For most children, television viewing was unrelated to achievement. In both their data and the present data, the inverse relationship between television viewing and achievement is strong among young people from whom the most would be expected, and it is weak, marginal or even reversed among those from whom the least would be expected. The pattern invites a proposition: Television viewing is inversely related to achievement when it displaces an intellectually and experientially richer environment, and it is positively related when it supplies such an environment. The stronger inverse relationships at the twelfth-grade level suggest that this pattern becomes increasingly discernible as the academic demands of schooling increase.

A year later, the California Assessment Program (1982) collected additional data from a probability sample of more than 15,000 sixth graders in 292 schools. As would be expected, the results for family socioeconomic status, television viewing, and achievement were consistent with those obtained a year earlier. The original results for television viewing, family socioeconomic status, and achievement were supported. In addition, three other relationships emerged:

- Television-centeredness is a meaningful way to distinguish among the families.
- The more children and teenagers viewed, the less selective they were and the larger the role of light entertainment in their viewing.
- Some minimum of television use is an index of alert participation in and coping with the environment.

Families in which television sets were present in the living room or in a child's bedroom were more likely to have a child who was a heavy viewer, who was likely to watch the same programs as his or her parents, and who was likely to discuss the programs with his or her parents; these households were television-centered. For most programs, heavy viewers were more likely to have watched than light viewers, but heavy viewers watched a much higher proportion of light entertainment while light viewers were more likely to watch news, documentary, or informational programs or more serious or sophisticated entertainment. Pupils who viewed no television scored lower than those recorded as viewing the minimal amount. Viewing television to some degree is a highly normative activity in the United States, and especially among children and teenagers; zero viewing, in these circumstances, is likely to reflect a set of circumstances and attributes not at all likely to facilitate achievement.

The role of television in the inverse relationship between viewing and achievement is far less clear than the fact that such a relationship exists. There are two possible explanations. The first is causation and the second is non-causative symptomatology.

In the first case, greater television viewing would have to contribute independently of all other variables to the lesser levels of achievement. Subsumed is the instance in which television would contribute indirectly by independently influencing some other variable which itself then independently contributes to lesser achievement. In both circumstances, television would be said to be a cause of lower achievement. In the second case, greater television viewing is simply the sign of the influence of some other factor such as lower intellectual ability, poorer prior grades in school, conflict with the family, estrangement from peers, and the like. In this case, however, television viewing would be a symptom whose relief conceivably could ameliorate some of the harmful effects of the underlying cause.

The inverse associations between amount of television viewed and time spent on homework, reading outside of assignments, and achievement imply that if television could be displaced by homework or outside reading among the heavier viewers, achievement might be increased. Thus, even if television could not be said properly to be the cause of lowered achievement, it remains part of the problem, and a part whose redress could reduce the negative influence on achievement of the underlying source.

Of the two, the latter explanation is somewhat more plausible. Television viewing is what children and teenagers (as well as adults) do when attention, presence, and time are not otherwise required. This leads one to suspect that if heavier viewers were not engaged in television viewing, they would be involved in something else — other than homework or reading — with similar low demands on involvement and intellectual effort and similarly distracting from real world obligations. From such a perspective, heavy television viewing nevertheless remains a symptom requiring treatment among low-achieving heavy viewers.

The actual evidence is mixed. Robert Hornik (1978), using data from Central America, concludes that television hampers acquisition of reading skills. Tannis Williams (1986) and colleagues, using Canadian data, reach the same conclusion. Donald Roberts and colleagues (Roberts, Bachen, Hornby, & Hernandez-Ramos, 1984), using California data, reach the opposite conclusion: There is no independent contribution of television viewing to lowered reading ability once the influence of other variables is taken into account.

Association is documented and a symptom requiring treatment identified, but whether or not television is a cause of lowered achievement remains moot. However, the explanation accompanying the conclusion of Williams and colleagues is certainly plausible. They propose that television displaces time that should be spent learning to read, and that such displacement is likely to permanently suppress scholastic achievement by leaving children as below-par readers. Learning to read, they argue, is hard work for a child and requires practice. Reading ability in America is ordinarily acquired within a certain age range, so that once a child has emerged from this period with a low level of reading skills, he or she is likely to be continuously hampered in scholastic achievement. Once reading skills are acquired, they are retained regardless of later amounts of television viewing; thus, amount of viewing at most age ranges would be unassociated with reading ability except to the degree that amount of viewing is positively correlated across age ranges (and there is a modest degree of such correlation). Those most affected would be those the least able to cope. Williams and colleagues write:

> Television provides a more attractive alternative, for most children, but especially for those who have most difficulty learning to read and who need to practice most, namely, those who are less intelligent (or have a learning disability). The brighter children either need less practice and get enough practice in school or practice more. (*The Impact of Television*, p.397)

This model also could readily apply to mathematical and writing skills. The principle advanced earlier has a variant: Television may take time away from other activities that academically and intellectually would help the child, and television viewing will not compensate for the displaced activities because the curriculum of television and that of the schools overlap only slightly.

Several psychologists have proposed that television has come to play a role in language acquisition. They include Erika Hoff-Ginsberg and Marilyn Shatz (1982), and Dafna Lemish and Mabel L. Rice (1986). They argue that television is important because of (a) the quantity of children's viewing, (b) the degree to which children's programs present child-pertinent dialogue, (c) the opportunity for children to learn the meaning of words from their use in program dialogue, and (d) the degree to which children borrow from television for things to say (and do) in play. Such views do not contradict the finding by Schramm, Lyle, and Parker (1961) that television does not significantly boost vocabulary over what it would otherwise have been. They merely designate that television is part of the process by which language is learned by children. This implies that the language employed by children and teenagers today is somewhat more grounded in popular entertainment than was the case before the introduction of television—a conclusion entirely in accord with the finding of Schramm, Lyle, and Parker four decades ago.

Television hardly can be said to be without implications for scholastic achievement. Although the knowledge it supplies ordinarily is not pertinent to the school curriculum, greater viewing predicts lowered achievement, and this outcome is particularly severe for those to whom television would be least likely to substitute profitably for other available experiences and sources of information. The displacement effect may be responsible for lowered achievement in mathematics, reading, and writing, but that is uncertain. It is certain that children and teenagers doing poorly in school and watching vast amounts of television somehow should be persuaded to spend their time otherwise. Television may well facilitate language acquisition. That merely becomes another testament to its pervasiveness in the lives of children.

Advertising

One category of television-pertinent knowledge, beliefs, and perceptions that have been the subject of extensive controversy concerns the influence of television advertising, and particularly advertising directed at young viewers. Four topics require coverage: (a) evolution of the issue, (b) points of contention, (c) empirical evidence, and (d) policy options.

Television advertising and its effects on young viewers were placed on the public agenda in the late 1960s and early 1970s by public interest groups. Particularly prominent were Action for Children's Television (ACT), a suburban Boston organization that has realized a national membership, and its founder, Peggy Charren, and a Midwestern zealot, Robert Choate. Previously, television advertising attracted almost no attention in connection with young viewers, although Saturday morning programming carried as many as 16 commercial minutes an hour as compared with an industry code limit at the time of 9.5 minutes per hour during primetime. As Les Brown (1977) recounts in *The New York Times Encyclopedia of Television:*

> Children's groups did not become aroused, however, until the networks began to deal excessively — in their competitive zeal — with monsters, grotesque superheroes and gratuitous violence to win the attention of youngsters. Advertisers, by then, were making the most of the gullibility of children by pitching sugar-coated cereals, candy-coated vitamins and expensive toys (some retailing for as much as $50) in shrewdly made commercials that often verged on outright deception.
>
> Such patent abuse of the child market — while Saturday morning grew into one of television's largest profit centers — prompted the formation of watchdog groups such as Action for Children's Television, whose pleas for reforms could hardly go unheeded by Congress or the Federal Communications Commission. (p. 83)

ACT emphasized the clutter, the quantity, the general undesirability, ostensibly dubious practices and techniques, and the alleged inherent unfairness or deceptiveness of advertising to a clientele many of whom were not old enough to understand the nature and purpose of advertising (readers will recall that print media generally warn adults about paid-for content that might be mistaken for legitimate news with the label, "advertising"). Choate emphasized the harmful behavior that advertising might encourage, and particularly the consumption of highly sugared and non-nutritious foods. Together, and with the help of many others, they achieved a reduction in advertising per hour that put children's programming on a par with primetime programming, ended advertising of drugs, such as vitamins, during children's programming, put restraints on the use of children's television personalities and characters as advertising spokespeople, led to tougher codes for children's advertising, and brought about at least some promises to reduce violence. Through appearances before congressional committees and through the media, Choate can be fairly credited with pressuring the giant cereal makers into nutritionally upgrading their products.

Later shifts in advertising practices in response to such efforts include so-called "bumpers," or brief segments that are neither program nor commercial that appear before and after commercials, that allegedly help children better identify advertisements and better distinguish them from program content. Eventually, in the late 1970s, ACT was successful in placing the demand for federally-imposed restraints and possibly a ban on television advertising directed at children on the rule-making agenda of the Federal Communications Commission and the Federal Trade Commission. More recently, ACT repeatedly asked the Federal Communications Commission to bar programs with characters or devices that are marketed as toys on the grounds that such presentations are program-length commercials.

There have been four principal points of contention. The first is the implications of the nature of advertising for children's imperfect comprehension. The critics of advertising argue that commercials directed at children are unfair and deceptive because children do not fully understand the self-interest represented by commercial content. The supporters of advertising argue that children quickly perceive commercials as differing from program content even if they cannot define what advertising is, and that children cannot be harmed even if unaware of advertising's self-interest because they do not have disposable income to act on urges or desires created by television commercials. They argue that ultimately only parents have that discretion.

The second is the possible harm inflicted by acceptance of the messages of television advertising. The critics argue that commercials promote unhealthy nutrition, misrepresent the performance of toys, and sometimes present examples of behavior that could be self-destructive to children (such as demonstrating chemically-dangerous household cleansers in commercials aimed at adults). The supporters argue that commercials may shape product choice but do not affect basic preferences, where parents and habit play the major roles; that puffery is inherent in advertising; and that the deviant response of a few children cannot be the criterion for television content aimed at adult consumers.

The third is family management. The critics argue that advertising directed at children creates product desires with which parents find it hard to cope, desires for products that parents believe undesirable, and conflicts over what will and will not be bought. The supporters argue that neither any influence on a child's desires nor any conflict between children and adults or parents attributable to television advertising directed at children is substantial enough to merit either remedial action or the label "pathology."

The fourth is the providing of television entertainment for children. The critics argue that advertising-supported television entertainment for children emphasizes audience-attracting features at the expense of educational and cultural content, so that the income broadcasters receive from vending children's attentiveness to advertisers will be maximized, and that the Federal Communications Commission could require broadcasters, as a condition of license renewal, to present a minimum number of hours of children's programming without commercials. The supporters argue that the popularity among children of television entertainment designed for them simply documents that it is what they want, that the power of the Federal Communications Commission to so specifically mandate programming is open to question, and that a Federal Communications Commission remedy is unlikely because the agency has never mandated programming on such a scale.

The most comprehensive examination of the evidence on the effects of television advertising on children remains that performed by Richard Adler and his many colleagues (Adler et al., 1980). It is a task force effort evaluating dozens of empirical studies supported by the National Science Foundation to contribute to the resolution of the controversy. Although completed almost a decade ago, it remains useful and valid today because commercials have remained essentially the same and not much new research has been performed in the interim. It should be taken as presenting a somewhat conservative perspective since its advisory committee contained a full spectrum of interested parties — public interest groups such as ACT, advertisers, and broadcasters.

Adler and colleagues conclude that:

- The ability to distinguish commercials from programs and an understanding of the nature of advertising increases with age, as would be expected, but a "substantial proportion of children, particularly those below age 7 or 8, do not draw upon the concept of selling intent in defining commercials, in distinguishing them from programs, or in explaining their purpose.

suggesting little comprehension and/or low salience of persuasive intent as a critical feature of advertising (p. 214)."

- Disclaimers may not be understood by children if phrasing is not simple, or if they employ only captions, and there is not joint use of audio and visual elements; thus, the disclaimers may be cosmetic instead of effective.

- The evaluation of a product by children will shift positively or negatively in accord with the viewer's evaluation of the endorser.

- No associations have been found between exposure to television commercials and children's and teenagers' use of illicit drugs; however, commercials for proprietary drugs do appear to create favorable impressions of those drugs.

- From food product advertising, children learn and recall the claims made and come to believe them.

- Although children come to understand the self-interest of advertising as they grow older, product desires and requests do not significantly decline with age.

- Children learn brand names, but repetitive exposure beyond the first or second time does not significantly increase such learning.

- Parents play only a small role in governing their children's television viewing or in discussing commercials with them; they become mediators only when product requests occur and "disappointment, conflict, and anger" occur when requests are denied (p. 219).

On the whole, the investigators conclude that television advertising directed at children is "at least moderately successful in creating positive attitudes toward a product and in stimulating requests for the product" (p. 222).

The types of research behind these conclusions fall largely into two categories, laboratory-type experiments and surveys. The former are exemplified by the work of Marvin Goldberg and Gerald Gorn (1978). They exposed children to programs with and without commercials and then asked them to make a choice of playing with the product or with friends or parents. Exposure to commercials markedly increased the proportion preferring the product. The latter are exemplified by the work of John Rossiter and Thomas Robertson (1977). They repeatedly queried a sample of children about toy choices during the pre-Christmas advertising season. They found that preferences shifted in favor of advertised toys and cognitive defenses that earlier made some children comparatively immune to the appeals decreased in effectiveness as Christmas Day approached.

When the Federal Trade Commission held joint hearings with the Federal Communications Commission in the late 1970s on the possibility of rule-making on television advertising directed at children, they considered various proposals as alternatives to a complete ban on such advertising (Federal Trade Commission, 1978a, 1978b, 1978c). These included:

- A ban effective only when children below some specified age constituted more than "x" percent of the audience.
- The elimination of advertising whose "dominant appeal" was to children below a specific age.
- The elimination of advertising for products appealing primarily to or purchased primarily for children below a specific age.
- Limitations more stringent than industry codes (which at the time had a ceiling of 9.5 commercial minutes per hour) on number and frequency of advertisements directed at children below a specific age.
- The elimination of advertising for specific product classes, such as heavily-sugared foods, designed to appeal to children.

Among the more specific remedies considered was a ban (a) on all advertising of heavily-sugared foods when children under age 12 were predominant in the audience on the grounds of a risk to their health, and (b) on all advertising directed at children below age eight on the grounds that it is unfair and deceptive to advertise to those who do not understand what advertising is.

In the end, the Federal Trade Commission concluded that while the evidence indicated that television advertising directed at children involved some risks, represented a social ill, and was a legitimate cause for concern, there were no practical, effective remedies open to federal policy-making. The practical barriers were (a) the difficulty of specifying what constitutes a child audience at risk (i.e., the ages, numbers, or proportions at which a policy restraint would become effective), and (b) the unpredictability of broadcaster response (i.e., lowering the quality of children's programming to reduce costs or cancelling it altogether in favor of some newly more profitable program category). The Federal Communications Commission gave no indication that it would ameliorate the second by mandating programming for children.

In effect, the FCC formally endorsed a "no such action" position later when, after extensive hearings, it declined to issue a rule requiring broadcasters to provide weekday programming of cultural and educational value for children. Since then, it has consistently declined any rule-making in regard to children's programming.

As a result, restraints on television advertising directed at children have rested solely with the various codes, guidelines, and practices formulated within the advertising and broadcasting businesses. These do not merit dismissal as having been either hypocritical, for they have been acknowledged as a means to prevent public displeasure and criticism and to minimize the likelihood of federal intervention, or as having been entirely ineffective, since when applied they have imposed on individual advertisers much stricter standards as to the what and how of advertising than the advertisers presumably would have imposed on themselves. As for the content of these codes, the historical record makes it quite evident that as long as the principle and the fact of being able to advertise to children are not threatened, the advertisers and broadcasters are willing to make numerous adjustments and reforms in response to federal, public, or public interest group displeasure. The reasons are quite simple: First, the effectiveness of commercials is not dependent on one or a few techniques (such as making toys seem huge or alive), and allegedly exploitative commercials can be readily jettisoned. Second, the elimination of one or a few product categories other than food or drink (such as children's vitamins) will not seriously impair the profitability of children's programming because other advertisers will enter the market to take up the slack.

The path chosen has been industry self-regulation. However, the forcefulness of codes and guidelines has become severely weakened by the large-scale withdrawal of the networks from their enforcement. Many in the advertising business would prefer the reinstatement of network vigilance precisely because of the protection it affords against federal intrusion and public criticism; others delight in the new latitude. In any case, controversies about children and television advertising directed at them are likely to continue because the circumstances which gave rise to them remain essentially unchanged. The process described by the title of Turow's history of American network children's television, *Entertainment, Education, and the Hard Sell* (1981) has if anything escalated. Throughout its history, children's programming has become increasingly oriented toward the marketplace. It began as low-key, not necessarily profitable, broadcasting, became modestly profitable, and now has entered a further stage in which new techniques make it lucrative. One is the so-called "program-length commercial," in which a series is designed to present characters and props suitable for vending in retail outlets as toys. These have proliferated recently, and the FCC has exempted them from consideration as commercials. As one critic has observed, the agency does not seem to be able to distinguish between a program built around long famous, revered icons of childhood, such as Mickey Mouse, Cinderella, and the like, and newly-concocted programs designed solely to merchandise goods licensed or manufactured by those responsible for them. Another is the promotion of "interactive" toys. Although so far rejected by the networks, independent stations carry children's programs that emit signals to which expensive toys respond, or that otherwise offer scenarios for the use of such toys. Children can fire upon televised villains and have their hits recorded; rocket fire and other clashes of weaponry occur between figures on the screen and plastic playthings on the living room floor.

The most recent legislative attempt to address some of the controversies arising from children's programming and advertising was vetoed by President Reagan in 1988. It merely would have set modest restrictions on advertising and would have required broadcasters to serve the needs of children. Thus, at the end of the 1980s, the use of television to market goods to satisfy the tastes of children and the restrictions appropriate to such marketing remained a topic of debate.

Behavior

The most persistent of all questions regarding television and young viewers has concerned one category — aggressive, antisocial, or delinquent behavior and their link, if any, with violent television entertainment. Attesting to this fact is the recent appearance of a review in *Psychological Bulletin* by Jonathan Freedman (1984) asserting that the many psychology textbooks that teach that television violence facilitates such behavior are wrong. There are almost 20 volumes advocating such a view, including the 9th edition of *Introduction to Psychology* by Rita L. Atkinson, Richard C. Atkinson, Edward Smith, and Ernest Hilgard (1987), and the 5th edition of *The Social Animal* by Elliot Aronson (1988). In fact, the recounting of Freedman of such texts is impressive evidence of the degree to which experts accept such a proposition:

- Darley, J. M., Glucksberg, S., Kamin, L. J., & Kinchla, R. A. (1981). *Psychology.*
- Kagan, J., & Havemann, E. (1980). *Psychology: An Introduction.*.
- McConnell, J. V. (1980). *Understanding Human Behavior.*
- Mischel, W., & Mischel, H. N. (1980). *Essentials of Psychology.*
- Smith, R. E., Sarason, E. G., & Sarason, B. R. (1982). *Psychology: The Frontiers of Behavior.*
- Jones, R. A., Hendrick, C., & Epstein, Y. M. (1979). *Introduction to Social Psychology.*
- Myers, D. G. (1983). *Social Psychology.*
- Oskamp, S. (1984). *Applied Social Psychology.*
- Penrod, S. (1983). *Social Psychology.*
- Perlman, D., & Cozby, P. C. (1983). *Social Psychology.*
- Elkind, D., & Weiner, I. B. (1978). *Development and the Child.*
- Evans, E. D., & McCandless, B. R. (1978). *Children and Youth*
- Hetherington, E. M., & Parke, R. D. (1979). *Child Psychology: A Contemporary Viewpoint.*
- Kopp, C. B., & Krakow, J. B. (1982). *The Child: Development in a Social Context.*
- Liebert, R. M., & Wicks-Nelson, R. (1979). *Developmental Psychology.*

The first five represent introductory psychology; the second five, social psychology; and the third five, child development. Could so many so varied in background be so wrong? Let us see.

The behavioral influence of violent television entertainment has been an issue since the late 1950s when the medium of television began to shift toward violent serials as the staple of evening programming. It was the subject of a hearing before a House of Representatives committee as early as 1952, and has been the subject of innumerable House and Senate hearings since then. It has also been the subject of two major task force inquiries. In 1969, the National Commission on the Causes and Prevention of Violence included among its many conclusions about the factors responsible for violent urban racial conflict, the judgment, based on reviews of the available research, that television violence contributed to aggressive and antisocial behavior. In 1972, the Surgeon

General's Scientific Advisory Committee on Television and Social Behavior concluded, based largely on new research conducted in its behalf, that the aggressive and antisocial behavior of at least some young viewers was increased by television violence (Comstock, 1983, 1986b, 1988).

The publication in 1963 of the first two experiments documenting that exposure to violent television portrayals could enhance aggressive behavior was recounted in the last chapter. Between then and the report of the Surgeon General's Committee (Surgeon General's Scientific Advisory Committee on Television and Social Behavior, 1972; Comstock, Rubinstein, & Murray, 1972a, 1972b; Murray, Rubinstein, & Comstock, 1972; Rubinstein, Comstock, & Murray, 1972), about 50 such experiments had been published with largely (if not wholly) supportive results. These experiments typically have followed a similar format:

- By some means, at the outset a degree of anger or frustration is induced in subjects so that there is some minimal level of arousal that can be influenced by a television or film portrayal. Typically, in the case of very young children, this is achieved by denying them access to attractive toys; in the case of college-age subjects, by a hostile remark, negative comment, insult, or unnecessarily harsh administration of minor discomfort, such as an electric shock or noxious noise. There are one or more treatment conditions, in which violent portrayals hypothesized to have some effect on aggressive behavior are viewed. Subjects are assigned to these conditions randomly — that is, at the beginning everyone participating has an equal chance of being assigned to any one condition, and assignment occurs as a result of a coin toss or other neutral gambit — which ensures that the groups will be comparable except for the inevitable differences attributable to chance.

- After the portrayals, behavior is measured by a means that disguises its true purpose — to assess the level of aggressiveness. With very young children, this is typically accomplished by secretly observing them at play. With college-age subjects, this typically is achieved by asking them to administer minor discomfort, such as an electric shock or noxious noise, as feedback to inform someone when they have made an error in solving a puzzle or completing a task. Typically the person who provokes the subjects initially is the same person to whom they later deliver discomfort, thereby ensuring that there is an appropriate target for the expression of hostility.

These circumstances permit causal inference. Because the experience of each group is identical and the groups comparable except for the experience manipulated by the experimenter, any differences great enough not to be attributable to chance variation in behavior or outlook among the groups subsequent to that experience can be attributed to the manipulation.

Such experiments, although convincing enough that such effects occurred within the setting of laboratory-type experiments, merited some skepticism regarding the applicability of their results to everyday life because of the inherent nature of laboratory experimentation:

- The viewing experience is brief and not continuous (if irregular and disrupted) as in the home setting.
- The experimental experience is itself extraordinary and may elicit atypical responses.
- The short time span between exposure and measurement, together with the absence of distracting, intervening, and possibly counter communicatory stimuli, may exaggerate effects.
- The absence of the possibility of retaliation removes the most common of factors inhibiting the kind of behavior under scrutiny.

From the perspective of evidentiary interpretation, the primary contribution of the research conducted in behalf of the Surgeon General's Committee was data not party to the same weaknesses. These new data came from surveys of everyday teenage television exposure and everyday teenage aggression. Today, there is evidence from many more laboratory-type experiments, some field experiments, and a much larger number of surveys. Those 1963 experiments now stand as the initiation of investigation varied in method, wide-ranging in focus, and complementary in regard to challenges as to generalizability to the everyday, or what psychologists call "external validity."

First, it should be clear that the many laboratory-type experiments that record enhanced aggressive or antisocial behavior as a consequence of brief exposure to violent television portrayals demonstrate that television can affect such behavior in such settings. Even skeptics about the everyday influence of television violence on aggressive and antisocial behavior such as Freedman make such an acknowledgement.

It is an axiom that when real-life circumstances resemble those of an experiment, the usual challenges to external validity do not apply and the results have a strong claim to generalizability to the everyday. That is the case here with the many experiments demonstrating effects on children of nursery school age. Children at that age lack the concept of experimentation that would lead them to behave atypically, and the experience of watching television and then playing (when behavior is measured) while under adult supervision is hardly unusual for them. For this one subject population, the experimental results by themselves are convincing.

In addition, the experimental evidence as a whole, including experiments in which subjects are of college-age as well as those in which they are younger, has become much more convincing as it has become more numerous. The many experiments are, on the whole, so consistent in outcome, so complementary and plausible in leading to explanations for the effects of television violence on aggressive and antisocial behavior, and so logically linked to and consistent with the outcome of research on other kinds of media effects and on topics other than media effects (such as general learning principles, psychotherapy, and public information campaigns) that the challenges to external validity have become much reduced in force. That is, as a body of evidence, experimental findings are not static in their claim to such validity but increase with replication, explanation, and linkages to and consistencies with other bodies of evidence.

Second, the surveys of male and female teenagers conducted for the Surgeon General's Committee permit a strong test of whether or not the findings of these experiments can be applied validly to everyday life (Chaffee, 1972; Lefkowitz, Eron, Walder, & Huesmann, 1972; McIntyre & Teevan, 1972; McLeod, Atkin, & Chaffee, 1972a, 1972b; Robinson & Bachman, 1972). They do so by having three characteristics:

- They obtain for sizable samples of boys and girls measures of everyday television viewing, including scores that for each boy or girl reflect the amount of violent programming viewed.

- They obtain for these same samples of boys and girls measures of everyday aggressiveness that reflect what each boy or girl actually has done.

- They include measures of other variables that might be responsible for an observed correlation between exposure to violent television and aggressive behavior.

The surveys thus provide answers to two important questions: Is there a positive correlation between media exposure and behavior that would be necessary for the experiments to apply to everyday life? If there is such a positive correlation, can it be attributed to anything other than media influence? In this particular instance, the survey data give hitherto-absent support to the experimental data:

- Exposure to television violence was positively correlated with aggressive and antisocial behavior, as would be necessary for a general, non-sporadic effect of the medium.

- The correlation was not wholly attributable to some third variable associated with both violence exposure and such behavior, which precluded the dismissal of television as irrelevant.

- In particular, neither the preference for violent entertainment among antisocial and aggressive youths nor frustrating experiences in schooling explained the correlation.

The last point requires some explanation, and provides an excellent example of how survey data, although not by themselves compelling because of their inability to establish unambiguously whether the ostensible "cause" preceded the alleged "effect," may figure importantly in causal inference. The alternative explanation that aggressive behavior predicted a preference for violent entertainment could be tested by obtaining data on preferences as well as exposure. If preference is responsible, then preference should be an equal or better predictor of the behavior in question. In fact, that did not turn out to be the case. Frustration over poor school performance easily could explain a television viewing and aggression correlation, with those doing poorly watching more television and behaving more aggressively. That too failed to fully explain the correlation. These are examples of testing an original association for spuriousness or attributability to a third variable. The more of such tests that an association can survive, the more credible it is as evidence of causation, and particularly so when these tests involve plausible explanations, as in the present instance.

Third, the pattern evident in these early surveys has been repeated again and again in additional surveys since the Surgeon General's inquiry. The early evidence has survived repeated tests. The least ambiguous documentation of a positive association between exposure to violent television entertainment and aggressive behavior is the panel study sponsored by NBC and conducted by J. Ronald Milavsky, a sociologist, and his colleagues (Milavsky, Kessler, Stipp, & Rubens, 1982). Over three-and-a-half years, they obtained data on viewing and behavior from cadres of elementary school boys and girls in two American cities at repeated intervals. The result is 12 separate instances, six for boys and six for girls, in which there are statistically significant positive correlations.

It must be acknowledged that not all investigators report or interpret survey data as documenting a positive correlation between media exposure and behavior. For example, despite those 12 statistically significant positive correlations, Milavsky and colleagues adopted a mode of analysis that permitted them to offer a null interpretation. The general principle that data are often open to more than one interpretation, and that one must choose among them on the basis of the varying rationales offered, is well illustrated here. Thomas Cook, a Northwestern University social psychologist, and colleagues (Cook, Kendzierski, & Thomas, 1983) reexamined the same data as Milavsky and colleagues and reached essentially an opposite conclusion!

What is important is not the interpretation of a single set of data, but the pattern of which any one set is a part. To make such an interpretation in this instance, it is necessary to introduce three concepts:

- Magnitude of association, or "effect size," refers to the degree of association recorded between two variables, which can be either negative (higher scores on one variable predict lower scores on the other) or positive (higher scores on one variable predict higher scores on the other) in sign and can vary from being perfect (ranking on one variable is equivalent to ranking on the other) to zero (no degree of association) or maximal to null.

- Sampling variability refers to the fact that any measure obtained from a survey, including correlations between variables, will vary with each sample drawn; the measures successively obtained will cluster about a mean that is the best possible estimate of the population measure.

- Implied central tendency refers to the population measure implied by the measures obtained by successively drawn samples or by a number of samples representing independent (but comparable, as opposed to distinctly different) populations.

In the present case, the recorded correlations range from about null (one would not expect a zero even if that were the true population measure because of sampling variability) to modestly positive, and are small in size. Almost all of the correlations are positive, with a positive average. The majority of these positive correlations achieve statistical significance — that is, they are big enough so that in these individual cases they cannot be attributed to sampling variation. The implied central tendency is thus positive. For it to be null, the correlations would have to distribute themselves roughly equally between positive and negative outcomes. The explanation for some null findings is simply that the underlying associations for the population are modest or small in magnitude, so that sampling variability would lead to some falling within the null range. The evidence from the varied surveys, then, is quite convincing that in real life young people who view greater amounts of television violence also behave more aggressively.

There are two reasons for suspecting that these obtained correlations underestimate the real-life association. One is that the measures of exposure and behavior are imperfect or, in jargon, have a degree of unreliability, and to the extent that correlated measures are imperfect or unreliable, the correlation observed will be diminished. The other is that television exposure is so common that any comparison involving frequency of exposure is limited to the high and moderate, and such a truncated distribution will lead to a correlation lower than would occur were low or zero scorers present.

Fourth, these patterns have been confirmed by the quantitative aggregation of the evidence. The technique has been meta-analysis, introduced by the University of Colorado educational researcher Eugene Glass (Glass, McGaw, & Smith 1981). Meta-analysis essentially is defined as the arithmetic averaging of the results of two or more studies. In meta-analysis, each study supplies information analogous to the way in which the respondent to a public opinion poll supplies information. The information can include not only the results, but study characteristics. In one case, the Canadian sociologist F. Scott Andison (1977) tabulated the results of 67 published studies of television violence and aggression, and found not only that a majority of experiments and surveys reported positive associations, but that almost all surveys reported positive correlations. Susan Hearold (1986), a student of Glass, examined 165 survey findings and found a distinctly positive average association; she also examined 290 findings of laboratory experiments and found the same. The number of findings are more than four times the actual number of studies examined because any single experiment or survey may produce more than one finding. These results for the experiments do not disappear when the analysis is confined to those of the highest quality or those that in procedure most closely duplicate real world conditions. This latter outcome supports the view that the experimental results cannot be dismissed on the ground of artificiality of the surrounding circumstances in which they were obtained.

Fifth, it is widely acknowledged that the several field experiments which have been conducted are uninterpretable as a body of evidence. For example, Cook and colleagues (1983) dismiss these studies as being divided in outcomes and without characteristics that encourage the analyst to prefer one to another. Hearold in her meta-analysis calculates the average outcome as about zero. In short, some investigators report effects, others do not, adjudication among them is problematic, and the average outcome approximates zero.

The problem is that the experimental paradigm in this instance has not transferred well from the laboratory to the outside world. Random assignment has seldom been possible, and the use of intact groups has sharply reduced the likelihood that control and treatment groups are comparable. Manipulations of everyday viewing are difficult, and may be resented — especially when one or another group is forced to watch television its members would not watch voluntarily. For example, when a group that would ordinarily watch much violent entertainment is forced to watch something else to create a control condition, the result may be frustration — which itself may increase aggression, thus confounding the manipulations. Finally, what in the abstract may appear to be a stunning design because of its realism on closer examination may prove highly insensitive to detecting realistic effects.

An example of the latter is provided by a field experiment conducted by the late Stanley Milgram and R. Lance Shotland (1973) under the sponsorship of CBS. They created various versions of a *Medical Center* episode in which the protagonist steals from a hospital charity box. In one version, he is punished. In another, he gets away. They showed these versions along with a neutral episode at a New York preview house, thereby creating control and treatment conditions. Finally, they invited people by mail to a midtown Manhattan premium center to receive a free radio as a reward for evaluating what they had seen. The dependent measure was whether or not those who had seen the portrayed theft stole from a similar charity box while left alone in the premium center office. The outcome was null. However, a little reflection leads to the conclusion that for an effect to occur a sizable proportion — perhaps 15% — of the subjects would have had to have been influenced by a 30-minute portrayal seen several days earlier. If television effects were so powerful, one would see them reflected each morning in the news as viewers acted out the previous evening's primetime transgressions.

In any case, results of the field experiments do not point clearly in one or another direction although partisans can find supportive studies. It is thus a major error to treat these field experiments as additional tests of a real-life relationship that can be crudely averaged with the outcomes of surveys because their mixed and on the average null outcomes appear to be attributable to the method itself.

In sum, laboratory-type experiments document causation in the laboratory context, and surveys extend external validity to these results by recording positive correlations between television exposure and behavior not readily explainable by factors other than media influence. Field experiments, if taken as the best test of the influence of television, would lead to a conclusion of null influence, but such an assumption is not justified (a) because of the high likelihood that the mixed results represent unresolved methodological problems, and (b) because of the mutually supportive evidence from laboratory-type experiments and from surveys, which unlike the field experiments do not appear to suffer from fundamental methodological problems.

The evidence is most convincing in regard to "interpersonal aggression" — fighting, hitting, name-calling, and troublemaking. This is because this is the kind of aggression that has been measured most often in the surveys, so that most of the recorded associations between television and behavior reflect interpersonal aggression. However, evidence is not absent in regard to criminal and seriously harmful antisocial behavior. First, the types of interpersonal aggression measured in specific instances easily could cross the threshold of the seriously harmful. Second, when delinquency, property damage, and physical violence against others have been measured, the pattern has not differed in kind from that for interpersonal aggression. What is different is that the number of recorded associations are fewer, and thus the pattern less striking.

The most compelling evidence in regard to criminal and seriously harmful antisocial behavior is provided by the survey of more than 1,500 London males between the ages of 12 and 17 conducted by William Belson (1978). His sample is not only very large but is as representative of the London teenage male population as research techniques permit. He obtained the crucial portions of his data by lengthy, probing clinical interviews rather than by impersonal (and more easily falsifiable) questionnaires, and his measures of antisocial behavior ranged from the comparatively trivial ("I wrote in big letters on the side of a building") to the truly criminal and seriously harmful ("I broke into a house and smashed everything I could find," "I stabbed another boy," "I threw the cat into the fire") and all gradations in between ("I deliberately smashed a school window," "I slashed the tires of some cars"). He found greater degrees of regular viewing of violent television positively associated with greater frequencies of antisocial behavior at all levels of seriousness. His strongest finding was that the very few youths who regularly viewed a great deal of television violence committed several more antisocial acts of the most serious and harmful variety over a period of several months than did youths equivalent in other characteristics except that they viewed far less violent television. Because the frequency of such acts even among these youths is comparatively rare, the proportionate increase his data attribute to the heavier viewing of violent television entertainment is large — 50%! He concludes:

> The evidence gathered through this investigation is very strongly supportive of the hypothesis that high exposure to television violence increases the degree to which boys engage in serious violence. Thus for serious violence by boys: (i) heavier viewers of television violence commit a great deal more serious violence than do lighter viewers of television violence who have been closely equated to the heavier viewers in terms of a wide array of empirically derived matching variables; (ii) the reverse form of this hypothesis is *not* supported by the evidence. (*Television Violence and the Adolescent Boy*, p. 15)

It is not necessary to accede to a causal interpretation to attach great importance to these data. The rationale for a causal inference is the statistical model employed which holds constant all variables except those of interest. This is presumptive evidence of causality, but not compelling, because there is no way to fully resolve issues of time-order and alternative explanations. Survey evidence never can fully do so. What it can do is raise or lower the plausibility of a causal link. In the present case, there is no justification to fully dismiss Belson's data. It can be unambiguously and conservatively interpreted as documenting that the associations between interpersonal aggression and violence viewing so often reported hold for far more serious, harmful, and criminal behavior. Thus, the laboratory experiments can be said to be validated by surveys not only of aggressive behavior but of criminal and seriously harmful antisocial behavior.

The evidence also is more convincing for very young children than for teenagers or young adults. The reason is the exemption of experiments in which subjects are young children from challenges over external validity. Thus, the evidence that unambiguously leads to causal inference is especially convincing in their case, and the fact that for young children play is the context of most aggression — and can be the setting for very seriously harmful acts — further strengthens this view.

However, the case for effects on teenagers and young adults is a solid one. First, young children affected by violent television are very likely to carry over their aggressive habits into the teens and adulthood. Second, teenagers and young adults demonstrably have their behavior changed by violent portrayals within experiments, and are documented as behaving more aggressively in everyday life if they also are higher in exposure to violent television programming.

Two issues remain. One is the explanation for these effects. The second is the range of phenomena to which such an explanation applies.

The psychology by which entertainment becomes information provides the answer to the first. Effects rest on the fundamental and encompassing dimensions of efficacy, normativeness, pertinence, and susceptibility, with the first three reflecting impressions attributable to the content of the portrayals and the fourth representing the state of the viewer. The lengthy catalogue of circumstances on which effects have been demonstrated to be contingent are only the empirically tested few of a probably infinitely larger number of specific facilitating circumstances. Most, and possibly all, of these would fall under one or more of the four dimensions.

Three major theories explain why these dimensions and the more specific contingent conditions make a difference. Social learning theory emphasizes the role of observation in learning (a) new ways of behaving, (b) the circumstances appropriate to their display, and (c) the likely consequences. Disinhibition and cue theory emphasizes the role of observation (a) in raising or lowering internal thresholds over displaying one or another kind of behavior and (b) in identifying signals indicating whether or not a particular kind of behavior is appropriate.

Arousal theory emphasizes the role of observation in heightening states of physiological arousal which may intensify subsequent behavior or push it beyond the threshold of restraint.

More recent elaborations by Albert Bandura (1986) and Leonard Berkowitz (1984) have expanded the predictive range of the concepts. Bandura has introduced "social cognitive" as a replacement for social learning theory, and Berkowitz has argued in behalf of "cognitive neoassociation" as embracing disinhibition and cue theory. These two perspectives are highly complementary. What they have in common is an increased emphasis on cognitive processing. Bandura argues that observation not only teaches the what, the when, and the why, but rules and stratagems for consciously changing behavior. That is, viewers incorporate not simply responses but modes of coping from what they observe. This carries viewer psychology a step farther because it extends it to acquiring principles of learning. Berkowitz focuses on the role of observed events in developing linkages between stimuli and appropriate responses, and such responses and subsequent responses. He argues that "semantic neoassociations" link such elements to create scenarios that people enact in real-life situations. That is, viewers not only have internal thresholds and responses to specific cues altered, but these become incorporated by autonomic mental associations into chains of behavior that, because of the probabilistic nature of association, are not fully predictable. Stimuli invoke labels, labels guide behavior by making one or another alternative more readily retrievable from the repertoire of responses or seem more appropriate, and the outcome leads to a new set of stimuli where associations again occur. Television plays a role in contributing to what is symbolized by the labels, and thereby to the behavioral sequence that will occur. This carries viewer psychology a step farther because it applies it to extended sequences of behavior rather than specific acts. Taking these views into account along with the evidence examined leads to a three-factor theory of media effects:

- The media influence behavior through the building up of mind sets that play a major role in governing displayed behavior, and they do so through the consistency of their portrayals.

- The media influence behavior through their establishing of linkages between stimuli and behavior, and they do so through the consistency of their portrayals.

- The media influence behavior when they deviate from the redundant, the stereotypic, and the already-learned.

Can we have it so vulgarly both ways, with both consistency and deviation of portrayals affecting behavior? We must, because that is the way media in fact function. The first two represent the continuing, cumulative, long-range influence of television. The third represents the well-documented influence of portrayals that deviate in some forceful or distinct way from the norm. Any specific example of a portrayal falling into the first category is unlikely by itself to have much influence, and any specific example of a portrayal falling into the third category will be somewhat limited in its possible effects by working against the tide.

Finally, there is the role of frustration. It is frequently argued that because many of the laboratory-type experiments demonstrating causation involve the provocation or frustration of subjects prior to the manipulation, the aggressive or antisocial behavior is dependent on or in some way outside the ordinary boundaries of human behavior. One reply is subjective. The experimentally-induced provocations are of a minor sort encountered daily by everyone, such as an insult, small pain, or denial of access to something pleasurable, and they hardly make the experiments an exception to what ordinary viewers would experience. Another is quantitative. Hearold's (1986) meta-analysis records the largest effect size for instances in which treatment subjects only are frustrated; the next largest when treatment and control subjects are both frustrated; and, a smaller but still decidedly positive effect size when neither are frustrated. Frustration is thus a facilitating but not a necessary condition. The media experience adds to what frustration accomplishes and can have an effect in its absence.

The range of phenomena to which these explanations apply is extremely wide. The question of the effects of television violence on aggression has been the context for the development of theories that apply broadly. Two examples will suffice.

There are a number of laboratory experiments examining the effects of television portrayals that cannot be said to contain violent, aggressive, or antisocial content. These portrayals typically present behavior that most, or at least many, would agree merits the label "prosocial," such as altruism; acceptance of others; social interaction; the engaging in of some non-antisocial activity; behavior in accord with safety, health, or conservation; book buying; obeying norms; respecting the law; cooperation; and the like. The results have been analogous to those for violent portrayals. Hearold's meta-analysis records that exposure to prosocial portrayals is much more strongly associated with prosocial behavior than is exposure to antisocial portrayals with antisocial behavior, an outcome probably attributable to the fact that most of the treatments in the prosocial instance were designed to influence, whereas many more of those in the antisocial instances were drawn from entertainment produced with no such intention, and to the fact that in the prosocial instances, the measured behavior much more often was similar or identical to what had been portrayed. Hearold also recorded an intriguing symmetry between the effects of anti- and prosocial portrayals; the former were associated with heightened antisocial and diminished prosocial behavior, while the latter were associated with diminished antisocial and heightened prosocial behavior. This implies that there are not one but two social costs to violent children's programming — increases in aggressive and antisocial behavior, and decreases in constructive behavior that could be but is not facilitated by television.

The theoretical basis for numerous present-day multi-million dollar U.S. government health information programs in various communities is the "health belief model" (Becker, 1974; Comstock, 1983). This model holds that health practices can be changed by depicting the preferred practices as efficacious, normative, and pertinent, and by increasing individual susceptibility to such arguments. The latter is accomplished by convincing individuals that they are at some risk, and that there are effective means of reducing that risk. One of the many means of achieving these goals is through the use of television and other mass media. The conceptual forerunner and basis of the health belief model is social learning theory. Thus, principles developed at Stanford by manipulating the exposure of children of nursery school age to violent television portrayals are being applied — with some apparent success — to changing the way Americans live their lives.

This wide range of applicability illustrates the principle of transferability. Concepts, explanations, and theories developed in one context can be transferred readily to another when — and only when — they reflect underlying fundamentals. When that is the case, their usefulness is not only increased by the extended range, but the extended range further reinforces the validity of the original research by demonstrating that its premises apply elsewhere when put to the test.

8

Impact

The empirical investigation of the role of television in American society has confirmed what many surmised, as well as occasionally documenting what many feared. Its message is essentially one of power, although power whose observable influence is frequently subtle. Television has changed the way Americans live, and to think of it otherwise would be myopic. It is intricately entwined in the braid of life, so much so that it is easy to mistake it for an entirely passive servant. What is most striking about television is that its power is exercised almost beyond the control of anyone — viewer, celebrity, anchorperson, writer, producer, actor, or network executive.

Necessary Duality

The varying emphases on the public at large and on the individual in assessing the impact of television in America inevitably raises the question of the comparative validity of sociology and psychology, or the macro- versus micro-analysis of social life. The partisan of one or another invariably speaks with a forked tongue, for each method has its advantages and disadvantages for addressing a particular question.

Social factors, even of the broadest magnitude, can hardly affect thought and behavior unless they impinge on the individual consciousness. Political upheavals, economic hard times, the opinions of friends, and the demands of parenting, doctoring, or janitoring enter the personal filter described by such concepts as anxiety, expectation, perception, reinforcement, and cognition. Conversely, the makeup of these components for any individual is the product of the behavior of people as a group, class, or society, and much of that to which the individual psyche must respond is determined by the character of these entities. This character is not sensibly construed as the sum of the attributes of the individuals encompassed, but derives from the particular pattern exemplified by the collectivity in question. Psyche, the individual, is governed by the social, whose force is expressed not simply in numbers but primarily in the relationships among those who make up that number.

This exchange between the individual and the social entities among which the individual moves occurs whether we think in terms of such abstractions as attitudes, values, and beliefs or something so concrete as the behavior in a particular instance of a single person. Such abstractions are a property of the person, the group, and the society. An infinite number of them, which we reduce to a more manageable quantity in deference to our limited powers of comprehension, equal at any moment the individual as well as the social collectivities that constitute the human world. In shifting from the concrete to the abstract, we do not escape from the interaction that occurs constantly between a single psyche and its social environment. We instead merely shift from complex wholes, persons, groups, and societies, to the elements into which they can be artificially dissembled. What is constant is that the specific and the singular are never freed from the collective.

Psychology and sociology exemplify the unavoidable dichotomy of focusing either on the individual or on a social entity. Obviously, television — like the automobile, industrialization, fascism, and democracy — can be comprehended only from both perspectives. The same dichotomy applies to the many other modes of thought and investigation on which we must call. For example, child development as a field emphasizes the individual; political science can be roughly grouped with sociology. The dichotomy is absurd if seen as separating truth from error, but it is real enough in distinguishing different bodies of knowledge.

The two approaches can be readily reconciled when we think about the behavior and thought of people, for one leads soon to the other. Partisanship nevertheless remains justified because the approaches serve different ends and identify problems and issues that are not at all the same. A focus on the social leads to questions of the homogenization of culture; changes in the conduct of politics; alterations in leisure; and — on a more intimate level of human interaction — to arrangements that typify parenting, family life, socialization, and the relationships that develop among couples. A focus on the individual leads to questions of learning; specific decisions about purchases, politics, and behavior; and the internal processes of mind and response on which these are contingent. The two approaches also lead to somewhat different strategies of reform or prescription, for apart from simply changing television programming itself, the one leads to a concern with the institutions that can complement, supplement, or counter the influence of television, while the other leads more directly to a clinical concern with the welfare of the individual.

Broadcasters, although they study and think about their audiences in the mass, in fact approach them, as British sociologist Denis McQuail (1979) once pointed out (p. 228), as if they were operating "a large laboratory in which millions of volunteer subjects are exposed to calculated stimuli designed to maximize the length of stay of subjects and hence the income of the laboratory." Thus, the difference between the approaches lies not in the quantity of persons assessed or in the mode of investigation, but in the theories that are introduced to explain phenomena and in the concepts which these theories employ. The social and the individual do not represent different approaches to the same subject, but different subjects. That is why the topics they address, for the most part, are so distinct.

McQuail perceived media research as plagued by an "inconsistency of vision", with the perspective on television as "a social-cultural phenomenon produced by, and in turn shaping, the history of America" in conflict and largely incompatible with the frequent treatment of television as "a mass consumption industry to be described in marketing terms." He is correct, and correct too in the implication that broadcasters on the whole have not cared much about the first, which from their perspective has for them a decidedly secondary role. What must be added to McQuail's formulation is that television is also a set of recurring stimuli constantly impinging on and sometimes affecting the individual in a way that can best be understood in terms of the psyche. Again, the two poles, the sociological and the psychological, the social and the individual, although inevitably in some opposition, must not be allowed to distract us totally from one or the other.

What we must confront in thinking about television is a constant duality of vision. We must examine the glass not only from above but from below. Otherwise, we shall be like the three blind men who each reached out for a different part of the elephant and came to three wrong conclusions about the beast.

Attention

The most obvious contribution of television to American life is its absorption of time that otherwise would be spent differently. By taking time away from other activities, television has changed the character and availability of other options as well as colored the way each day is lived out in the average home. The extensive attention to the mass media, for which television is in good part responsible, represents one of the defining characteristics of life in the second half of our century.

The mass media, in entertainment and in news, have their own language that is often, if not invariably, pared of individuality, intellectual depth, or subtlety. The media are inherently exploitative, sometimes of the best in us, but more often of something considerably less than that. Television serves curiosity, the will to experience and understand, the longing to enter the imaginary, the impulse to engage the imagination and the mind in something that is real enough yet distant enough from everyday life to strengthen and enrich them; but it also serves materialism, vulgarity, the reduction of life to simple motives and single dimensions, and the urge to flee from ourselves and those about us. Television has made the particular kind of secondary experience represented by the media an integral part of our lives, from shortly after birth to death, an achievement that was beyond the printing press, the phonograph, the radio, or the movie camera.

Television not only has changed the way politics is conducted and made entertainment in its manufactured form a more prominent part of life, but it has also created new galaxies of heroes and heroines. In many ways, they are no different from those who captured public admiration and passion in the more primitive days of the media — the trench-coated foreign correspondents with the recurring bylines from European capitals and from Latin American revolutions, the great stars of Hollywood, the idolized bandleaders and singers. Yet, there are certain shifts that suggest that what we have is not more of the same multiplied, but a phenomenon that is, in essence, different. No longer does public acclaim rest on deeds; instead, it is the product of mere presence in our living rooms. This change amounts to another evolutionary step in the quality of our vicarious participation in life. Television seldom leaves us breathless. It is by turns charming, amusing, diverting, and occasionally compelling, but the singular thrust by which it has held the attention of its subjects has been through orderly, dependable repetition. Marshall McLuhan (1964) has made much of the immense degree to which the medium has increased our use of the visual in comprehending the world, and psychologists have emphasized the degree to which it has made vicarious experience a source of influence, but another dimension of television is its implicit celebration of the mundane and the ordinary. The men and women of the media once could be said to be larger than life. Now they more nearly approximate our neighbors.

These modular celebrities are more insistently with us than their predecessors. The newer ones come and go, infinitely replaceable as popularity wanes, while the older and more permanent figures — sometimes survivors from the previous age of movies and radio — are recycled from one vehicle and one *persona* to another. They are not only at hand daily or weekly when they perform, but the medium constantly repackages them for use in transient passages, with entertainers a mainstay of talk shows.

The contribution of television has been one of reverse alchemy. The observation of the gods and goddesses has become the giddy coverage of human foibles among the mighty and powerful, or at least the famous as exemplified by *People* and *Us.* The genius of this supermarket journalism is to treat people as characters in a sitcom or guests on a talk show. Like *USA Today,* they are the transfer of a television format to print. Their print success was pioneered by television's cultivation, by snapshot comedy and the personal revelations of the talk shows, of audience sensibility and taste. *Lifestyles of the Rich and Famous* and *Entertainment Tonight* derive from the same sources. The underlying message is that some may have it (much) better but no one is superior. Hollywood's age of movies made no similar impression on print journalism because its genres were more varied and far less sharply distilled and therefore were far less successful in shaping the expectations of the audience about what other media should deliver.

Just as attention goes to *Chez Panisse* (Berkeley), which invented the gourmet pizza (duck breast instead of pepperoni), while the bulk of the American dining-out dollar goes to fast foods and their variants in steak-and-salad-bar and theme restaurants evoking religious orders, sailing ships, and railroad yards, television has made its most striking claims on the public in its deviations from the routine. When television can take a naturally occurring event and treat it as a spectacle is a major example. Recent editions include the marriage of Diane and Charles, the Iran-Contra ("Iran-gate") hearings, and the *Challenger* space shuttle disaster, but the genre extends to the early days of television and includes the Republican and Democratic conventions, the Army-McCarthy hearing, the Kennedy assassinations, and the first moon landing. What they have in common is the attraction of an abnormal number of viewers for an event that television translates through its treatment into a performance. These phenomena represent a cessation of normal activity for a sizable proportion of the public. Empirically, any one can be described precisely by their four necessary components—the actual event, the television coverage, the atypicality of the assembled audience, and public opinion about it. Sociologist Elihu Katz (1988) describes them:

> These media events include Sadat's coming to Jerusalem, the Pope's pilgrimage to Poland, the astronauts landing on the moon, the Kennedy funeral, the Olympics, the Watergate hearings, and other 'historical ceremonies' in which the media interrupt the flow of our lives. They say, 'Stop everything! We take you away from your regular schedule of living, away from our regular schedule of broadcasting, to something you can't afford to miss.' People do stop and watch when these programs are on, and they expect others to do so. What's more, they dress up (rather than undress) for the occasion. They celebrate, they invite friends, they serve refreshments, they respond affectively. They do all the things that some theorists would suggest are not typical of everyday television viewing. They're . . . not just letting the programs flow onward. They're intent, they're concentrated, they are with others, they are discussing, they contemplate values that the events bring into focus . . . . In addition, viewers take a role as they participate . . . citizen . . . mourner . . . fan . . . loyal subject . . . . They are participating, not just as television viewers, not just as family members, not even as consumers, but in socially definable roles that have some of the quality of mindfulness . . . . (p. 370)

Empirical documentation of qualitatively different viewing comes from interviews representing a national sample of about 1,700 households at the time of the 1984 Olympics by Eric Rothenbuhler (1988) of the University of Iowa. He found that more planning than ordinarily was the case preceded viewing, viewing was more often done with a group, food and drink were more likely to be served, and that on the whole the event resembled a major holiday such as Christmas and Thanksgiving. This documentation that these events represent for a sizable number an experience distinct from ordinary television should not lead us astray from the realization that for many in the audience, these events are received with no more attention, interest, or festivity than any other programming — as something to do when there is nothing else that must be done.

In their impact on society, they take three quite different directions. In the case of the political conventions, the attention of television has changed the event itself. Television in this instance meddles with the symbols of history. In the case of space shots, television contributes to a common experience on which the whole society will draw for years to come. The medium in this instance acts as an integrative influence in the society, as it does so often in its everyday programming. The most typical way in which audiences for these events are atypical is in their size, but often it is their continuing attention and interest and the degree to which they depart from the usual daytime or primetime audience in makeup. In the latter case, television becomes a means by which individuals and groups certify their identity. Congressional inquiries attract the politically interested, a political party's nominating convention attracts more of the party's supporters than those of the opposing party, royal weddings appeal more to females than males, and surely, the diplomatic adventure in Jerusalem was of particular interest to the Jewish community. In these cases, television takes on the less typical role of cultivating cultural variation and differences within the larger society.

Entertainment and regularly scheduled sports also occasionally achieve temporary peaks of attention that break the normal pattern. These departures from the ordinary levels of attention also vary in the degree to which they provide a common experience for the disparate segments of society or nurture the variation that exists. *War and Remembrance,* the Super Bowl, and the Kentucky Derby exemplify television events that cross the boundaries that make groups distinct while at the same time attracting extraordinary proportions of those with an intense interest in their subject matter. However intensely personal the viewing of such national celebrations may be, they also constitute the symbols by which people express a common interest and on which social cohesion rests.

Whether these media events represent fiction, fact, drama, or sport is irrelevant. They take their social importance from their reformulation of the ordinary television audience, and by that step make a contribution to national experience. Yet, in the dual character of their influence, they should not be taken as unique. The same distinction, to a lesser degree, can be made for the rest of television. Soap operas and daytime game shows, with their predominantly female audiences, and *Late Night With David Letterman,* which attracts the young and irreverent, cultivate existing differences within the society; primetime television, and especially situation comedies with their near-universal appeal, provide a common, unifying experience. Thus, media events exemplify at a heightened level what television does ordinarily.

Communications scholar George Gerbner and colleagues have pointed out that religion, education, and mass media are all systems by which the public is acculturated, or introduced, to the norms, conventions, and taboos of society (Gerbner, Gross, Morgan, & Signorielli, 1986; Morgan, 1989). What sets religion and mass media apart from schooling is their continuing, repetitious presence throughout life.

One might expect that the great quantity of time consumed by television would infringe on time devoted to religion. The multi-nation comparison of time use (Szalai, 1972) by television set owners and nonowners in various societies at a time when set ownership was far from universal suggests that television slightly reduced the amount of time per week devoted to conventional religious observance. What does seem clear is that in the case of cultures in which traditional religious observances have a visible and important place, television is one of the central components of modernization that channels public energies toward secular pursuits. Elihu Katz and Michael Gurevitch (1976) have documented this phenomenon in Israel by tracing the changes in religion and leisure over the years subsequent to the introduction of television. Television viewing not only conformed to the expected pattern of taking patronage away from other media and other leisure activities, but appeared to be part of a drift away from participation in celebrations and activities associated with Jewish religious practice. The prime symbol of this shift was the Sabbath itself. Television broadcasting was initially prohibited during this period. In response to public demand, the prohibition was lifted. Television claimed another broadcast day.

Gerbner and colleagues suggest that television in the United States can be looked upon as an institution that has assumed some of the functions of a dominant religion, and thus might be thought of as the successor to conventional religion. This is an intriguing perspective (Gerbner & Gross, 1976; Comstock, 1982a). The television business, of course, represents a concentration of economic power, as historically does religion, but economic power is common to many institutions. Where television particularly resembles religion is that the basis of this power is the voluntary acceptance of its communications by the intended audience. Television also would appear to resemble religion in the communication of values and interpretation of the world. Television does not do so explicitly as does religion (except in religious and other exhortatory programming), but does so implicitly. It has been argued with great plausibility by Gerbner and his colleague Larry Gross (1976) that television drama as a whole presents, through its violence, a text on the attributes associated with success, power, and dominance, and, through the high frequency with which persons fall victim, another on the hostile and dangerous nature of the world. Similarly, the attributes of figures chosen to appear as entertainers, newscasters, or the subjects of interviews in a favorable context are implicitly identified as the equipment of prominence and success. Television inherently presents winners, and winners represent values.

The connection does not end with the common dissemination of values. Television also establishes a mechanism for the giving or withholding of status. Television's preeminent figures function much like priests in guiding those who watch them to people and things fit for their scrutiny. In this respect, television has become the arbiter of acceptability. CBS news correspondent Charles Kuralt saw things exactly this way when he criticized ABC's Barbara Walters for the sentimental and circumspect interview with President and Mrs. Carter shortly after the 1977 inauguration by characterizing Walters as "the female pope of television" giving benediction to the new secular leader. However, television as a religion is more heuristic metaphor than insight. As J. Mallory Wober (1988), the British social psychologist, has pointed out, even if television meets one test of being a religion, that of prescribing ways of behaving, their conventionality probably makes television more of a servant and reinforcer of established religion than a challenger, and that it surely fails another test — that of identifying a deity or supernatural power as their source.

The assumption by television of some of the functions traditionally performed by religion is a quite different topic from the use of television for the dissemination of theology. Religious television in the United States in recent years has attracted considerable attention. It has been controversial by seemingly offering competition to established, traditional religions, by presenting sometimes flamboyant figures, by its salesmanship in behalf of contributions, and sometimes by emphasizing political and social issues within its theology. Religious television has been thought to attract huge and ever-growing audiences. More recently, it has become the subject of scandals over the sexual and financial acrobatics of some of its most prominent performers.

Recently, three excellent examinations of the phenomenon have appeared — Peter Horsfield's *Religious Television* (1984), William Fore's *Television and Religion* (1987), and Razelle Frankl's *Televangelism* (1987). They make it clear that:

- The size of the audience for religious television reached a peak in the late 1970s, has been fluctuating since, and by no means has there been the phenomenal growth in the 1980s that supposedly has drawn so much attention to such programming.

- The size of the audience for religious television is really quite modest, although as usual much depends on the definition of audience. It is estimated that only about four million, or less than 2% of the total population, watch one or more hours of religious programming per week, and that only about 13 million, or about 6% of the population, watch 15 minutes or more per week.

- The audience is drawn largely from church members, and very few in the audience could be said to be new recruits to religion.

- There is considerable variety in thematic emphasis within religious television, and several of its major figures would be more fairly described as unconcerned or indifferent to issues other than personal needs rather than as politically oriented.

- Religious television in Frankl's phrase depends on "economics, television, and theology," with the first two, and especially the first, dictating program production.

These varied factors lead these authors to question both the legitimacy of the notoriety achieved by religious television and its religious effectiveness. As Horsfield (1984) writes:

The research casts doubt on the validity of the goal of evangelism in the use of television. Evangelism in this regard is defined as establishing contact with those outside the Christian faith, bringing them to a realization of the relevance of the Christian faith for their lives, and establishing them in a process of continuing growth in faith and service within a Christian community. Though television does provide some contact with those who are otherwise religiously uninterested or uncommitted, because of the randomness of television viewing in general or the use of religious television to satisfy other needs than religious needs, research indicates that religious programs consistently reach only a small and segmented portion of this population. (*Religious Television*, p. 175)

Another arena where television has earned some notoriety has been in its coverage of terrorism. American television has been accused of being intrusive, unethical, and contributing to the commission of future terrorist acts by its sometimes intensive coverage. One of the apparent phenomena of modern life is the tendency of terrorist acts and outbreaks of violence of a particular kind to occur in a series. Such clustering suggests that one factor is the coverage given these events by the mass media. It would be silly to hold television responsible apart from other mass media — newspapers, radio, and news magazines. This is not solely because these other media also disseminate information about such events, but because the values expressed in television news derive largely from the values of journalism as a whole, although clearly modified by the particular demands of television as a medium.

Nevertheless, television does occupy a special place among the media in regard to terrorism. Television coverage is our preeminent symbol of public attention, and reportage of one event may encourage similar acts because of the apparent assurance of subsequent attention from the medium. At the same time, television coverage may provide helpful clues for the commission of antisocial acts. Its often vivid camera portrayals supply concrete examples of daring, a sense of actuality, and a realism, which by themselves not only may be instructive, but which may serve as the compelling axis around which the typically more detailed and inevitably drier accounts of newspapers and magazines will be organized and assigned enhanced meaning by potential perpetrators. *The Doomsday Flight* experience gives credence to such a view.

The Stanford psychologist Albert Bandura (1986) makes the case in his *Social Foundations of Thought and Action*:

Airline hijacking provides a graphic example of the rapid diffusion and decline of aggressive tactics. Air piracy was unheard of in the United States until an airliner was hijacked to Havana in 1961. Prior to that incident, Cubans were hijacking planes to Miami. These incidents were followed by a wave of hijackings, both in the United States and abroad, eventually involving over 70 nations. Thereafter, hijackings declined in the United States but continued to spread to other countries so that international air piracy became relatively common. An inventive hijacker, D. B. Cooper, devised an extortion technique in which he exchanged passengers for a parachute and a sizable ransom. He then parachuted from the plane in a remote area. (p. 173)

Others, inspired by his success, copied the hijacking technique but were captured with the aid of signal devices planted in the parachutes to allow easy tracking by pursuing planes. The Air Force announced publicly that this failure should serve as a lesson to others. It did. The next hijacker brought his own parachute aboard and, after sending the interceptor planes astray by casting off the bugged parachute, bailed out safely with half a million dollars. (p. 331)

Sometimes it is the fictional media that furnishes the salient example . . . . The (made-for-television movie) *Doomsday Flight* provides an excellent illustration because of its novel modeled strategy. In this plot, an extortionist threatens airline officials that an altitude-sensitive bomb will be exploded on a transcontinental airliner in flight as it descends below 5,000 feet for its landing. In the end, the pilot outwits the extortionist by selecting an airport located at an elevation above the critical altitude. Extortion attempts using the same barometric-bomb plot rose sharply for two months following the telecast. Moreover, a day or two after the program was rerun in different cities in the United States and abroad, airlines were subjected to further extortion demands . . . to get the extortionist to reveal the placement of altitude-sensitive bombs . . . . Planes were rerouted to airports at high elevations, and some extortion demands were paid by airline officials, only to learn that the airliner contained no bomb. A rebroadcast of the program in Anchorage made an Alaskan viewer $25,000 richer, and a rerun in Sydney made an Australian instantly wealthy, after collecting $560,000 from Qantas. He added considerable force to his threat by directing Qantas officials to an airport locker where he had placed a sample barometric bomb he had built. (p. 173)

Television coverage also may be a factor on which the course of events is contingent. Television coverage occasionally is a condition for safe treatment of hostages or the conduct of negotiations. The access to public attention implied by television may distort the decisionmaking and behavior of those involved. The concept of all the world as a stage is heightened by television coverage. In some cases, it may restrain behavior by the apparent guarantee of exposure to public scrutiny. In others, it may exacerbate dreadful events by giving participants a sense of playing roles in high drama.

Non-political crime, a category into which many airline extortion plots fall, probably exceeds terrorism in its susceptibility to influence by the mass media both because of its independence from ideology and the wealth of opportunities for its commission. Unresolved political tensions, although common enough, are far less common than greed or personal desperation. Banks, gas stations, and supermarkets are everywhere. In those incidents in which hostages are taken, the media — particularly television because it so often transmits events directly to the public — may become a central element in their resolution, for people may act differently when their deeds are on public display. Television enjoys an advantage over other media in its potential for inspiring crime not only for the superior instruction of its visual depiction but because it may be the sole medium reaching many potential perpetrators. In the language of psychology, the successful bank robbery is no more than a portrayal of rewarded antisocial behavior, and we should not be surprised if such stories encourage emulation. Epidemics of crime sometimes may be the chance conjunction of independent events, but they also may constitute a chain whose links are fashioned by the very attention focused by the media on such behavior.

"The whole world is watching!" Television coverage may be a calculated outcome rather than the concomitant of organized displays of dissatisfaction and unrest. Apart from its symbolic value in representing the achievement of public attention, there is the actual political worth of that attention. It is a standard tactic for disaffected groups to seek public sympathy through publicity. Less often, they may attempt to manipulate the course of events by provoking reprisals from those in authority that, when covered by the media, will gain them sympathy and support. The medium of television probably has raised the stakes in such tactics not only because of its access to the public but because of its immediacy and the visual drama it imparts to the events in question.

Such tactics hinge on the expectations held by perpetrators. Their target may be the masses, or the elite that wields power. They may hope to sway public opinion, or to preempt it through the anticipatory response of those in authority. Exposure of the public to shocking events is the immediate fact, but in the arsenal of political action, it is a sword that cuts differently in different circumstances. The tactics themselves are often based on media coverage of earlier terrorist acts. Even failures may be instructive and encourage emulation when, as in Bandura's example, they identify a poor technique that can be improved upon. When the goal is primarily media coverage, the concept of failure — in the sense of apprehension or death — loses all meaning unless the media do the unthinkable — ignore a dramatic, highly compelling, newsworthy event.

Ethics have become an issue in a number of respects. Media coverage of terrorist news conferences, public displays of hostages and their testimonials, and interviews with terrorist leaders in clandestine circumstances place the media in the position of advancing terrorist causes, while to ignore such events would place them in the position of failing to report what is newsworthy. "Checkbook journalism," by which the media pay a fee to an informant or finance an event, has an aura of the unsavory but hardly amounts to making things up. The great prominence given to early U.S. airline hijackings to foreign destinations almost certainly encouraged subsequent hijackings, but the continuing policy of the media in giving scant attention to the kidnapping of airliners in the absence of the seizing of hostages has almost eliminated the media as a factor in such events. By their very nature, the media can serve the end of social tranquility only imperfectly in these circumstances, because they are in the business of purveying the news — a commodity not only far from tranquil itself but equally distant from tranquility in its consequences.

These varied possible outcomes of television coverage stand in contrast to the benefits of an informed public. The rights and privileges of the press rest on the service that it renders the public, and television is in no way dishonored by the power and behavior peculiar to it. What we must recognize is that the price of an unfettered press, which we accept as the surest safeguard for an informed public, is sometimes an outcome not only unintended but also unwelcome by the press, as well as by almost everyone else. We would err to accept the myth so compatible with the practice of journalism that news and events are synonymous, with the former merely reflecting the latter. Events make news, but news also surely makes events, and television news influences events in its particular way — through the behavior it is so well equipped to encourage, through the emotions it so powerfully evokes, and through the anxieties and misgivings on the part of those in authority these powers often invoke.

Family Life

Television has introduced a new set of experiences to the American household quite apart from what is viewed. The films of families viewing television document that attention is commonly discontinuous — people wander in and out of a room, children play and fight, meals are consumed. It would be a mistake, however, to conclude that because television is not often treated as a theater performance it is irrelevant to the life lived around it, for the large number of hours that the set is on each day in the average household makes it the framework within which human interaction occurs.

Less time was devoted to conversation by those who possessed television sets in the multination time-use study. This gives support to the speculation that it reduces interaction among family members. Television has also reduced slightly the time parents devote to child care — by distracting them from children, by providing an impersonal babysitter, by substituting for the reading of bedtime stories by a mother or father.

A large majority — about three-fourths — of American households have two or more television sets. About 90% of all households have a set in a principal social area, the living room or the "family" room. About 70% of multiset households have a second set in a bedroom, and, contrary to the belief that the second set belongs to the children, most of these bedroom sets are in adults' bedrooms.

Multiple sets in the home are a mark of individual and national affluence, but their effect is to increase the privitization of the television experience and to alter the social aspects of viewing. Viewing alone increases, joint viewing by two or more family members decreases, viewing by the entire family decreases, and viewing by children with adults not present increases. The consequence is to further separate adult and child experience. These effects are a second step in the privitization of experience begun with the apparent declines in conversation and child care.

Nevertheless, family members frequently must decide among themselves on what to view. The most frequent circumstance is a decision that is perceived as mutual. When the choice is not mutual, decisions follow the norms of status and majority rule: Fathers tend to prevail over children and mothers; older children tend to prevail over younger; and among adult couples, males tend to prevail over females. What television has added to family life in this decisionmaking is a new if minor arena for the delineation of roles and exertion of authority.

Robert Bower in 1985 described changes in public opinion during television's first three decades that would appear to document a decided rise in parental concern over the medium. In almost every respect, the public at large and parents in particular have come to express increased doubts about the benefits that television brings to children and to make a greater effort to regulate children's viewing.

There has been an increase in the number of parents who assert that they impose rules on their children's television viewing. Nevertheless, rule-making is strongly related to level of parental education. A good majority of those with a college education impose restrictions compared with only about a fourth of those whose education did not go beyond elementary school.

Children between seven and nine years of age are somewhat more often the focus of rule-making than those younger or older. This makes sense, because they would have greater access to and comprehension of adult programming than those younger, yet would be considered as more vulnerable, impressionable, or otherwise "at risk" than those older.

A good majority of parents assert that they "often" restrict the viewing of children to special hours, and almost half assert that they often limit amount of viewing. About half assert that they often choose the programs their children can watch and often forbid watching certain programs, while a startling 60% assert that they often change the channel when something objectionable is on. This represents a doubling of the figure recorded 10 years earlier. Mothers and fathers zapping what they perceive as lurid would seem to express a truly sharp degree of anxiety and dislike over what children may view.

Less than 10% assert they often encourage these children to watch television either to keep them occupied or to keep them at home, with about a half saying they "never" do the former and about three-fourths saying they "never" do the latter. The figures representing those who would encourage children to view have fallen by about a third from what they had been a decade earlier. Only slightly more than one out of ten parents name its capacity as a babysitter as one of television's advantages for children, a figure that is less than half what it was two decades earlier. Finally, the proportion of the public who choose "better off without" over "better off with" television is about four out of ten, a stunning rise from one out of four a decade earlier (although a majority, about six out of 10, still chose "better off with"). Chief among the alleged disadvantages is exposure to something inappropriate ("see things they shouldn't"), cited by about half of the respondents, with violence and crime mentioned far more often than the runner-up, sex or suggestiveness. The second most frequently named disadvantage was that television took up time that could be better spent ("keeps them from doing things they should"), cited by almost one out of three. These opinions are held in conjunction with the view that one of television's major advantages is its educational capability.

When these results are set against those from the national Roper poll sponsored by the Television Information Office (1985), in the late 1980s, the underlying cause becomes apparent. Of 12 activities judged as to whether parents placed "too much," "too little," or "the right amount" of emphasis on them, two-thirds of those polled said parents place too little emphasis on the amount and kind of television their children watch. This was the top score for "too little" emphasis. Television was followed by "kinds of food eaten," "cultural activities," "exercise," and "kinds of friends they have"—all of which were said to receive too little emphasis by between 50 and 60% of the public. When asked whether there were "enough television programs suitable for children," 54% said "not enough," and only 29% agreed that there was "about the right amount." Thus, a principal source of dissatisfaction and concern in regard to children and television is the perceived lack of suitable programming. This is exemplified in the data described by Bower (1985) when parents were asked,

"Which of the programs your (child watches/children watch) do you think are the best programs for (him/her/them)?"

The top eight choices in 1980 apparently exhausted the list, with only 6% naming the last choice on the list, *Eight is Enough.* The top scorers were *Sesame Street* (39%) and *The Electric Company* (12%), followed by *Little House on the Prairie* (11%), *Mr. Rogers* (10%), *Walt Disney* (8%), *Captain Kangaroo* (7%), and *Happy Days* (7%). The 1970s saw the development of *Sesame Street,* a public television offering, and there was no comparable innovation on either public or commercial television in the 1980s.

In sum, there has been a shift toward increased parental concern. This has been exemplified by an increase in rule-making and strictures, a greater willingness to prescribe and proscribe programs, and an increased readiness to turn off the television set. The public believes that what children view and how much they view deserves greater parental attention, and there is a widespread public conviction that there are not enough programs suitable for children — a viewpoint confirmed by the short list and low percentages that emerge when parents are asked to name programs that are particularly good for children.

Three Investigations

Three very recent investigations make a strong case for the influence of television on thought and behavior. Each is different in method and focus. One is a time series that takes advantage of a mammoth experiment inadvertently designed by the U.S. government, another is a real-life test of the effectiveness of an entertainment program designed to change people's minds, and a third employs the late arrival of television in an isolated community as a treatment in a three-community experiment.

In the early 1950s, the U.S. government halted the licensing of television stations while it reviewed certain technical questions about spectrum space and its effective allocation. The consequence was that for several years there was a sizable portion of the country that could receive television signals and a sizable portion that could not. As part of a project directed at Northwestern University by the philosopher of scientific inquiry Thomas Cook, Karen Hennigan and colleagues (Hennigan et al., 1982) took advantage of this circumstance to examine the influence of the introduction of television on crime rates — a natural topic given the controversy over the influence of television violence.

Hennigan and colleagues sorted U.S. cities into two categories — television cities and non-television cities at the time of the initial halt of licensing. They then did the same for states. This was done on the basis of the proportion of households with television sets, and it was easy to create samples of cities and states with low or high proportions because once signals became available, television set ownership increased rapidly and before they were available, it essentially was nil.

They next examined annual government crime rate statistics for four kinds of lawbreaking:

- Violent crime of all kinds.
- Burglary — theft accompanied by breaking and entering.
- Auto theft.
- Larceny theft — defined as "the unlawful taking, carrying, leading, or riding away of property from the possession or constructive possession of another. Thefts of bicycles, automobile accessories, shoplifting, pocket-picking, or any stealing of property or article which is not taken by force and violence or by fraud. Excluded embezzlement, 'con' games, forgery, worthless checks, etc." (p.465)

In this design, the television cities and states became the treatment groups and the non-television cities and states the control groups. When the researchers compared the statistical trends across the years for the treatment and control cities, they found that two types of crime increased significantly in the treatment cities — auto theft and larceny theft. When they made the same comparison for the states, they found the same thing — auto theft and larceny theft increased in the television states to a degree unmatched in the non-television states.

Hennigan and colleagues next compared the trends several years later when the license halt was ended. The treatment and control cities now trade places. The original treatment cities and states become the control groups because they long ago experienced the introduction of television. Any effect that might have taken place would have already occurred. The original control cities and states become the treatment groups because they are experiencing television for the first time. When trends for treatment and control sites were compared, the investigators found that among both the cities and states one type of crime increased in the treatment sites to a degree unmatched in the control sites — larceny theft.

This is a very strong design because it subjects any effect to four separate tests — two wholly independent tests with the switching of treatment and control roles, and two largely independent tests by the city and state data (there would obviously be a modest degree of overlap) at each point in time. It is called a "time series with switching replications" because of the way in which the treatment and control sites trade roles at the second point in time.

Because the auto theft effect did not replicate at the second point in time, Hennigan and colleagues decline to interpret the apparent effect at the first point in time. However, it is probably wise to reserve judgment because the greater proximity to World War II and its ban on civilian auto production would have made autos far more susceptible to any influence on antisocial behavior in the earlier time period (except for television itself, it is hard to think of anything that attracted more attention in the postwar years than the arrival of new models at auto showrooms). The researchers have no such qualms about larceny theft.

The actual increase in larceny theft is estimated as at least 5%. Why did this happen? There are at least two possibilities:

- Relative deprivation. By introducing through its programming and its commercials an enormous increase in exposure to materialistic well-being, television created dissatisfactions that could be remedied by minor seizures of property. Television itself could have played a major role in this, because by present day standards, sets were quite expensive and their extreme desirability would have dramatized for some their "have not" status.

- Social learning. Television in its drama presented a great deal of violence and numerous instances in which desirable goals were pursued by illegal and antisocial means. Viewers conceivably emulated these lessons.

Hennigan and colleagues prefer the former, because violent crime did not increase despite the large quantity of violence portrayed on television. However, it is equally plausible that the high level of portrayed violence had only a low level social effect because such law-breaking would minimize the violation of norms, the likelihood of apprehension, and the severity of punishment if apprehended.

The real-life test of the effectiveness of an entertainment program in changing people's minds involved an extraordinary element — all three network outlets in a sizable market were persuaded to simultaneously and voluntarily broadcast an entertaining but educational program. However, the outcome is equally striking.

The Great American Values Test was a 30-minute information-style program featuring Ed Asner and Sandy Hill, then anchor on ABC's *Good Morning America*. It was broadcast by ABC, CBS, and NBC outlets in the "tri-cities" area of eastern Washington state (Richland, Pasco, and Kennewick) between 7:30 p.m.-8 p.m. on a weekday during the winter. The program was written and produced, and the research designed by a well-known psychologist, Milton Rokeach, and a well-known sociologist, Sandra Ball-Rokeach (Ball-Rokeach, Rokeach, & Grube, 1984).

The first half of the program defined in news and documentary style the concept of "values," described their measurement, and presented interesting statistics drawn from national samples on the importance Americans attach to 18 different values, and discussed how differences in values are associated with sex, race, socioeconomic status, and age. The flavor is conveyed by Asner's introductory voice-over accompanying visuals of people walking and talking:

> These are people. Like you and me. Americans who work, relax, and live life with all of its anxieties and pleasures . . . all of us, no matter what we do or who we are, have a definite set of human values. For the next 30 minutes . . . *The Great American Values Test* will help us find out what our own values are and how similar or different they are from the values of other Americans. (p. 73)

In the second half of the program, the two hosts directed the attention of viewers to possible conflicts among their values, and in particular attempted to create dissatisfaction with the value viewers placed on two of the 18 — equality and the environment. The treatment of equality counterposed it to freedom. Asner said:

> Americans feel that freedom is very important. They rank it third. But they also feel that equality is considerably less important . . . they rank it twelfth. Since most Americans value freedom far higher than they value equality, the question is: What does that mean? Does it suggest that Americans as a whole are much more interested in their own freedom than they are in freedom for other people? Is there a contradiction in the American people between their love of freedom and their lesser love for equality? (p. 74)

Later, in commenting on the fact that persons who agreed with the statement that "he brought it on himself" in regard to the assassination of Martin Luther King, Jr. ranked equality far lower than those who felt sad, angry, or ashamed, Hill said:

> This raises the question of whether those who are against civil rights are really saying they care a great deal about their own freedom but don't care that much about other people's freedom. (p. 75)

The environment was treated analogously, with the valuing of "a world of beauty" counterposed with the valuing of "a comfortable life."

The calculated intent with both equality and the environment was to instill in viewers dissatisfaction with their valuing of each, thereby initiating shifts in attitude and behavior that would restore the viewers' self-esteem — that is, shifts favoring equality and the environment. Those familiar with social psychology will recognize the application of a "balance" or "equilibrium" theory which holds that the human organism will attempt to restore a satisfying psychological state from which it has been dislodged. In the present instance, those made uncomfortable about their valuing of equality and the environment could restore self-esteem if they increased the value placed on each. If values, as Rokeach and Ball-Rokeach argue, to an important degree govern attitude and behavior, changes in these too would be expected.

They tested the effectiveness of their program and the validity of the thinking behind it by a field experiment. They obtained by mail questionnaire data on values, attitudes, and behavior from representative samples of about 2,750 persons, about a third of whom resided in a control city also in eastern Washington state (Yakima). The other two-thirds resided in the Tri-Cities treatment site. In the control city, value and attitude data were obtained by mail questionnaire from equal-size samples of different individuals before and after the date of the broadcast. In the Tri-Cities treatment area, the before-and-after sampling was weighted 70%-30% in favor of post-broadcast data collection to increase the reliability and sensitivity of analyses comparing viewers of *The Great American Values Test* with non-viewers in the same community. Values were measured by ranking 18 "end states" (generally defined as the goals toward which people strive) such as equality, freedom, and a world of beauty. Attitudes were measured by such items as:

- White people have a right to keep blacks out of their neighborhoods if they want to, and blacks should respect that right (agree strongly, agree somewhat, not sure, disagree somewhat, disagree strongly).
- Schools should pay more attention to preparing boys for careers than girls (agree strongly, agree somewhat, not sure, disagree somewhat, disagree strongly).
- Continued economic growth is necessary even if it means some sacrifice of environmental quality (agree strongly, agree somewhat, not sure, disagree somewhat, disagree strongly).

In an important addition, they measured possible behavioral influence of the 30-minute program by separately mailed solicitations for funds by three actual organizations promoting racial minority rights, equal treatment of women, and protection of the environment through support of a ban on nonreturnable bottles.

One or more persons in one-fourth of the households in the Tri-Cities treatment sample watched the program. This was about two-thirds of all those watching television between 7:30 p.m. and 8 p.m. The other five-eighths of the chosen treatment sample were doing something else — eating, shopping, running errands, and the like. The most compelling finding, then, is the comparison of the entire samples in the treatment and control sites in regard to response to the financial solicitations. Although the positive response of 8.3% in the treatment site was hardly sensational, it was substantially larger — 60% or so — than the 5.2% for the control city, and the difference between the two meets the conventional criteria for statistical significance (that is, it is not reasonably attributable to mere sampling variation).

This result is compelling because it rests on the comparison of all people sampled in the treatment and control sites when only about a fourth of the households in the treatment site were tuned-in to the program. This implies a rate of favorable response to the financial solicitations of as great as almost one in five viewing households, or four times greater than that for the control site. Such a comparison pinpoints a strong effect on a few, and an effect difficult to attribute to anything other than the program because the whole samples would be entirely comparable since each would have been randomly drawn and there would be no self-selection or attrition.

Such methodologically rigorous comparisons of whole samples did not yield any statistically significant differences in before-after responses on the attitude and value measures between the treatment and control sites. However, if differences were small they would be masked by the irrelevant scores from those in the treatment site who did not view the program. The question of effects on attitudes and values was therefore further pursued by examining the viewers in the treatment site by degree of attention. If the program affected attitudes and values as well as behavior, then scores for all three should be greater among those who devoted the most attention to the program.

When those who identified themselves as full viewers, interrupted or partial viewers, and non-viewers were compared, changes in values and in attitudes were as hypothesized. Further confirmation of behavioral change was provided by decidedly higher average financial contributions from full viewers (as compared to those from interrupted or partial viewers and non-viewers).

Ball-Rokeach and Rokeach reject the term "manipulation" so frequently employed by psychologists and prefer to term *The Great American Values Test* as educative on the grounds that it invited the viewer to voluntarily inspect and evaluate his or her beliefs. Yet, they recognize that the technique of creating dissatisfaction with the valuing of one or another end state surely could be turned to outcomes noxious, evil, or at least undesirable to some — as was surely the case for even the two values on which this enterprise focused. As they write, "We thus end this discussion with a far greater feeling of uneasiness than we had in ending earlier discussions about the possibility that our work might be used for evil or ignoble or antidemocratic or self-serving purposes" (pp. 171-172). *The Great American Values Test* empirically supports what most people in broadcasting believe — that a well-designed program intended to influence people can do so. It also raises an interesting question: If television passes such an influence test, can those who run television pass the values test and avoid "evil or ignoble or antidemocratic or self-serving purposes"?

The third investigation, involving the examination of actual communities within an experimental design many years after the introduction of television in North America, is far easier to propose than achieve. The rapid diffusion of television quickly rendered the required non-television community a rarity; probably no other innovation in history (including the swivel-handled vegetable peeler) has ever been adopted so rapidly and universally. Finding communities similar enough to serve as convincing treatment and control sites would be problematic since not having television itself would suggest some highly unusual attribute. External events other than the introduction of television could have effects that could be mistaken for those from television, for an experimental comparison of two or three communities does not provide the protection against the intrusion of one or more unique factors afforded by large samples of states, communities, or individuals. Data collection from populations going about their everyday lives would be an enormous burden, and the interpretability of results would depend on the adroit choice of the right thing to measure. Finally, such a real-life experiment might fail to capture effects that are cumulative or delayed, and might record effects that are merely short-term.

Nevertheless, it is precisely such an experiment that Tannis MacBeth Williams and a dozen colleagues describe in *The Impact of Television* (1986). In the mid-1970s, they found an isolated logging and farming community in northwest Canada unable to receive television signals but scheduled soon to be able to receive one channel, the government-owned Canadian Broadcasting Corporation (CBC). "Notel," as it is labeled in their research, had a population of about 650 and became the treatment site. For one control site, they chose a place nearly identical in size, economic activities, average income, proportion of English-speaking households, and other circumstances that had been receiving the same Canadian channel for several years. This community, about 55 miles from Notel, they labeled "Unitel." For another control site, they chose a community several hundred miles from the first two and much nearer the U.S. border. It was slightly larger but otherwise highly similar to Notel and Unitel, and received the CBC and all three American networks — ABC, CBS, and NBC — thereby making it possible for the data to suggest whether television effects, if any, were dependent on availability of the medium or the quantity and diversity of the medium available. This community was labelled "Multitel."

Data on children and adults were collected two years apart, before and after Notel began receiving the CBC, Unitel added a second CBC channel, and Multitel continued to receive its four channels. The findings represent a plausible account of television effects on the community level that importantly adds to and confirms previous research.

A pattern of major interest is the frequency with which, at the beginning, measures for Unitel resemble those for Multitel more than they resemble those for Notel. It is as if television is homogeneous and a regular amount of any kind is sufficient for its effects to occur. In fact, it is somewhat more complicated. The CBC, although broadcasting less violent entertainment than the U.S. networks, is not without violent entertainment, and its commercials are essentially the same as in the United States. When whatever amount of television that is offered by different sources is similar, amount and diversity available does not matter much in the effects the medium will have. Thus, this apparent phenomenon of "some is enough" does not imply that content is irrelevant but that Canada and the United States (and other modern societies, too) use television in similar ways.

The experiment also replicates the rapid diffusion and near-universal adoption of television. People were eager for television in Notel, and by the end of two years, almost every household had a set.

The data support the prior research on television violence and aggression, in which laboratory experiments demonstrate causation and catalogue the factors on which real-life effects might be contingent and surveys of everyday aggression and television viewing among adolescents document that those higher in violence viewing are also higher in aggressive behavior. In this case, we have a real-life experiment and the authors recorded increases in real-life verbal and physical aggression with the coming of television to Notel. These increases were recorded for both boys and girls.

The data also suggest that television to a small degree lowered the scores of both children and adults on standard psychological measures of creativity and problem-solving. The authors speculate that television, by its conventional plots and formulas, may hamper an individual's search for novel alternatives and persistence in finding solutions. They found children's reading ability reduced by television and they speculate that television is an escape from study and from the practice of reading for some children so that they never or only poorly master this skill. The important lesson is that parents and teachers must take care that television does not displace the time essential for the mastery of basic skills. Once gained, such mastery cannot be lost, but if not gained at the appropriate point in schooling, it is unlikely to be achieved.

Sex-role stereotyping appears to have been increased by television. The authors argue that an effect of this kind is remarkable since television admittedly only reflects the conventions of everyday life and it is surprising that it should have any independent effect.

A major social effect was the reduction in participation in social, recreational, and community activities. This occurred for young people, where attendance at sports events and dances was reduced. It also occurred among adults, and especially among those 55 years of age and older. Television does not displace many activities in the home because they can be easily done while also attending to it, but if it is to be attended to it does require one to be at home, and the people of Notel — at least during their first years of television — wanted to give it more attention than their prior schedules would have permitted.

There is, of course, the question of cultural differences. Do these Canadian communities provide data with implications for the effects of television upon Americans or upon more urban North American populations? The answer, on the whole, would appear to be yes. The television is comparable, and the effects involve fundamental elements of thought and behavior difficult to construe as somehow culture-bound. These factors argue for substantial generalizability.

Each of these three investigations presents evidence that television has been the cause of a change in thought or behavior. The first documented an increase in larceny theft with the introduction of television, the second found changes in behavior and beliefs as a consequence of viewing an entertaining television program designed to achieve those ends, and the third recorded a series of changes in the beliefs and behavior of children and adults with the introduction of television in an isolated community. Their strength is that the designs they employ justify attributing the recorded changes to the influence of television. Although each naturally invites dismissal as outlandish and unlikely because of the strong effects reported, this very design factor combined with their high degree of internal consistency (in the first, among several analyses; in the second, between and within conditions; and in the third, across initial comparisons and over time) and consistency with previous research makes them important as well as intriguing instances of the apparent documentation of television effects.

Cultivation

A new topic was introduced into research on the effects of television when George Gerbner, then dean of the Annenberg School at the University of Pennsylvania, and his colleagues began in the 1970s to report positive associations between amount of television viewed and perceptions of real-world conditions (Gerbner & Gross, 1974, 1976, 1980; Gerbner, Gross, Morgan, & Signorielli, 1980). He called the presumed effect "cultivation" — the continuing, cumulative, subtle shaping of public beliefs by the content dominant and typical in television programming.

His basic technique was to ask people to estimate some social statistic, such as the proportion of U.S. citizens employed in entertainment, health, or law enforcement; the proportion of persons in the world who are U.S. citizens or who are non-white; or the probability of falling victim to crime or assault. He would divide these replies into those representing heavier and lighter viewers of television. By using his own annual content analyses of one representative week of fall programming, he was able to supply figures describing television programming, and from standard statistical compilations, he could supply figures representing the facts. Invariably, he found that persons whose television viewing was greater gave answers that on the average were closer to the television figure than to that representing the real world. These differences persisted regardless of amount of education, exposure to other media, and sex.

Since then, cultivation has become the subject of extensive research by Gerbner and colleagues (Gerbner, Gross, Morgan & Signorielli, 1986) and by many others, and of controversy between Gerbner and colleagues and some of these other investigators (Gerbner et al., 1981a, 1981b; Hirsch 1980a, 1980b, 1981a, 1981b; Hughes, 1980). Cultivation has caught on, probably because the effect it hypothesizes is intuitively plausible. The highly diverse and varied bodies of data appear to present a coherent pattern which can be described in terms of two distinct outcomes, fearfulness versus pessimism, and two distinct relationships, association versus causation.

As Gerbner's work progressed, he began to concentrate on "mean world" effects (Morgan, 1989). He reasoned that the quantity of violence on television provided a continuing barrage of depictions of the world as unsafe and treacherous. In particular, he began to employ as a major measure of belief and perception a widely used scale of "anomie," or alienation from society, that asked people whether other people could be trusted, officials worked in the public interest, the world was a fit place to have a baby, relationships with foreign countries were problematic, or there were places nearby where they were afraid to go. Gerbner's most discussed and striking finding has been the consistency with which television exposure predicts higher scores on this "mean world" scale.

The scale would appear to include two distinct components (Comstock, 1982a):

• Pessimism. Examples would include high or exaggerated estimates of the crime rate and the likelihood of others falling victim to crime or attack, and skeptical or mistrustful beliefs about the quality of life and human behavior.

- Fearfulness. Examples would include fear of engaging in some common behavior, such as walking somewhere, and exaggerated estimates of oneself falling victim to crime or attack.

The former is decidedly more cognitive because it reflects broad conceptions of reality, while the latter is more affective in nature because it concerns personal safety. In examining the possible influence of television on these two categories of thought, we will wish to examine the evidence in behalf of two distinctly different relationships:

- Association. Do such beliefs and perceptions vary with amount of television viewed?
- Causation. Are such beliefs and perceptions cultivated or caused by exposure to television?

There is no doubt that in North America beliefs and perceptions in accord with the "mean world" scale are more common among those who view more television. This has been documented repeatedly. When the data are examined separately for fearfulness and pessimism, the picture becomes much more complex.

The analysis of large, representative national samples by Michael Hughes (1980), a political scientist, in *Public Opinion Quarterly* provides the best example. Scores for the one item representing fearfulness appeared to increase somewhat as television viewing increased, but did not do so sufficiently for the relationship to achieve statistical significance — it could be due to chance. Scores for the other four items representing pessimism all increased with greater television exposure, and to statistically significant degrees. These data constitute definite, strong evidence for association, but it is far greater for pessimism than for fearfulness. In fact, the observed association between fearfulness and television exposure does not exceed the threshold required for interpreting the association as real.

The plausibility if not the certainty of causation can be addressed by examining the role of other influences in the relationship between television exposure and beliefs and perceptions. That is, we cannot address the question of causation directly with survey data because of the impossibility of determining time order, but we can ask whether any measured variable is associated with both television exposure and beliefs and perceptions, and thereby explains the association of the latter two with exposure. Hughes simultaneously held constant 14 variables. This is a much more rigorous test than that employed by Gerbner, who held constant one variable at a time. The variables held constant by Hughes included age, sex, and socioeconomic status, employment status, and memberships in organizations. The first three are particularly important, because it is known that they independently not only predict greater exposure to television but also higher scores on the "mean world" scale (those over age 55, females, and the socioeconomically less well off typically watch more television and score higher). When he did so, there were two major findings:

- The relationship between fearfulness and exposure was reversed, with fearfulness greater among those who viewed less television.
- The number of pessimism items associated with television exposure to a statistically significant degree dropped from four to three.

In short, there is no presumptive case for any causal contribution of television exposure to fearfulness. There remains the possibility that television exposure contributes to a pessimistic outlook.

The validity of this pattern gains support from the surveys conducted by Tom Tyler (1978) at the University of California at Los Angeles. By telephone interviews with a sample of about 1,600 adults in Chicago, Philadelphia, and San Francisco and by door-to-door interviews with a Los Angeles sample of about 225 adults, he obtained measures of fear of crime, exposure to crime in the media, the community crime rate, and actual experience with crime as a victim. The major findings were highly consistent. Fearfulness was unrelated to exposure to crime in the media, but was related to actual experience with crime. Higher estimates of the crime rate — a measure of pessimism as the term is used here — were related to such media exposure. Higher estimates of the community crime rate were unrelated to fearfulness. These data strongly support the view that fearfulness and pessimism are not affected alike by the media.

Research on the topic of cultivation verifies that there is an association between television exposure and certain beliefs and perceptions, and that this association is clear only for those of a cognitive cast, to which the label of pessimism has been applied here. It does not totally disabuse us of the hypothesis that television exposure causes such beliefs and perceptions, but it does confine any causation to pessimism. That is, to cognitive outcomes. The rise in estimates of the community crime rate with exposure to crime news, and the failure of vulnerability or fearfulness to increase with such estimates, supports the view that media effects are more common for cognitive than affective responses.

The findings strongly imply that it is beliefs about the world in general that the media principally convey. What people feel about their safety will have far more to do with their personal experience, and their ability to avoid dangerous circumstances in their daily lives. Thus, the East Side luxury apartment dweller in New York may have his or her estimate of subway crime affected by the evening's newscast, *The New York Times,* or even an episode of a crime series, but it will not affect fearfulness as long as that dweller can use transportation other than the subway.

Secondary Influence

The research on the influence of television inevitably places the medium at the forefront of attention. It would be a mistake to transfer a focus that serves the ends of scientific inquiry to our understanding about real-life events. Television is much more sensibly thought of as a secondary rather than a primary influence. An exception, of course, are effects traceable to the introduction of the medium. Even here, it is more in accord with what is known about human behavior to believe that an effect occurred than to believe that it was of great magnitude, and to believe that the effect was at least somewhat contingent on factors other than television. Ordinarily, television in its continuing influence will interact with other factors, and typically will play a definitional role — that is, it will give shape to behavior largely driven and motivated by factors other than television.

The television business itself perpetuates the myth of television as the primary factor in any influence it may have by its reaction to any evidence that some of the medium's effects may be unwelcome. It does so by consistently rejecting evidence that television has any influence whatsoever beyond that which the business espouses — the providing of entertainment, news and information, and the attracting of public attention. This response, rooted in the same insensitive assessment of evidence that marks the response of the tobacco industry to the health risks of cigarette smoking, is exemplified in the responses to the 1972 report of the Surgeon General's advisory committee that concluded that violent television contributed to aggressive behavior by some young viewers, and of the report of a National Institute of Mental Health special committee that confirmed the 1972 conclusion and raised the possibility of more wide-ranging effects (Pearl et al., 1982a, 1982b). It is also exemplified by the frequency with which industry spokesmen appear at conferences and at professional meetings (such as the annual meetings of the American Psychological Association) to present "an industry view," which essentially is that the social and behavioral sciences have not made much of a case in regard to television's social role. The consequence has been a continuing debate over media effects that has kept the medium unnecessarily in an adversarial position. It would be more intellectually honest and more to the benefit of television to accept the wide range of possible effects with the caveat that television is rarely a major factor. This would substitute knowledge and understanding for vested self-interest, and the result could only improve the framework within which television produces and disseminates its products. Television violence provides a good example. Are we likely to produce "better television" if we reject entirely the argument that violent portrayals may have some adverse influence or if we accept the possibility, know about the factors on which effects are contingent, and make and market television that reflects such knowledge and understanding?

That this should be so is ironic on two grounds. The first is that the research itself strongly encourages a highly qualified view of the influence of television. The second is that, although the effort recently has become diminished, the networks for years have monitored programs and commercials to ensure that they meet acceptable standards. Giving no offense surely has taken precedence over risking some harm to viewers, yet the latter standard has been far from completely ignored. The television business in fact has ignored the evidence it has attempted to refute, yet has behaved as if even more has been demonstrated than is in fact the case.

The psychology of those blocks that spread northwest of Rockefeller Center, of course, has always been that of Chicken Little. The sky is seen daily as falling, and the response is usually suited in its judiciousness to the perception. Religious fundamentalists criticize television for sex and violence, child advocates want to ban commercials aimed at children and oppose product-based programs on the grounds that they are program length commercials, health advocates want to ban beer and wine commercials, educators want educational and cultural programming for teenagers and children on weekday afternoons, and scholarly experts argue that the evidence on television violence is credible. Each is taken as a dire threat to profits, audience size, artistic freedom, and the manageability of the entire enterprise. What seems to be forgotten is that except for a very few stipulations by the FCC, in the absence of new legislation by Congress or new regulatory measures by the FCC, either of which almost certainly would have to survive challenges in the courts, the television business can produce and disseminate whatever it chooses under the protection afforded by the First Amendment. Pressure from some group is a poor excuse for abrogating aesthetic, moral, or social judgments. More importantly, such an anxiety-ridden outlook ignores the force of the television paradigm in America and its enormous ability to keep television much the same except for the inevitable changes attributable to new technology.

The psychology of behavioral effects does not imply that every portrayal influences a sizable portion of viewers, nor does it imply that effects are wholly detrimental to viewers even though its empirical foundation has been the study of aggressive behavior. It simply posits a set of principles that identify attributes of the television portrayal, the circumstances, and the viewer likely to facilitate or deter effects. The accompanying evidence of a positive correlation among adolescents between quantity of violent programming viewed and everyday aggressiveness in real life certainly should not be interpreted to mean that factors other than television do not have an important and probably superordinate role.

The issue that has drawn the most attention in the United States in connection with television has been its possible contribution to delinquency, crime, and other seriously harmful antisocial acts. The evidence supports the proposition that the viewing of television violence increases the likelihood of subsequent aggressiveness on the part of the young, and the analogous proposition that viewing violence increases violations of the law and seriously harmful antisocial acts, but gives much stronger support to the former than to the latter.

The acceptance of the second proposition is contingent on the assumption that television's demonstrated contribution to aggressiveness augments the frequency of serious transgressions, where behavior would be governed by deeply ingraining inhibitions and fears of punishment or disclosure of shame. Albert Bandura (1986), whose experiments and theories have contributed so much to our understanding of the psychology on which any behavioral influence of television rests, places television third behind family and social milieus in which a person resides as a source of influence. He further argues that any actual display of behavior is likely to be strongly dependent on immediate circumstances, such as the perceived likelihood of success and, in the case of aggression, frustration and deprivation. Bandura finds that the consistent expression of any kind of behavior will depend on the reinforcement it receives and how effectively it serves the ends sought by the individual. Such a perspective fits everything we know about human behavior. It is more plausible to argue that seriously harmful or criminal antisocial acts are somewhat shaped by television than that they are very often instigated by it, because such a view accepts the ability of television to enhance capability to perform an act by providing a model without requiring that it overcome major psychological and social restraints. Aggressive or antisocial behavior that falls closer to or — perhaps for a few — within the borders of acceptability is somewhat more likely to be instigated by a portrayal, and far more likely to be shaped by television.

There is not a great deal of evidence directly linking exposure to television with the commission of criminal or seriously harmful antisocial acts. *The Doomsday Flight* is the most persuasive instance, but others include newspaper accounts of acts apparently in imitation of a television or film portrayal, press accounts of admissions that a television or film portrayal inspired a criminal act, and the museum theft committed a number of years ago by Miami beach boys (led by a fellow known as Murph the Surf) that took as its model the popular film *Topkapi* (MGM, 1964). The sole direct experimental test, the field experiment conducted in New York by Stanley Milgram and R. Lance Shotland (1973), found no evidence of a link, but this negative finding is not very persuasive because the rate of antisocial behavior required in this instance for statistical significance was far in excess of that necessary for significant social impact — which would require only the influencing of a minute proportion of viewers. However, the sparsity of direct evidence is not pertinent because it is implausible that such "monkey see, monkey do" imitation would be frequent or widespread. The variety of factors — individual, situational, and societal — involved in criminal or seriously harmful acts are so many and so intertwined that any direct connection to television is unlikely to be readily demonstrable.

When such circumstances make a direct test implausible, the alternative is to test propositions consistent with the supposedly untestable proposition. This, in effect, is what has occurred in the experiments on violence viewing (which demonstrate a number of ways in which violent portrayals may increase subsequent aggressiveness) and the surveys that provide positive correlations between prior violence viewing and aggressiveness. Of the latter, the most powerful in the present context is the survey of London teenage males in which criminal and seriously harmful antisocial acts were decidedly more frequent among boys who were heavy viewers of television violence than among boys alike in other characteristics except for their viewing of markedly less television violence. Thus, the case in behalf of television violence contributing to criminal and seriously harmful antisocial behavior rests on (a) laboratory experiments demonstrating that exposure to television violence can cause an increase in aggressive responses by young adults, (b) surveys of teenagers that document a positive association between such exposure and everyday aggressive behavior not readily explainable except by the influence of the media, with the behavior of a type that could play a part in serious deviance, and (c) a major survey of teenagers that documents the identical relationship for criminal and seriously harmful antisocial behavior.

Thus, it cannot be said with certainty whether the contribution of television violence to seriously harmful antisocial behavior is great, substantial, modest, negligible, or null. The evidence, however, is supportive of some contribution — probably modest but perhaps more substantial, and conceivably through increasing the frequency of such acts, but more probably by shaping them.

There also is the possibility that continual exposure to violence in entertainment may make viewers less sensitive to violence in real life, and as a consequence, less ready to assist or intervene when others are hurt or threatened, and perhaps more willing themselves to inflict punishment. Psychologists long ago demonstrated that people become progressively less emotionally aroused as they observe someone suffering pain. The same progressive desensitization has been convincingly demonstrated in responsiveness to repeated exposure to sexually invigorating stimuli. Might not such desensitization occur through television viewing? Victor Cline and his colleagues (Cline, Croft, & Courrier, 1973) found that children who were heavy television viewers exhibited less physiologically measured emotional arousal when shown a violent portrayal on television. Ronald Drabman and Margaret Hanratty Thomas (1974) found that exposing children to a violent television episode delayed their response when children whose play they had been assigned to monitor by television became destructive. Thomas, Drabman, and two colleagues subsequently found that the physiologically measured arousal of emotionality induced by television scenes of real-life violence in 8-10-year-old children and in college students was lower after they had seen a sequence from a violent police drama than after they had viewed clips of a non-violent volleyball game (Thomas, Horton, Lippincott, & Drabman, 1977). Edward Donnerstein and colleagues (Donnerstein, Linz, & Penrod, 1987) describe numerous studies in which exposure to erotica, violent erotica, or violence against women in a sexual context variously has been followed by one or another desensitized response by male and in some instances female undergraduates. Such stimuli become judged as less violent or less pornographic, more enjoyable, and more acceptable for broadcast or viewing by children. More lenient sentences are assigned to perpetrators of rape. Males become more accepting of the rape myth (the belief that women secretly desire forced intercourse with males), and evaluate victims of rape as less injured and less worthy, and more readily endorse callous statements about females such as, "Pickups should expect to put out."

These four studies document that heavy viewers are somewhat different in their capacity to be aroused, identify exposure to a portrayal as responsible for lessened readiness to intervene, demonstrate reduced reactivity after seeing a violent episode, and find increased acceptance of portrayals of violence and sex and decreased sensitivity to women after repeated exposure to films in which women are brutally victimized. They thereby support the view that the viewing of television violence is desensitizing. However, they leave ambiguous the degree to which the subject of that desensitization is the media or real life. In each case, the violent experience to which the subjects were less responsive was introduced by the media. We know that the meaning people attach to what they experience depends on cues, and a major cue in these instances was the mediated character of the experience. The evidence is more clearly in support of desensitization toward further media than real-life experience. Conceivably, violent programming reduces sensitivity to the violence actually around us, but it almost certainly dulls our reaction to what we experience in the media. There is thus a psychological as well as a social explanation of changing norms for increasing emphasis in television and films on violent and sexual encounters, for people need ever-stronger fare to achieve the same degree of pleasurable excitement.

What the research does not demonstrate is any likelihood that media portrayals would affect the response to injury, suffering, or violent death experienced firsthand. The mock trial data suggests that evaluation of the fate of others may be affected, but not direct response to the plight of a victim. This is in line with much psychological research. Distant violence against others can be justified by portraying them as unworthy, less than human, and deserving of punishment. Bandura (1986) draws on this research in arguing that the dehumanizing of a victim by the media or otherwise permits the infliction of punishment and suffering that otherwise would be impermissible. This is what nations have long done, and with considerable success, in regard to wartime enemies, and what has been done often within societies to justify violence by one ethnic, religious or political group against another.

Television certainly provides countless examples of violence, but it also provides countless examples of intervention. Just as televised examples of violence may, by various means, encourage aggressive behavior by a viewer, so, too, may televised examples of helpful intervention encourage that kind of behavior, for the same psychology applies to both. It is true that violence in entertainment may have the advantage in achieving some impact, but this does not mean that portrayals of constructive behavior are totally ineffectual. They simply will suffer in effectiveness when they do not match a violent portrayal in attracting and holding attention, inducing physiological arousal, being understood, falling within the behavioral capabilities of the viewer, and there arising in the viewer's environment an opportunity to behave in such a way. It is more plausible to believe that the kind of violent programming common on television, with its rescues and bravery, has increased the likelihood of intervention and decreased the possibility that an incident in real life would traumatize an observer to the point of ineffectuality (although both effects would surely be extremely modest in degree) than to believe that television stands in the way of people helping each other. Nevertheless, the progressive desensitization of taste does imply that television and films will present increasingly vivid portrayals of violence that may contribute to antisocial behavior on the part of some of those in the audience.

Several hypotheses have been offered about very broad effects of television on the beliefs and perceptions held by the public. What they have in common is a focus on changes in the texture, diversity, and outlook that characterizes the public mainstream. Three of these hypotheses are succinctly characterized by their central concept:

- Reinforcement — the hypothesis that television strengthens the position of those social strata already predominant.
- Assimilation — the hypothesis that television inculcates people with primarily middle-class values.
- Homogenization — the hypothesis that television makes everyone more like everyone else in outlook.

George Gerbner and colleagues have argued that television is a powerful reinforcer of the status quo (Morgan, 1989). The ostensible mechanism is the effects of its portrayals on public expectations and perceptions. Television portrayals, and particularly violent drama, are said to assign roles of authority, power, success, failure, dependence, and vulnerability in a manner that matches the real-life social hierarchy, thereby strengthening that hierarchy by increasing its acknowledgment among the public and by failing to provide positive images for members of social categories occupying a subservient position. Gerbner and colleagues believe that the status quo derives support not only from the authority and power that they argue is implied for those who commit violence, who typically are white males in the prime of life already privileged in the real-life social hierarchy, but also from the kind of distorted outlook that the frequency of violent portrayals may stimulate. They argue that a belief in a mean or threatening world is conducive to support for stricter laws, punitiveness against transgressors, and expanded license for agencies of law enforcement.

One of the attributes of a television society is the historically unprecedented sharing of the same experience. The only comparable sharing prior to television, except for the more limited popularity of radio, was religious and patriotic rites. Although amount of viewing and attitudes toward television vary by social strata, with viewing and favorability of attitude inversely related to education, viewing is sufficiently similar for television to be considered a national experience. Leo Bogart (1972) has hypothesized that the consequence, because of television's attachment to the acceptable, is to reduce tolerance of deviation and, because of the emphasis on middle-class values, to assimilate blue-collar and other subgroups to a middle-class perspective.

There is substantial evidence in behalf of the view that television contributes to the way people perceive the world and that the result is a somewhat more commonly held way of thinking and behaving. William Belson (1978), for example, found that socioeconomic differences in the activities engaged in by families in England were somewhat reduced once they possessed a television set. Prominent among these, of course, is the amount of time all strata spend watching television, which in turn reduces the amount of time that can be spent doing other things in which diversity might appear among social strata. In the United States, other investigators found that turning to television to learn something is markedly more common among those of less education, among the elderly, among the poor, and among blacks. Presumably, the gratifying of this motive would encourage a commonality of outlook. Melvin DeFleur and Lois DeFleur (1967) found that beliefs based on television were more uniform among children and parents than those derived from other sources. Television presents stereotypes, so what is learned is limited in diversity. W. Russell Neuman (1982) found that the thoughts people entertain while viewing primetime entertainment are similar in content and focus regardless of strata, and do not vary in quantity across such strata except for a greater number among those comprising an educational extreme — college humanities professors. In any specific instance, television portrayals in entertainment, news, and sports are open to numerous interpretations — in Robert Allen's (1985) term, they are "malleable" — and these differing interpretations surely vary systematically by socioeconomic status, race, age, culture and other viewer characteristics, as Elihu Katz has argued, but television to a large degree on the whole also engenders responses that are fairly similar in both quality and content across social strata.

During its several decades of existence in America, television for many has undeniably broadened experience by occasionally exposing viewers to places, events, and examples of human interaction that they would not otherwise have encountered. It is this very fact that has made it at times offensive and threatening to some. Because of the inevitable allegiance of television to the perspective of the urban, educated class in whose hands it rests, entertainment, sports, and news have encouraged the classic liberal value of tolerance. The process that is justifiably labelled homogenization has lessened, not deepened, allegiance to traditional ties and convictions, in the sense that people have become more rather than less accepting of beliefs and behavior on the part of others that they disdain for themselves. Such influence is likely to have been modest in the specific instance or for any individual because of the well-known propensity of people to interpret what they experience in a manner consistent with previously held beliefs. Nevertheless, given the continuing exposure of viewers to unfamiliar experiences and the inculcation of new generations that grow up with television, its influence in a liberalizing direction has been profound.

The reinforcement of the status quo, homogenization, and assimilation to middle-class values are plausible effects (but because of their broadness not provable) that revolve around the very great heterogeneity of American society. It is this heterogeneity that makes it possible to give credence both to the views of Gerbner and colleagues, whose argument about the status quo implies some resistance and hostility to deviant behavior, and to the view that television has encouraged a tolerant, liberal outlook, and to believe that the three—reinforcement, assimilation, and homogenization—coalesce in a mainstream influence.

Social distinctions are rooted in education, income, occupation, and ethnic and family background. These are not attributes erased by the adoption either of isolated new values, such as tolerance, or of a common source of diversion, such as television. For all that television has done and might do, the social hierarchy remains, if altered somewhat in its evolution, and quite possibly in significant ways, by television. Homogenization and assimilation to middle-class values, and in particular the acceptance of thought and behavior at variance with one's own, do not represent a diminution of the social hierarchy or a disruption of the status quo, but the reinforcement of the values on which the hierarchy rests. The two function in behalf of stability and the status quo.

The convergence of perspective that has apparently occurred, and if so, is certainly likely to continue, in fact tempers the hostilities that ordinarily would emanate from social distinctions. Class warfare has never been absent from the American experience, and at times, in monetary and economic disputes, in labor strife, and in ethnic clashes, it has had a prominent role. However, it has not been a defining characteristic of American life or a pervasive condition which Americans have accepted as a basis for their behavior. Television has moved us, if ever so slightly, a further step away from such a state of mutual siege.

Yet, in some respects, television also disrupts the social order. It certainly does so through any contribution it may make to acts of crime and violence. By stimulating aggressiveness that falls within the boundaries of acceptability, it also would make the minute social interactions on which the conduct of our lives depends somewhat more sharp and, occasionally, less pleasant. By continually exposing at least a portion of its audience to affluence, possessions, and modes of life beyond their economic and social resources, it almost certainly has encouraged dissatisfaction with what American society offers. Some have been alienated, others angered. These feelings sometimes may translate into very constructive behavior, either on the personal or political level, but they also may leave many, with no recourse to solve their predicament, confused, unhappy, and bitter. The outcome occasionally but all too frequently will be an act of crime, violence, or seriously harmful antisocial behavior. Television will have had a role as a highly secondary factor.

By sometimes being manipulated by the dissident few in their attempt to reach the many, and by the exploitation of extremism — social and political — that is the inescapable product of the values by which newscasters select stories from events, television certainly upon occasion exacerbates hostilities within America. The television coverage of the civil rights marches in the South, and later the Vietnam protests, surely aided these causes by drawing support to them, but it also aroused strong feelings among their opponents. When television emphasizes symbols that threaten, it sharpens antagonisms and delays their resolution. Thus, television is a force in behalf of a society whose members have more rather than less in common, as well as a force in behalf of society's occasional division and inflammation.

World Model

Television in America is a product of the decisions made in the 1930s about the role of government in broadcasting, and the three attributes that characterize it so well and constitute the television paradigm — non-paternalism, entertainment, and competition — have their foundation in what took place more than a half-century ago. One of the silliest of beliefs, encouraged at every turn by those whose business is broadcasting, is that the American system is the only sensible or feasible arrangement. There is much that can be said in its favor, certainly. It has always been a meritocracy in which individual success — whether it is network management, station operation, or creative endeavor in production, writing, or acting — has hinged on the ability to deliver what is required. One is justified, however, in questioning whether popularity and the assembly of a mass audience in behalf of advertisers are particularly praiseworthy requirements.

In the commercial broadcasting that so dominates present arrangements, television has been self-supporting. If, in regard to public service, it has never been profligate, it would be unfair to label it as niggardly. Risk, in terms of audience appeal, has not been absent, although it has not been typical. The hunger for profits, visible in so many decisions made by broadcasters, has continually been compromised not only by the statutory requirement of providing public service that is a condition of station licensing but also by the aspirations of those who work in broadcasting. The worldwide popularity of American programming, a by-product of the quantity of material produced for the American market and of the rich production budgets that its lucrativeness has justified, has made a positive if not grand contribution to our balance of payments. We have had the privilege, rare in the world, not only of seeing a national administration conclude that television in its news and public affairs coverage presented an antagonistic and contrary voice, but of seeing that administration essentially powerless to take corrective action. None of these facts, however, should blind us to the simple truth that what we have had and will have in the way of television is something we invented. We might have invented differently.

We have arranged for advertisers to pay directly for our programming, and we pay indirectly by our purchase of products. This has resulted in programming that is acceptable to many, but seldom extraordinarily attractive to anyone in particular. As Les Brown of *Channels* magazine has written, broadcasters speak of the public as if it were one, but in fact the exchange of time and money that begins with the purchase of advertising time and ends with purchases at the supermarket, department store, fast food outlet, and automobile dealer is based on the continuing attention during primetime of a central segment of the American population who regularly watch television — those cajoled subjects in the endless experiment. The foundation of television's wealth is the minority of heavy viewers who consistently can be shifted back and forth across channels and programs. Television *is* a national experience; it crosses every demographic boundary imaginable, but paradoxically its dependable middle — the essential core of its audience — is a passive crowd of onlookers who surpass the A. C. Nielsen Company averages in their weekly attention.

We have been, in all this, somewhat more clever than we conceivably could have imagined. By placing financial support in the medium's own hands, we have avoided the problem that increasingly confronts those systems dependent on fees levied on viewers. In such systems, the set owner pays the equivalent of a tax to support the production and broadcast of programming. As is the case in Great Britain, television supported by the sale of advertising may co-exist in the same marketplace. The political problem with such fee-based systems even in democratic countries is maintaining independence from government or the dominant political party. The economic problem is inflation. The costs of operating the system inevitably rise more quickly than the revenue from fees, because the size of the levy is a decision contingent on popular support. People naturally oppose an increase in household expenditure, and politicians are disinclined to oppose them. The result is that these systems face a progressively declining ability to serve their audiences as they have in the past. The price of our accidental prescience, and one that we have paid for over the past four decades, is the priority that is given to profits and popularity in programming decisions and the secondary and sometimes entirely absent place occupied by social and artistic conscience.

There will be no need to change the terms by which we describe the basic character of television in America, but over the next decade as we approach the year 2001, television nevertheless will change. Network television will continue to be weakened by the alternative means of dissemination offered by satellites, by the increased programming made available by cable and pay-services, and by the new latitude that videocassette recorders give to viewers in treating television with the selectivity associated with books, magazines, recorded music, and theatrical experiences. Television financed by advertising certainly will remain with us. Some price that advertisers will pay willingly can be established for time on any video product, however small the audience; thus, any television, including that disseminated by cable and pay services, is subject to becoming an advertising vehicle. This trend is exemplified by the frequent inclusion on videos for in-home use of "promos" for other videos or broadcast television series. On the assumption that commercials make a program somewhat less appealing, the question from the viewpoint of the telecommunications businessman who has alternatives is the extent to which he will wish to rely on advertising revenue instead of that from subscriber fees. Profit maximization is the criterion, and commercials will accrue until total revenue begins to decline. From the larger perspective of telecommunications as a whole, the question becomes one of the pattern of advertiser-supported, free, broadcast, cable, fee, in-home playback, and videocassette recorder television that will evolve as each competitor seeks profit maximization.

The networks will remain able to assemble profitable audiences for two reasons. First, many segments of the population will not be able or willing to spend the money that will give them the diversity offered by the new technology. Second, some genuinely popular programming may not fit any other means of dissemination so well as a financial investment. For example, the Olympics are certain to draw a huge audience on broadcast television, but it is not so clear that they would fare nearly as well on a pay basis, even if all homes were equipped for such service. The reason is that the audience for the Olympics, entranced though it becomes by what it sees, is not an audience of impassioned partisans. People will not necessarily pay to witness a media event. The audience for team sports, both professional and collegiate, and for championship boxing, is made up of fans who await the confrontations with zeal. This devotion, missing from the motive of those who assemble for the Olympics, ensures a sizable number who would pay to see a 90-yard run or a title defense. Even so, for fan intensive sports that can attract large audiences, network television will remain the principal source of dissemination because the advertising revenues produced by reaching the larger broadcast audience will generally exceed the sum of revenues from advertising and pay-per-view fees from the smaller cable audience. This means that rather than a substantial shift of major sports to non-broadcast sources there will be minor reallocations that for each sport will serve the twin purposes of avoiding so many presentations that the broadcast audience will become diluted and of maximizing profits by drawing revenue from a new source. The sport with a small but devoted following that has had a minor place in broadcast television will find a vastly enlarged role on cable, as exemplified by ESPN's *Thoroughbred Digest* and that cable network's live coverage of major horse races.

The new technology that apparently will make so much available to the individual viewer will not necessarily improve television except in the sense that a Big Boy hamburger provides a change from a Big Mac. As the networks grudgingly surrender portions of their audience to programming from other sources, the audience which they can offer advertisers will become smaller and, because less affluent, less desirable in composition. Their declining revenues will accelerate competition for viewers, and may very well impel the networks toward sensationalism and the video equivalent of the tabloids that adorn supermarket checkout stands. Such a trend will be encouraged by the increasing predominance in the audience for "free" broadcast television of those with lesser education and intellectual discernment.

The sole exception, besides some sports and mini-series certain to draw huge audiences, is likely to be made-for-TV movies, which now command multi-million-dollar budgets and have a degree of polish far beyond those of a few years ago. Made-for-TV movies, which have a proven capability to attract very large primetime audiences, may be able to resist incursions on the network audience because of their ability to be accepted as special events.

The availability of quality programming from non-network sources remains problematic. It is not clear that the audiences that can be assembled by them will be large enough to attract enough advertising revenue, or that they will be able or willing to pay enough directly, to support new production. This is the problem that has faced cable, and has left it with modest amounts of original programming that for the most part is no different from what the networks are offering. Certainly, the promises of highly specific narrowcasting to small target audiences, enormous diversity, and programming high in artistic and cultural quality will go unmet for many years beyond 2001. At the same time, the available stock of material — reruns and theater movies — that now seems so plentiful will become increasingly familiar. Series episodes do not remain eternally fresh, although certainly some series have proven extraordinarily enduring, and the conventions peculiar to each genre of movie — action-adventure, comedy, science fiction and horror — become stereotypic across many of the titles produced annually. What once seemed bountiful may eventually become tiresome. We can expect more of the same from the new technologies and a greater disparity between the occasional triumphs and obdurate trivia of network television programming.

This is not to say that the new technology has not brought something of value into the home, increased the diversity of programming available, and enlarged the alternatives available to viewers. It has decidedly done so, and thereby has improved in a small way the daily lives of those who have access to the various components of that technology. The networks were once so predominant that they were for all practical purposes sole suppliers, and that is now far from the case. Independent stations and other non-network sources increasingly consume larger proportions of viewing time. The 24-hour news programming of the Cable News Network makes a significant difference in the availability of televised coverage, and its specialized segments provide television coverage of topics largely ignored by the three networks and local broadcasters. Much the same can be said for ESPN and for other cable services. There surely will be increases in the diversity of programming in the future, and increases in the quality of that diversity. What has not transpired and will not transpire in the foreseeable future, and certainly not in the next decade, is the revolutionary transformation of television as we have known it into the video analog of Scribner's Bookstore on New York's Fifth Avenue.

The new technology also introduces a troubling question of equity. Undeniably, it has the capacity to serve audiences too small to have been of much interest to commercial broadcasters — for example, children of a specific age, ethnic minorities, the elderly, and those seeking education or high culture. Whether it will do so depends on economic feasibility. However, if it does, the redemption of the golden promise of television for some will mean the continuing voiding of the claims of others. Households of lower socioeconomic status will have to do without, or with less of whatever is available, because use of cable, pay-services, videodiscs, cassettes, and in-home playback and recording is contingent on the ability to pay. For the foreseeable future, the new technology will mean greater inequality in access to entertainment and information.

If it in fact does disseminate programming arguably more congruent with the public interest, then many will wonder whether the exclusion of those already less privileged economically is not intolerably in conflict with that interest. Broadcast policy in the United States, however slow, clumsy, or imperfect in execution, has been guided by the principle of maximum public access, and it is that principle which the new technology contravenes. Admittedly, no one worried much that recorded music, the theater screen, and the live stage have not been freely available to all, but television is accorded a different status in our society analogous to that of education, where policy is committed to minimizing inequities. The new technology is creating for television the problem that the public library was devised to solve for print media — involuntary exclusion — and it is a problem that will become the more, not the less, disquieting the better the new technology performs in providing programming for interests and motives relatively ignored in the past by the oligopoly of commercial broadcasting. It is the old conundrum the new technology poses so sharply: Whether and how to meddle in the evolution of the mass media in behalf of a social ideal.

What is easy to overlook is that television itself, from the beginning, has been a technology with its own imperatives. The next decade may bring a new stage in its evolution in the United States, but there are certain trends that have been observed worldwide that make the American system in some ways the most prominent example of what television inevitably is and will be. Thus, the relationship that American television has to television in other societies is paradoxical. American television stands in contrast in the minor role it has accorded to the philosophy of public communication in which popularity has a subordinate place, but illustrates in certain respects the direction in which technology drives television everywhere, whatever the prevailing philosophy of those who are supposedly its masters.

Broadcast television is a costly mass medium that, once in place as a system with production capability, transmitting facilities, and television sets accessible to almost everyone, overcomes every barrier of literacy and isolation that restricts the flow of other media and experience. Radio did much the same, but with the reduced power of an aural medium. Newspapers, books, and magazines were never in the same class in their ability to reach a mass audience.

Television's character around the world derives from the twin facts of its enormous reach and ability to communicate. Once television as a system is in place, there is created — from the public and from political leaders — pressure to employ it to the utmost. Thus, the drive toward popularity, toward satisfying the interests of the masses, continually reduces the proportion of programming that can said to be cultural or directed to a small segment of the audience. The hours of broadcasting increase with the passage of time. One or two channel systems expand to take further advantage of the available audience. The content, the broadcast day, and the number of channels of broadcasting — all have been driven by the potential of the technology. That is not only the underlying factor behind the evolution of television in the United States but also elsewhere. At the same time, as broadcast television conformed to the appetite of the broadest possible range of the potential audience, the public itself came to think of it more and more as a medium of triviality and diversion, and to expect and demand less and less from it.

We see everywhere those signs that are so amplified in the American system. There is everywhere on the part of those responsible for television a concern with popularity, so that the high cost of the system can be justified by the attention that the public devotes to it. The result is that everywhere — in communist and socialist as well as in mixed and capitalist societies — the same demographic pattern marks the audience.

When first introduced in some of the eastern bloc nations, more time was spent viewing television by those of higher socioeconomic status and greater education than those lower in those attributes. In the United States, the demographic picture from the beginning has been for those lower in socioeconomic status and with less education to view more television. The explanation is two-fold. In the United States, the rapid diffusion of set ownership made the medium quickly a mass medium, and programming from the inception was aimed at a mass audience. In the eastern bloc nations, television set diffusion was far, far slower because of the comparatively enormous cost, sets were far more frequent among the affluent and better educated, and as a result, programming at the inception was aimed more at an elite audience and gave more emphasis to culture and information.

Certainly, entertainment television is not going to change substantially in response to the scientific evidence that it has some effects on children and teenagers. This is not a function of the quality of the research or character of the subjects examined. It reflects three factors. The first is television as a business enterprise. It functions in terms of its profitability. The second is that the implications of the research are not always clear, especially to those who are untrained in the social or behavioral sciences. Third is the fact that the members of television's creative community, analogous to those in news, constitute a subculture in which values other than possible harmful effects or even beneficial effects are not of much concern. It is not that they don't care; they simply care about other things — such as telling a compelling story, and for some, a story that says something important about people or society. Stuart Fischoff (1988), a psychologist who also writes for television and movies, made the point well at the annual meeting of the American Psychological Association:

> Let's propose, for a moment, a perfect scenario. Let's suppose the results, the conclusions were incontrovertible — TV and film modelling of aggression and other anti-social values has significant effects on the viewing audience. Would it really make any difference to the gate keepers of media fare in Hollywood and New York? I submit the answer is. . . not on your life!
>
> An important principle of psychology can help clarify such pessimism: *The more far-reaching and costly the consequences of accepting a message, the more facts needed before an audience will be persuaded as to the accuracy of the message — and the more energy will be expended in denigrating both the message and the messenger in order to maintain existing belief. . .*
>
> For the studios, networks, producers and writers to buy our research findings would open them up to constraints which are antagonistic to prevailing methods of filmmaking — and, possibly very costly in terms of receipts and ratings. . .
>
> In Hollywood, like the tobacco industry, if research is against you, discount it. The nature of research is that it is almost always probabilistic in its conclusions and almost always criticizable in terms of generalizability to the real world. . . (p. 3)

> Fundamental to all consideration of the problem is the fact that films and TV are part of show business with the emphasis on *business*, the motto of MGM, Ars Graits Artis, *"Art for Art's Sake,"* notwithstanding. (p. 5)

As the television system became more thoroughly entrenched, programming changed to employ unused hours of broadcast time and to consume the hours unfilled by viewing at the disposal of the public. The demographic pattern soon came to resemble that in the United States. For example, in the Soviet Union today, there are not only game shows that emulate the western system at its most trivial (if harmless), but the demographics of the audience match those of the United States — greater viewing by women, the less educated, blue-collar workers, the elderly, and children. In Israel and Australia, a complementary shift has been observed. Broadcasting has not only become more devoted to entertainment, but the people themselves have changed in what they expect from the medium. In both countries, people anticipated much more in the way of cultural enrichment before they saw television firsthand. Once they had spent a few months or years with the medium, their outlook changed.

The television experience in our homes is undeniably the product of the system we have established, and different systems will produce different kinds of television, but television as a medium is also in part its own master. In the United States, it has simply been given a particularly free rein. The evolution of American television has thus become the model for the world.

References

Adler, Richard P., Lesser, Gerald S., Meringoff, Laurene K., Robertson, Thomas S., Rossiter, John R., & Ward, Scott. (1980). *The effects of television advertising on children: Review and recommendations.* Lexington, MA: Lexington Books.

Alexander, Alison, Wartella, Ellen, & Brown, Dan. (1981). Estimates of children's television viewing by mother and child. *Journal of Broadcasting, 25*(3), 243-252.

Allen, Charles. (1965). Photographing the audience. *Journal of Advertising Research, 5,* 2-8.

Allen, Robert. (1985). *Speaking of soap operas.* Chapel Hill: University of North Carolina Press.

Alper, S. William, & Leidy, Thomas R. (1970). The impact of information transmission through television. *Public Opinion Quarterly, 33*(2), 556-562.

Altheide, David L. (1977). *Creating reality: How TV news distorts events.* Beverly Hills, CA: Sage.

Altheide, David L., & Snow, Robert P. (1979). *Media logic.* Beverly Hills, CA: Sage.

Anderson, Daniel R. (1985). Online cognitive processing of television. In L. F. Alwitt & A. A. Mitchell (Eds.), *Psychological process and advertising effects: Theory, research, application* (pp. 177-199). Hillsdale, NJ: Lawrence Erlbaum.

Anderson, Daniel R., Field, Diane E., Collins, Patricia A., Lorch, Elizabeth Pugzles, & Nathan, John G. (1985). Estimates of young children's time with television: A methodological comparison of parent reports with time-lapse video home observation. *Child Development, 56*(5), 1345-1357.

Anderson, Daniel R., Lorch, Elizabeth Pugzles, Field, Diane E., Collins, Patricia A., & Nathan, John G. (1986). Television viewing at home: Age trends in visual attention and time with TV. *Child Development, 57*(4), 1024-1033.

Andison, F. Scott. (1977). TV violence and viewer aggression: A cumulation of study results. *Public Opinion Quarterly, 41,* 314-331.

Aronson, Elliot. (1988). *The social animal* (5th ed.). San Francisco: Freeman.

289

Atkinson, Rita L., Atkinson, Richard C., Smith, Edward E., & Hilgard, Ernest R. (1987). *Introduction to psychology* (9th ed.). New York: Harcourt Brace Jovanovich.

Baldwin, Thomas F., & Lewis, Colby. (1972). Violence in television: The industry looks at itself. In G. A. Comstock & E. A. Rubinstein (Eds.), *Television and social behavior: Vol. 1. Media content and control* (pp. 290-373). Washington, DC: U.S. Government Printing Office.

Ball-Rokeach, Sandra, Rokeach, Milton, & Grube, Joel W. (1984). *The great American values test.* New York: Free Press.

Bandura, Albert. (1973). *Aggression: A social learning analysis.* Englewood Cliffs, NJ: Prentice-Hall.

Bandura, Albert. (1986). *Social foundations of thought and action: A social cognitive theory.* Englewood Cliffs, NJ: Prentice-Hall.

Bandura, Albert, Ross, Dorothea, & Ross, Shiela A. (1963a). Imitation of film-meditated aggressive models. *Journal of Abnormal and Social Psychology, 66,* 3-11.

Bandura, Albert, Ross, Dorothea, & Ross, Shiela A. (1963b). Vicarious reinforcement and imitative learning. *Journal of Abnormal and Social Psychology, 67,* 601-607.

Banham, Reyner. (1971). *Los Angeles: The architecture of four ecologies.* New York: Harper and Row.

Barnouw, Eric. (1975). *Tube of plenty: The evolution of American television.* New York: Oxford University Press.

Barwise, Patrick, & Ehrenberg, Andrew. (1989). *Television and its audiences.* Newbury Park, CA: Sage.

Bechtel, Robert B., Achelpohl, Clark, & Akers, Roger. (1972). Correlates between observed behavior and questionnaire responses on television viewing. In E. A. Rubinstein, G. A. Comstock, & J. P. Murray (Eds.), *Television and social behavior: Vol. 4. Television in day-to-day life: Patterns of use* (pp. 274-344). Washington, DC: U.S. Government Printing Office.

Becker, Marshall H. (Ed.). (1974). The health belief model and personal health behavior. *Health Education Monographs, 2*(4).

Belson, William. (1978). *Television violence and the adolescent boy.* Westmead, England: Saxon House, Teakfield Limited.

Berkowitz, Leonard. (1962). Violence in the mass media. In L. Berkowitz, *Aggression: A social psychological analysis.* New York: McGraw-Hill.

Berkowitz, Leonard. (1984). Some effects of thoughts on anti- and prosocial influences of media events: A cognitive-neoassociation analysis. *Psychological Bulletin, 95*(3), 410-427.

Berkowitz, Leonard., & Alioto, J. T. (1973). The meaning of an observed event as a determinant of its aggressive consequences. *Journal of Personality and Social Psychology, 28,*206-217.

Berkowitz, Leonard., & Geen, Russell G. (1966). Film violence and the cue properties of available targets. *Journal of Personality and Social Psychology, 3,* 525-530.

Berkowitz, Leonard, & Rawlings, Edna. (1963). Effects of film violence on inhibitions against subsequent aggression. *Journal of Abnormal and Social Psychology, 66,* 405-412.

Beville, Hugh Malcolm, Jr. (1989). *Audience ratings: Radio, television, cable* (rev. ed.). Hillsdale, NJ: Lawrence Erlbaum.

Bogart, Leo (1962). American television: A brief survey of research findings. *Journal of Social Issues, 18*(2), 36-42.

Bogart, Leo (1972). *The age of television* (3rd ed.). New York: Frederick Ungar.

Bogart, Leo (1989). *Press and public* (rev. ed.). Hillsdale, NJ: Lawrence Erlbaum.

Bower, Robert T. (1973). *Television and the public.* New York: Holt, Rinehart, and Winston.

Bower, Robert T. (1985). *The changing television audience in America.* New York: Columbia University Press.

Brown, Les. (1971). *Television: The business behind the box.* New York: Harcourt Brace Jovanovich.

Brown, Les. (1977). *The New York Times encyclopedia of television.* New York: Times Books.

Bybee, Carl, Robinson, Danny, & Turow, Joseph. (1982). *Mass media scholars' perceptions of television's effects on children.* (Paper presented at the Annual Convention of the American Association for Public Opinion Research, Hunt Valley, MD.).

By the numbers (1989, Oct. 9). *Broadcasting* p. 14.

Cain, James M. (1978a). *Double indemnity.* New York: Random House.

Cain, James M. (1978b). *The postman always rings twice.* New York: Random House.

Cain, James M. (1978c). *Mildred Pierce.* New York: Random House.

California Assessment Program. (1981). *Student achievement in California schools. 1979-80 annual report: Television and student achievement.* Sacramento: California State Department of Education. (ERIC Document Reproduction Service No. ED 195 559)

California Assessment Program. (1982). *Survey of sixth grade school achievement and television viewing habits.* Sacramento: California State Department of Education.

Cantor, Muriel G. (1971). *The Hollywood TV producer.* New York: Basic Books.

Cantor, Muriel G. (1972). The role of the producer in choosing children's television content. In G. A. Comstock & E. A. Rubinstein (Eds.), *Television and social behavior: Vol. 1. Media content and control* (pp. 259-289). Washington, DC: U.S. Government Printing Office.

Cantor, Muriel G. (1980). *Prime-time television: Content and control.* Beverly Hills, CA: Sage.

Caplow, Theodore, Bahr, Howard M., Chadwick, Bruce A., Hill, Reuben, & Williamson, Margaret Homes. (1982). *Middletown families: Fifty years of change and continuity.* Minneapolis: University of Minnesota Press.

Carnegie Commission on the Future of Public Broadcasting. (1978). *The public trust: The landmark report of the Carnegie Commission on the Future of Public Broadcasting.* New York: Bantam.

Cassata, Mary, & Skill, Thomas. (1983). *Life on daytime television.* Norwood, NJ: Ablex.

Chaffee, Steven (1972). Television and adolescent aggressiveness (overview). In G. A. Comstock & E. A. Rubinstein (Eds.), *Television and social behavior: Vol. 3. Television and adolescent aggressiveness* (pp. 1-34). Washington, DC: U.S. Government Printing Office.

Chandler, Raymond. (1976). *The long goodbye.* New York: Random House.

Chandler, Raymond. (1977). *The big sleep.* New York: Ballantine.

Clarke, Peter, & Fredin, Eric. (1978). Newspapers, television and political reasoning. *Public Opinion Quarterly, 42,* 143-160.

Cline, Victor B., Croft, Roger G., & Courrier, Steven. (1973). Desensitization of children to television violence. *Journal of Personality and Social Psychology, 27,* 360-365.

Cole, Barry, & Oettinger, Mal. (1978). *Reluctant regulators*. Reading, MA: Addison-Wesley.

Comstock, George. (1982a). Television and American social institutions. In D. Pearl, L. Bouthilet, & J. Lazar (Eds.), *Television and behavior: Ten years of scientific inquiry and implications for the eighties: Vol. 2. Summary reviews* (pp. 334-348). Washington, DC: U.S. Government Printing Office.

Comstock, George. (1982b). The mass media and social change. In E. Seidman (Ed.), *Handbook of social intervention* (pp. 268-288). Newbury Park, CA: Sage.

Comstock, George. (1983). Media influences on aggression. In A. Goldstein (Ed.), *Prevention and control of aggression* (pp. 241-272). Elmsford, NY: Pergamon.

Comstock, George. (Ed.). (1986a). *Public communication and behavior: Vol. 1*. New York: Academic Press.

Comstock, George. (1986b). Television and film violence. In S. J. Apter & A. Goldstein (Eds.), *Youth violence: Programs and prospects* (pp. 178-218). Elmsford, NY: Pergamon.

Comstock, George. (1988, June). *Deceptive appearances: Television violence and aggressive behavior.* Invited address presented at "Television and Teens: Health Implications," a conference sponsored by the Kaiser Foundation, Los Angeles, June 22-24.

Comstock, George. (Ed.). (1989a). *Public communication and behavior: Vol. 2*. New York: Academic Press.

Comstock, George. (1989b). Television. In *The World Book Encyclopedia* (Vol. 19, pp. 110-128). Chicago: World Book, Inc.

Comstock, George., Chaffee, Steven., Katzman, Natam., McCombs, Maxwell., & Roberts, Donald. (1978). *Television and human behavior.* New York: Columbia University Press.

Comstock, George., & Paik, Hae-Jung. (1987). Television and children: A review of recent research. Syracuse, N.Y.: ERIC Clearing House on Information Resources.

Comstock, George A., & Rubinstein, Eli A. (Eds.). (1972a). *Television and social behavior. Vol. 1. Media content and control.* Washington, DC: U.S. Government Printing Office.

Comstock, George, & Rubinstein, Eli. (Eds.). (1972b). *Television and social behavior. Vol. 3. Television and adolescent aggressiveness.* Washington, DC: U.S. Government Printing Office. (ERIC Document Reproduction Service No. ED 059 625)

Comstock, George, Rubinstein, Eli, & Murray, John P. (Eds.). (1972). *Television and social behavior. Vol. 5. Television's effects: Further explorations.* Washington, DC: U.S. Government Printing Office. (ERIC Document Reproduction Service No. ED 059 625)

Cook, Thomas D., & Campbell, Donald. T. (1979). *Quasi-experimentation: Design analysis issues for field settings.* Chicago: Houghton-Mifflin.

Cook, Thomas D., Kendzierski, Deborah A., & Thomas, Stephen V. (1983). The implicit assumptions of television research: An analysis of the 1982 NIMH report on *Television and Behavior. Public Opinion Quarterly, 47*(2), 161-201.

Coover, Robert. (1979). *The origin of the Brunists.* New York: Bantam.

Darley, J. M., Glucksberg, S., Kamin, L. J., & Kinchla, R. A. (1981). *Psychology.* Englewood Cliffs, NJ: Prentice-Hall.

DeFleur, Melvin L., & DeFleur, Lois B. (1967). The relative contribution of television as a learning source for children's occupational knowledge. *American Sociological Review, 32,* 777-789.

Didion, Joan. (1971). *Play it as it lays.* New York: Bantam.

Dominick, Joseph R., & Greenberg, Bradley S. (1972). Attitudes toward violence: The interaction of television, family exposure, and social class. In G. A. Comstock & E. A. Rubinstein (Eds.), *Television and social behavior: Vol. 3. Television and adolescent aggressiveness* (pp. 314-335) Washington, DC: U.S. Government Printing Office.

Donnerstein, Edward, Linz, Daniel, & Penrod, Steven. (1987). *The question of pornography: Research findings and policy implications.* New York: Free Press.

Drabman, Ronald S., & Thomas, Margaret Hanratty. (1974). Does media violence increase children's toleration of real life aggression? *Developmental Psychology, 10,* 418-421.

Efron, Edith. (1971). *The news twisters.* Los Angeles: Nash.

Ekman, Paul, Liebert, Robert M., Friesen, Wallace V., Harrison, Randall, Zlatchin, Carl, Malmstrom, Edward J., & Baron, Robert A. (1972). Facial expressions of emotion while watching televised violence as predictors of subsequent aggression. In G. A. Comstock, E. A. Rubinstein, & J. P. Murray (Eds.). *Television and social behavior: Vol. 5. Television's effects: Further explorations* (pp. 22-58). Washington, DC: U.S. Government Printing Office.

Elkind, D., & Weiner, I. B. (1978). *Development and the child.* New York: John Wiley.

Emery, Edwin. (1976). Changing role of the mass media in American politics. *The Annals of the American Academy of Political and Social Science, 427,* 84-94.

Epstein, Edward Jay. (1973). *News from nowhere.* New York: Random House.

Evans, Ellis. D., & McCandless, Boyd. R. (1978). *Children and youth.* New York: Holt, Rinehart, and Winston.

Eyal, Chaim. (1979). *Time frame in agenda-setting research: A study of the conceptual and methodological factors affecting time frame content of the agenda-setting process.* Unpublished doctoral dissertation, Syracuse University, Syracuse, NY.

Federal Trade Commission. (1978a, February). *Staff report on television advertising for children.* Washington, DC: Federal Trade Commission.

Federal Trade Commission. (1978b, April). Children's advertising: Proposed trade regulation rulemaking and public hearing. *Federal Register, 43*(82), 17967-17972.

Federal Trade Commission. (1978c). *Federal Trade Commission news summary, 3*(24).

Feshbach, Seymour. (1961). The stimulating vs. cathartic effects of a vicarious aggressive activity. *Journal of Abnormal and Social Psychology, 63,* 381-385.

Feshbach, Seymour. (1972). Reality and fantasy in filmed violence. In J. P. Murray, E. A. Rubinstein, & G. A. Comstock (Eds.), *Television and social behavior: Vol. 2. Television and social learning* (pp. 318-345). Washington, DC: U.S. Government Printing Office.

Fischoff, Stuart. (1988, August). *Psychological research and a black hole called Hollywood.* Paper presented at the annual meeting of the American Psychological Association, Atlanta, Georgia.

Fore, William F. (1987). *Television and religion: The shaping of faith, values and culture.* Minneapolis, MN: Augsberg.

Frank, Richard. (1973). *Message dimensions of television news.* Lexington, MA: Lexington Books.

Frank, Ronald E., & Greenberg, Marshall G. (1980). *The public's use of television.* Beverly Hills, CA: Sage.

Frankl, Razelle. (1987). *Televangelism: The marketing of popular religion.* Carbondale: Southern Illinois University Press.

Freedman, Jonathan L. (1984). Effect of television violence on aggressiveness. *Psychological Bulletin, 96*(2), 227-246.

Freuh, Terry, & McGhee, Paul E. (1975). Traditional sex role development and amount of time spent watching television. *Developmental Psychology, 11*(1), 109.

Fuchs, Douglas. (1966). Election day radio-television and Western voting. *Public Opinion Quarterly, 30*, 226-236.

Gans, Herbert J. (1974). *Popular culture and high culture: An analysis and evaluation of taste.* New York: Basic Books.

Gans, Herbert J. (1979). *Deciding what's news: A study of CBS Evening News, NBC Nightly News, Newsweek, and Time.* New York: Pantheon.

Gaziano, Cecile. (1988). How credible is the credibility crisis? *Journalism Quarterly, 65*(2), 267-278.

Geen, Russell G. (1975). The meaning of observed violence: Real vs. fictional violence and consequent effects on aggression and emotional arousal. *Journal of Research in Personality, 9*, 270-281.

Geen, Russell G., & Stonner, David. (1972). Context effects in observed violence. *Journal of Personality and Social Psychology, 25*, 145-150.

Gerbner, George, & Gross, Larry. (1974). *Violence profile no. 6: Trends in network television drama and viewer conceptions of social reality: 1967-1973.* Unpublished manuscript, University of Pennsylvania, Annenberg School of Communications.

Gerbner, George, & Gross, Larry. (1976). Living with television: The violence profile. *Journal of Communication, 26*(2), 173-199.

Gerbner, G., & Gross, Larry. (1980). The violent face of television and its lessons. In E. Palmer & A. Dorr (Eds.), *Children and the faces of television: Teaching, violence, selling* (pp. 149-162). New York: Academic Press.

Gerbner, George, Gross, Larry, Eleey, Michael F., Jackson-Beeck, Marilyn, Jeffries-Fox, Suzanne, & Signorielli, Nancy. (1978). TV violence profile no. 8: The highlights. *Journal of Communication, 27*(2), 171-180.

Gerbner, George, Gross, Larry, Morgan, Michael, & Signorielli, Nancy. (1980). The "mainstreaming" of America. *Journal of Communication, 30*(3), 10-29.

Gerbner, George, Gross, Larry, Morgan, Michael, & Signorielli, Nancy. (1981a). A curious journey into the scary world of Paul Hirsch. *Communication Research, 8*, 39-72.

Gerbner, George, Gross, Larry, Morgan, Michael, & Signorielli, Nancy. (1981b). Final reply to Hirsch, *Communication Research, 8*, 259-280.

Gerbner, George, Gross, Larry, Morgan, Michael, & Signorielli, Nancy. (1986). Living with television: The dynamics of the cultivation process. In J. Bryant & D. Zillmann (Eds.), *Perspectives on media effects* (pp. 17-40). Hillsdale, NJ: Lawrence Erlbaum.

Gerbner, George, Gross, Larry, Signorielli, Nancy, & Morgan, Michael. (1986). *Television's mean world: Violence profile no. 14-15.* Philadelphia: University of Pennsylvania, Annenberg School of Communications.

Gitlin, Todd. (1983). *Inside primetime.* New York: Pantheon.

Glass, Gene V., McGaw, Barry, & Smith, Mary Lee. (1981). *Meta-analysis in social research.* Newbury Park, CA: Sage.

Goldberg, Marvin E., & Gorn, Gerald J. (1974). Children's reaction to television advertising: An experimental approach. *Journal of Communication, 1*(2), 69-75.

Goldberg, Marvin E., & Gorn, Gerald J. (1978). Some unintended consequences of TV advertising to children. *Journal of Consumer Research, 5*(1), 22-29.

Greenberg, Bradley. (1980). *Life on television*. Norwood, NJ: Ablex.

Greenberg, Bradley S., & Gordon, Thomas F. (1972). Social and racial differences in children's perceptions of television violence. In G. A. Comstock, E. A. Rubinstein, & John P. Murray (Eds.), Television and social behavior: Vol. 5. *Television's effects: Further explorations* (pp. 185-210). Washington, DC: U.S. Government Printing Office. (ERIC Document Reproduction Service No. ED 059 627)

Gunter, Barrie. (1987). *Poor reception: Misunderstanding and forgetting broadcast news*. Hillsdale, NJ: Lawrence Erlbaum.

Hearold, Susan. (1986). A synthesis of 1,043 effects of television on social behavior. In G. Comstock (Ed.), *Public communication and behavior: Vol. 1*, (pp. 66-135). New York: Academic Press.

Heffner, Richard D., & Kramer, Esther H. (1972). *Network television's environmental content*. Unpublished manuscript, Rutger's University, New Brunswick, NJ.

Hennigan, Karen M., Heath, Linda, Wharton, J. D., Del Rosario, Marilyn L., Cook, Thomas D., & Calder, Bobby J. (1982). Impact of the introduction of television on crime in the United States: Empirical findings and theoretical implications. *Journal of Personality and Social Psychology, 42*(3), 461-477.

Hetherington, Ellen M., & Parke, Ross D. (1979). *Child psychology: A contemporary viewpoint*. New York: McGraw-Hill.

Hickey, James. (1972, April 8). What America thinks of TV's political coverage. *TV Guide*, pp. 6-11.

Himmelweit, Hilde, Oppenheim, A. N., & Vince, Pamela. (1958). *Television and the child*. London: Oxford University Press.

Hirsch, Paul. (1980a). On Hughes' contribution: The limits of advocacy research. *Public Opinion Quarterly, 44*(3), 411-413.

Hirsch, Paul. (1980b). "Scary world" of the nonviewer and other anomalies: A re-analysis of Gerbner et al's. findings on cultivation analysis. Part one. *Communication Research, 7*, 403-456.

Hirsch, Paul. (1981a). On not learning from one's own mistakes: A re-analysis of Gerbner et al. Part two. *Communication Research, 8*, 73-95.

Hirsch, Paul. (1981b). Distinguishing good speculation from bad theory: A rejoinder to Gerbner et al. *Communication Research, 8*, 73-95.

Hoff-Ginsberg, Erika, & Shatz, Marilyn. (1982). Linguistic input and the child's acquisition of language, *Psychological Bulletin, 92*, 3-26.

Hofstetter, C. Richard. (1976) *Bias in the news: Network television coverage of the 1972 election campaign*. Columbus: Ohio State University Press.

Hollenbeck, Albert, & Slaby, Ronald. (1979). Infant visual and vocal responses to television. *Child Development, 50*, 41-45.

Hornik, Robert. (1978). Television access and the slowing of cognitive growth. *American Educational Research Journal, 15*, 1-5.

Horsfield, Peter G. (1984). *Religious television: The American experience*. New York: Longman.

Howe, Irving. (1976). *World of our fathers*. New York: Harcourt Brace Jovanovich.

Hughes, Michael. (1980). The fruits of cultivation analysis: A re-examination of the effects of television watching on fear of victimization, alienation, and the approval of violence. *Public Opinion Quarterly, 44*(3), 287-303.

Huston, Aletha, & Wright, John C. (1989). The forms of television and the child viewer. In G. Comstock (Ed.), *Public communication and behavior* (Vol. 2, pp. 103-159). New York: Academic Press.

Huston, Aletha, Wright, John C., Rice, Mabel L., Kerkman, Dennis, Seigle, J., & Bremer, M. (1983). *Family environment and television use by preschool children.* Paper presented at the biennial meeting of the Society for Research on Child Development, Detroit, MI. (ERIC Document No. ED 230 293)

Immerwahr, John, & Doble, John. (1982). Public attitudes toward freedom of the press. *Public Opinion Quarterly, 46,* 177-194.

Iyengar, Shanto, & Kinder, Donald. (1987) *News that matters.* Chicago: University of Chicago Press.

Johnston, Jerome, & Ettema, James S. (1982). *Positive images: Breaking stereotypes with children's television.* Beverly Hills, CA: Sage.

Jones, R. A., Hendrick, C., & Epstein, Y. M. (1979). *Introduction of social psychology.* Sunderland, MA.: Sinauer Assoc.

Kagan, Jerome, & Havemann, E. (1980). *Psychology: An introduction.* New York: Harcourt Brace Jovanovich.

Katz, Elihu. (1988). On conceptualizing media effects: Another look. In S. Oskamp (Ed.), *Applied social psychology annual: Vol. 8. Television as a social issue* (pp. 361-374). Newbury Park, CA: Sage.

Katz, Elihu, & Feldman, Jacob J. (1962). The debates in the light of research: A survey of surveys. In S. Kraus (Ed.), *The great debates: Kennedy vs. Nixon, 1960* (pp. 173-223). Bloomington: Indiana University Press.

Katz, Elihu, & Gurevitch, Michael. (1976). *The secularization of leisure.* Cambridge, MA: Harvard University Press.

Katz, Elihu, & Liebes, Tamara. (1985). Mutual aid in the decoding of "Dallas." In P. Drummond & R. Paterson (Eds.), *Television in transition: Papers from the first International Television Studies Conference* (pp. 187-198). London: British Film Institute.

Katzman, Natan. (1972). Television's soap operas: What's been going on anyway? *Public Opinion Quarterly, 36*(2), 200-212.

Kopp, Claire. B., & Krakow, Joanne. B. (1982). *The child: Development in a social context.* Reading, MA: Addison-Wesley.

Kraus, Sidney (Ed.). (1977). *The great debates: Kennedy vs. Nixon, 1960.* Bloomington: Indiana University Press.

Kraus, Sidney (Ed.). (1979). *The great debates: Carter vs. Ford, 1976.* Bloomington: Indiana University Press.

Kraus, Sidney. (1988). *Televised presidential debates and public policy.* Hillsdale, NJ: Lawrence Erlbaum.

Kuhn, Thomas S. (1962). *The structure of scientific revolutions.* Chicago: University of Chicago Press.

Lambert, Gavin. (1968). *Slide area.* New York: Dial Press.

Lang, Gladys Engel, & Lang, Kurt. (1968). *Politics and television.* Chicago: Quadrangle.

Lang, Gladys Engel, & Lang, Kurt. (1984). *Politics and television re-viewed.* Newbury Park, CA: Sage.

Lang, Kurt, & Lang, Gladys Engel. (1953). The unique perspective of television and its effects: A pilot study. *American Sociological Review, 18,* 3-12.

Larsen, Otto, Gray, L. N., & Fortis, John G. (1963). Goals and goal achievement in television content: Models for anomie? *Sociological Inquiry, 33,* 180-196.

Lazarsfeld, Paul F., & Merton, Robert K. (1971). Mass communication, popular taste, and organized social action. In W. Schramm & D. F. Roberts (Eds.), *The process and effects of mass communication* (pp. 554-578). Urbana: University of Illinois Press.

Lefcourt, H. M., Barnes, K., Parke, R. & Schwartz, F. (1966). Anticipated social censure and aggression-conflict as mediators of response to aggression induction. *Journal of Social Psychology, 70,* 251-263.

Lefkowitz, Monroe M., Eron, Leonard D., Walder, Leonard O., & Huesmann, L. Rowell. (1972). Television violence and child aggression: A followup study. In G. A. Comstock & E. A. Rubinstein (Eds.), *Television and social behavior: Vol. 3. Television and adolescent aggressiveness* (pp. 35-135). Washington, DC: U.S. Government Printing Office.

Lemert, James B. (1974). Content duplication by the networks in competing evening broadcasts. *Journalism Quarterly, 51,* 238-244.

Lemish, Dafna, & Rice, Mabel L. (1986). Television as a talking picture book: A prop for language acquisition. *Journal of Child Language, 13,* 251-274.

Levy, Mark R. (1978). The audience experience with television news. *Journalism Quarterly, 55,* 1-29.

Lichty, Lawrence W. (1982). Video vs. print. *The Wilson Quarterly, 6*(5), 49-57.

Liebert, Robert M. & Wicks-Nelson, Rita. (1979). *Developmental psychology.* New York: McGraw-Hill.

Linz, Daniel, Donnerstein, Edward, & Penrod, Steven. (1984). The effects of multiple exposure to filmed violence against women. *Journal of Communication, 34*(3), 130-147.

Lipset, Seymour Martin & Schneider, William. (1983). *The confidence gap.* New York: Free Press.

LoScuito, Leonard A. (1972). A natural inventory of television viewing behavior. In E. A. Rubinstein, G. A. Comstock, & J. P. Murray (Eds.), *Television and social behavior: Vol. 4. Television in day-to-day life: Patterns of viewing* (pp. 33-86). Washington, DC: U.S. Government Printing Office.

Lovibond, S. H. (1967). The effect of media stressing crime and violence upon children's attitudes. *Social Problems, 15,* 91-100.

Lowry, Dennis T. (1971a). Agnew and the network TV news: A before/after content analysis. *Journalism Quarterly, 48,* 205-210.

Lowry, Dennis T. (1971b). Gresham's law and network TV news selection. *Journal of Broadcasting, 15,* 397-408.

Loye, David, Gorney, Roderic, & Steele, Gary. (1977). Effects of television: An experimental field study. *Journal of Communication, 27,* 206-216.

Lucas, William A., & Adams, William C. (1978). Talking TV and voter indecision. *Journal of Communication, 28,* 120-131.

Lurie, Allison. (1975). *The nowhere city.* New York: Avon.

Lynd, Robert S., & Lynd, Helen Merrell. (1929). *Middletown: A study in American culture.* New York: Harcourt and Brace.

Lynd, Robert S., & Lynd, Helen Merrell. (1937). *Middletown in transition: A study in cultural conflicts.* New York: Harcourt and Brace.

MacDonald, Ross. (1959). *The Galton case.* New York: Alfred A. Knopf.

MacDonald, Ross. (1967). *Archer in Hollywood.* New York: Alfred A. Knopf.

Martel, Myles. (1981). Debate preparations in the Reagan camp: An insider's view. *Speaker and Gavel, 18*(2), 34-36.

McConnell, James V. (1980). *Understanding human behavior.* New York: Holt, Rinehart, and Winston.

McIntyre, Jennie J. & Teevan, James J. Jr. (1972). Television violence and deviant behavior. In G. A. Comstock & E. A. Rubinstein (Eds.), *Television and social behavior: Vol. 3. Television and adolescent aggressiveness* (pp. 383-435). Washington, DC: U.S. Government Printing Office.

McLeod, Jack M., Atkin, Charles K., & Chaffee, Steven H. (1972a). Adolescents, parents, and television use: Adolescent self-support measures from Maryland and Wisconsin samples: In G. A. Comstock & E. A. Rubinstein (Eds.), *Television and social behavior: Vol. 3. Television and adolescent aggressiveness* (pp. 173-238). Washington, DC: U.S. Government Printing Office.

McLeod, J. M., Atkin, C. K., & Chaffee, S. H. (1972b). Adolescents, parents, and television use: Self-report and other-report measures from the Wisconsin sample. In G. A. Comstock & E. A. Rubinstein (Eds.), *Television and social behavior: Vol. 3. Television and adolescent aggressiveness* (pp. 239-313). Washington, DC: U.S. Government Printing Office.

McLuhan, Marshall. (1964). *Understanding media: The extensions of man.* New York: McGraw-Hill.

McQuail, Dennis. (1979). End of an era. *Journal of Communication, 29,* 227-229.

Medrich, Elliott A., Roizen, Judith A., Rubin, Victor, & Buckley, Stuart. (1982). *The serious business of growing up. A study of children's lives outside school.* Berkeley: University of California Press.

Meltzoff, Andrew N. (1988). Imitation of televised models by infants. *Child Development, 59*(5), 1221-1229.

Mendelsohn, Harold. (1966). Election-day broadcasts and terminal voting decisions. *Public Opinion Quarterly, 30,* 212-225.

Mendelsohn, Harold A., & Crespi, Irving. (1970). *Polls, television and the new politics.* San Francisco: Chandler.

Mendelsohn, Harold A., & O'Keefe, Garrett J. (1976). *The people choose a president: Influences on voter decision making.* New York: Praeger.

Meyersohn, Rolf B. (1965). *Leisure and television: A study in compatibility.* Unpublished doctoral dissertation, Columbia University.

Milavsky, J. Ronald. (1988, August). *AIDS and the media.* Invited address, American Psychological Association, Atlanta, GA.

Milavsky, J. Ronald, Kessler, Ronald, Stipp, Horst, & Rubens, William S. (1982). *Television and aggression: A panel study.* New York: Academic Press.

Milgram, Stanley, & Shotland, R. Lance. (1973). *Television and antisocial behavior: Field experiments.* New York: Academic Press.

Mischel, Walter, & Mischel, Harriett N. (1980). *Essentials of psychology.* New York: Random House.

Morgan, Michael. (1989). Cultivation analysis. In E. Barnouw (Ed.), *International encyclopedia of communications* (Vol. 1, pp. 430-433). New York: Oxford University Press.

Mosco, Vincent. (1979). *Broadcasting in the United States: Innovative challenge and organizational control.* Norwood, NJ: Ablex.

Murray, John P. (1983). *Results of an informal poll of knowledgeable persons concerning the impact of TV violence.* Paper presented to the APA Monitor staff, American Psychological Association, Washington, DC.

Murray, John, Rubinstein, Eli, & Comstock, George. (Eds.). (1972). *Television and social behavior, Vol. 2. Television and social learning.* Washington, DC: U.S. Government Printing Office.

Myers, D. G. (1983). *Social psychology.* New York: McGraw-Hill.

National Commission on the Causes and Prevention of Violence. (1969). *To establish justice, to insure domestic tranquility.* Washington, DC: U.S. Government Printing Office.

Neuman, W. Russell. (1982). Television and American culture: The mass medium and the pluralist audience. *Public Opinion Quarterly, 46*(4), 471-487.

Newcomb, Horace, & Alley, Robert S. (1983). *The producer's medium: Conversations with creators of American TV.* New York: Oxford University Press.

Oskamp, Stuart. (1984). *Applied social psychology.* Englewood Cliffs, NJ: Prentice-Hall.

Paletz, David L., & Elson, Martha. (1976). Television coverage of presidential conventions: Now you see it, now you don't. *Political Science Quarterly, 9,* 109-131.

Patterson, Thomas. (1980). *The mass media election.* New York: Praeger.

Patterson, Thomas E., & McClure, Robert D. (1976). *The unseeing eye.* New York: Putnam.

Pearl, David, Bouthilet, Lorraine, & Lazar, Joyce. (Eds.). (1982a). *Television and behavior: Ten years of scientific progress and implications for the eighties. Vol. 1: Summary report* (DHHS Publication No. ADM 82-1195). Washington, DC: U.S. Government Printing Office.

Pearl, David, Bouthilet, Lorraine, & Lazar, Joyce. (Eds.). (1982b). *Television and behavior: Ten years of scientific progress and implications for the eighties. Vol. 2: Technical reviews* (DHHS Publication No. ADM 82-1196). Washington, DC: U.S. Government Printing Office.

Penrod, Steven. (1983). *Social psychology.* Englewood Cliffs, NJ: Prentice-Hall.

Perlman, Daniel, & Cozby, P. Christopher. (1983). *Social psychology.* New York: Holt, Rinehart, and Winston.

Pride, Richard A., & Clarke, Daniel H. (1973). Race relations in television news: A content analysis of the networks, *Journalism Quarterly, 50,* 319-328.

Pride, Richard A., & Richards, Barbara (1974). Denigration of authority? Television news coverage of the student movement. *Journal of Politics, 36,* 637-660.

Pride, Richard A., & Wamsley, Gary L. (1972). Symbol analysis of network coverage of Laos incursion. *Journalism Quarterly, 49,* 635-640.

Ritter, Kurt W. (Ed.). (1981). The 1980 presidential debates [Special issue]. *Speaker and Gavel, 18*(2).

Roberts, Donald F., Bachen, Christine M., Hornby, Melinda C., & Hernandez-Ramos, Pedro. (1984). Reading and television: Predictors of reading achievement at different age levels. *Communication Research, 11*(1), 9-49.

Robinson, John P. (1969). Television and leisure time: Yesterday, today, and (maybe) tomorrow. *Public Opinion Quarterly, 33,* 210-233.

Robinson, John P. (1971). The audience for national TV news programs. *Public Opinion Quarterly, 35,* 403-405.

Robinson, John P. (1972a). Television's impact on everyday life: Some cross-national evidence. In E. A. Rubinstein, G. A. Comstock, & J. P. Murray (Eds.), *Television and social behavior: Vol. 4. Television in day-to-day life: Patterns of use* (pp. 410-431). Washington, DC: U.S. Government Printing Office.

Robinson, John P. (1972b). Toward defining the functions of television. In E. A. Rubinstein, G. A. Comstock, & J. P. Murray (Eds.), *Television and social behavior: Vol. 4. Television in day-to-day life: Patterns of use* (pp. 568-603). Washington, DC: U.S. Government Printing Office.

Robinson, John P. (1977). *How Americans use time: A social-psychological analysis of everyday behavior.* New York: Praeger.

Robinson, John P., & Bachman, Jerald G. (1972). Television viewing habits and aggression. In G. A. Comstock & E. A. Rubinstein (Eds.), *Television and social behavior: Vol. 3. Television and adolescent aggressiveness* (pp. 372-382). Washington, DC: U.S. Government Printing Office.

Robinson, John P., & Converse, Phillip E. (1972). The impact of television on mass media usage: A cross-national comparison. In A. Szalai (Ed.), *The use of time: Daily activities of urban and suburban populations in twelve countries* (pp. 197-212). The Hague: Mouton.

Robinson, John P., Converse, Phillip E., & Szalai, Alexander. (1972). Everyday life in twelve countries. In A. Szalai (Ed.), *The use of time: Daily activities of urban and suburban populations in twelve countries.* The Hague: Mouton.

Robinson, John P., & Levy, Mark R. (1986). *The main source.* Newbury Park, CA: Sage.

Rogers, Everett M. (1986). *Communication technology.* New York: Free Press.

The Roper Organization, Inc. (1981a). *Public perceptions of the mass media, 1959-1981.* New York: The Television Information Office

The Roper Organization, Inc. (1981b). *Sex, profanity and violence: An opinion survey about seventeen television programs.* Conducted for the National Broadcasting Company. New York: Television Information Office.

The Roper Organization, Inc. (1985). *Public attitudes toward television and other media in a time of change.* New York: Television Information Office.

The Roper Organization, Inc. (1987). *America's watching: Public attitudes toward television.* New York: Television Information Office.

Rosekrans, M. A. (1967). Imitation in children as a function of perceived similarities to a social model of vicarious reinforcement. *Journal of Personality and Social Psychology, 7,* 307-315.

Rossiter, John R., & Robertson, Thomas S. (1977). Children's responsiveness to commercials. *Journal of Communication, 27,* 101-106.

Rothenbuhler, Eric W. (1988). The living room celebration of the Olympic games. *Journal of Communication, 38*(4), 61-81.

Rubinstein, Eli, Comstock, George, & Murray, John P. (Eds.). (1972). *Television and social behavior: Vol. 4. Television in day-to-day life: Patterns of use.* Washington, DC: U.S. Government Printing Office.

Salomon, Gavriel. (1981a). *Communication and education: Social and psychological interactions.* Newbury Park, CA: Sage.

Salomon, Gavriel. (1981b). Introducing AIME: The assessment of children's mental involvement with television. In H. Kelley & H. Gardner (Eds.), *New directions for child development: Viewing children through television* (No. 13, pp. 89-112). San Francisco: Jossey-Bass.

Salomon, Gavriel. (1983). Television watching and mental effort: A social psychological view. In J. Bryant & D. R. Anderson (Eds.), *Children's understanding of television: Research on attention and comprehension* (pp. 181-198). New York: Academic Press.

Schneider, Frederick P. (1985). *The substance and structure of network television news: An analysis of content features, format features, and formal features.* Unpublished doctoral dissertation, Syracuse University, Syracuse, NY.

Schramm, Wilbur, Lyle, Jack, & Parker, Edwin B. (1961). *Television in the lives of our children.* Stanford, CA: Stanford University Press.

Schulberg, Budd. (1957). *What makes Sammy run.* New York: Bantam.

Sears, David O., & Chaffee, Steven H. (1979). Uses and effects of the 1976 debates: An overview of empirical studies. In S. Kraus (Ed.), *The great debates: Carter vs. Ford, 1976.* Bloomington: Indiana University Press.

Shaw, Donald L., & McCombs, Maxwell E. (1977). *The emergence of American political issues: The agenda-setting function of the press.* St. Paul: West Publishing.

Singer, Jerry S., Singer, Dorothy G., & Rapaczynski, Wanda S. (1984). Family patterns and television viewing as predictors of children's beliefs and aggression. *Journal of Communication, 34*(2), 73-89.

Slife, B. C., & Rychiak, J. R. (1982). Role of affective assessment in modeling aggressive behavior. *Journal of Personality and Social Psychology. 43*(4), 861-868.

Smith, R. E., Sarason, Esther G., & Sarason, Barbara R. (1982). *Psychology: The frontiers of behavior.* New York: Harper and Row.

Stauffer, John, Frost, Richard, & Rybolt, William. (1983). The attention factor in recalling network television news. *Journal of Communication, 33*(1), 29-37.

Stein, Ben. (1979). *The view from Sunset Boulevard.* New York: Basic Books.

Steiner, Gary A. (1963). *The people look at television.* New York: Alfred A. Knopf.

Stevenson, Robert L., Eisinger, Richard A., Feinberg, Barry M., & Kotok, Alan B. (1973). Untwisting the news twisters: A replication of Efron's study. *Journalism Quarterly, 50,* 211-219.

Surgeon General's Scientific Advisory Committee on Television and Social Behavior. (1972). *Television and growing up: The impact of televised violence.* Report to the Surgeon General, United States Public Health Service. Washington, DC: U.S. Government Printing Office. (ERIC Document Reproduction service no. ED 057 595)

Szalai, Alexander (Ed.). (1972). *The use of time: Daily activities of urban and suburban populations in twelve countries.* The Hague: Mouton.

Tannenbaum, Percy H., & Kostrich, Leslie J. (1983). *Turned-on TV/Turned-off voters: Policy options for election projections.* Newbury Park, CA: Sage.

Tannenbaum, Percy, & Zillmann, Dolf. (1975). Emotional arousal in the facilitation of aggression through communication. In L. Berkowitz (Ed.), *Advances in experimental social psychology* (Vol. 8, pp. 149-192). New York: Academic Press.

Thomas, Margaret H., Horton, Robert W., Lippincott, Elaine C., & Drabman, Ronald S. (1977). Desensitization to portrayals of real life aggression as a function of exposure to television violence. *Journal of Personality and Social Psychology, 35,* 450-458.

Tuchman, Gaye. (1978). *Making news: A study in the construction of reality.* New York: Free Press.

Tuchman, S. & Coffin, T. E. (1971). The influence of television broadcasts in a close election. *Public Opinion Quarterly, 35,* 315-326.

Tunstall, Jeremy, & Walker, David. (1981). *Media made in California.* New York: Oxford University Press.

Turow, Joseph. (1981). *Entertainment, education, and the hard sell: Three decades of network children's television.* New York: Praeger.

Turow, Joseph. (1984). *Media industries: The production of news and entertainment.* New York: Longman.

TV's political coverage not so bad says book. (1988, Nov. 14). *Broadcasting,* pp. 76-77.

Tyler, Tom R. (1978). *Drawing inferences from experiences: The effects of crime victimization upon crime-related attitudes and behavior.* Unpublished doctoral dissertation, University of California, Los Angeles.

Vallone, Robert P., Ross, Lee, & Lepper, Mark R. (1985). The hostile media phenomenon: Biased perception and perceptions of media bias in coverage of the Beirut massacre. *Journal of Personality and Social Psychology, 49*(3), 577-585.

West, Nathaniel. (1975). *The day of the locust.* New York: Bantam.

Whiteside, Thomas. (1981). *The blockbuster complex. Conglomerates, show business, and book publishing.* Middletown, CT: Wesleyan University Press.

Williams, Tannis MacBeth (Ed.). (1986). *The impact of television: A natural experiment in three communities.* New York: Academic Press.

Wober, J. Mallory. (1988). *The use and abuse of television: A social psychological analysis of the changing screen.* Hillsdale, NJ: Lawrence Erlbaum.

Wright, Charles R. (1986). *Mass communication: A sociological perspective* (3rd ed.). New York: Random House.

Zillmann, Dolf. (1971). Excitation transfer in communication-mediated aggressive behavior. *Journal of Experimental Social Psychology, 7,* 419-434.

Zillmann, Dolf, & Bryant, Jennings. (1982). Pornography, sexual callousness, and the trivialization of rape. *Journal of Communication, 32*(4), 10-21.

Author Index

Subject Index

About the Author

GEORGE COMSTOCK is S.I. Newhouse Professor of Public Communications at Syracuse University. He was a senior social psychologist at The Rand Corporation, Santa Monica, CA., and science adviser and senior research coordinator for the Surgeon General's Scientific Advisory Committee on Television and Social Behavior. He is an editor of the five volumes reporting research commissioned by the Surgeon General's inquiry, *Television and Social Behavior* (1972); a contributor to the update a decade later, *Television and Behavior: Ten Years of Scientific Inquiry and Implications for the Eighties* (1982); senior author of *Television and Human Behavior* (1978); and editor of the (more or less) annual series *Public Communication and Behavior* (1986, 1989, in press). He holds a Ph.D. and an M.A. from Stanford University and a B.A. from the University of Washington.